365 MORE SIMPLE SCIENCE EXPERIMENTS

365 MORE SIMPLE SCIENCE EXPERIMENTS

with everyday materials

By E. Richard Churchill,
Louis V. Loeschnig, and
Muriel Mandell

Illustrated by Frances
Zweifel

BLACK DOG
& LEVENTHAL
PUBLISHERS

Designed by Liz Trovato

Published by
Black Dog & Leventhal Publishers, Inc.
151 West 19th Street
New York, NY 10011

Distributed by
Workman Publishing Company
708 Broadway
New York, NY 10003

Manufactured in the United States of America

ISBN 1–57912–035–0

h g f e d

CONTENTS

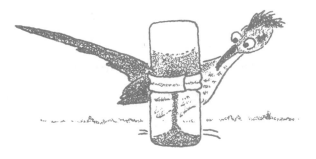

INTRODUCTION

365 Simple Science Experiments was the first book in this series and it taught many people about science. Science, however, includes so many topics that we needed to create *365 More Simple Science Experiments*. Now you can fill more of your days with fun and entertaining activities. All of these experiments have a surprise in them. Some of them will surprise you because of how they work. Others are surprising because of what happens.

These experiments come in the form of projects, stunts, tricks and even games. The one thing that they all have in common is that they are based on scientific principles. This book helps you to put scientific ideas to work in ways that may seem impossible, but which are always interesting and enjoyable.

The first seven chapters talk about physics. It's a marvelous world that we live in. A world filled with rainbows and rockets, with echoes and electric sparks, with atomic particles and planets, and with invisible forces and vibrations that affect you without your even knowing they exist.

Physics comes from the Greek word *physica*, meaning "natural things." Learning about the natural things of this world, what is happening every second all around us, is what physics is all about. What better way to learn about physics than in our everyday laboratory—the world itself—where it can be experienced and not just studied.

These hands-on experiments put the natural world at your fingertips. And you don't have to spend time and money at the store buying expensive equipment and supplies. You can do all of these experiments using just odds and ends that you probably have around your home. (If you don't have an eyedropper, use a straw. See instructions on page 44.) Use whatever you have available and, if necessary, adjust or substitute using the experiment's instuctions as a guide. Most likely the experiment will work just as

well. And if it doesn't, with some thought you'll discover why it doesn't and be well on your way to becoming a problemsolver (someone who gets things done no matter what).

Several of these experiments require the use of heat. Where possible, the heat needed comes from a 100-watt light bulb with a foil shade (the shade makes its easier on your eyes and the light bulb is safer to use). A symbol reminding you to be careful marks those experiments using heat.

The next eight chapters focus on learning about science using everyday foods. What makes you hungry or thirsty? Does water always boil at the same temperature? Why is a tomato called a fruit? Is a raw carrot healthier than a cooked one? Why do we cry when we peel an onion?

These are a few of the questions the experiments in this section will answer. We'll be working with carbon, hydrogen, oxygen, nitrogen, phosphorus and sulphur—the elements that play a leading role in the chemistry of the kitchen. They combine to make up the food we eat: carbohydrates such as sugars and starches; fats and oils; proteins such as meat and eggs; and water.

When we cook, we're actually preparing chemical compounds in a form our body can use safely—with enough good taste so that we're willing to eat them. This book will help you discover both the how and the why of doing this. The eating is a bonus!

The experiments in the next seven chapters relate to time. Through these exciting projects you will learn all about the history of the earliest time-telling devices and clocks, how the sun, the moon and the stars all determine time, and why time, at one place in the world registers differently—at the same moment—than time in another place in the world.

The seven chapters that follow help to explain some puzzling and interesting ideas about nature. You may not realize it but you are related to the dragonfly. You are also related to the pine tree and the mushroom. In fact, all living organisms are related to each other in some way. We depend on members of the plant and animal kingdoms for our food, building and clothing materials, and for our enjoyment. Plants and animals depend on each other for their survival, too. In fact, all plants and animals (including human beings like you and me) are part of a complex survival system, commonly called ecology, with every other member of the plant and animal world.

The activities in this section are designed to help you explore and understand nature, and to appreciate the connections that exist between all living things and the world around them. You will discover that you alone can do a lot to help the environment. That is the way we learn to really appreciate the plants and animals with whom we share this world, and can ensure that we will be able to enjoy them for years to come.

This is a book of discovery. All of the activities are hands-on, fun to do, and use only simple, easy-to-obtain materials. Some activities will take only a few minutes; others will last several days or weeks. Most of the activities are open-ended—meaning there are no right or wrong answers. You can do as many of the experiments as you wish, again and again, or for as long as you want. You are the scientist.

Several of the activities suggest that you keep a journal or notebook to record your observations. Scientists always do this. Buy a spiral notebook and mark it "My Nature Journal." Use your journal to keep track of the growth of a plant, the animals you see in a certain area, or how much rain fell on a certain day. Your journal will be an important record of what you did and observed during an experiment so that you can compare it to what happens when you do the same experiment again several weeks or months later.

It's smart to be careful in whatever you do. A few of these experiments or activities call for the use of a stove, a knife, or a sharp scissors—times when you might want to ask an adult for help. Watch for the "safety bee" in some if the experiments to remind you, and do be careful.

The final chapters help you explore the science of space. Space travel came from man's imagination. The French writer Jules Verne (1828–1905) set down his dream of going to other worlds in a book entitled FROM THE EARTH TO THE MOON. It was a story about traveling in rockets.

Sir Isaac Newton's Law of Motion gave modern space scientists the principle that every rocket is based upon: for every action, there is an equal and opposite reaction. In 1926, an American, Robert Goddard, built and launched the first successful fueled rocket.

In the 1940s, while the Germans developed working long-range ground missiles, the Russians worked on building larger rockets, powerful enough to thrust them towards their dream of outer space. In 1957, the Russians launched *Sputnik* I, the first unmanned satellite to go into orbit around the Earth. They continued their lead in space exploration by, in 1961, placing the first human being in orbit, a cosmonaut named Yuri Gagarin.

Americans finally pulled ahead in the space race when, on July 20, 1969, Neil Armstrong became the first human to step foot on the moon. Later, through 1972, there were several other manned moon landings (*Apollo* missions). Over the years since, the U.S. has taken part in many space missions, launched many satellites and space probes, and has placed several space stations in orbit. But it is the Russians that are credited with launching and maintaining in orbit the most impressive and largest space station to date, the *Mir*.

It is the purpose of this section to give future astronauts and flight and space scientists food for thought. Here is a chance to experiment, question, think, and dream. In this section, you'll learn about Bernoulli's Principle—without it, you'd never know the basic laws of flight. You'll design an airfoil, or airplane wing, construct a simple helicopter-like toy, learn about gravity and centrifugal/centripetal force. In addition, you'll

construct flight instruments, learn about hot-air balloons, and make a variety of gliders and planes to discover how they really work. You'll also make your own kites— with flight and aerodynamics in mind. You'll even learn about the orbits and sizes of the planets, and do some great experiments to explain it all!

As space scientists, you'll learn about conditions on the moon, how conditions in outer space and lack of gravity affect space flight, and how astronauts reenter Earth's atmosphere and maintain orbit. You'll design, construct and launch a simple rocket space shuttle—and, if that's not enough, you'll learn how NASA's future astronauts are selected and trained.

Most of the materials you'll need to do the many projects in this book are inexpensive and easy to find—usually simple, everyday household items. We'll let you know, though, about the few things you may need to hunt up. So get ready to have fun and learn all about the many mysteries of science. We wish you many hours of happy experiments!

BEATING THE HEAT

Heat is a form of energy. It is what happens when molecules move around within a substance. The faster the molecules move, the hotter the substance gets.

About Heat

All things have some heat. Heat passes freely from hot to cold things. For example, you pour a hot drink into a glass with ice cubes. The heat from the drink moves into the ice, melting it, and the drink is cooled, meaning that some of the heat has been removed.

Heat affects what kinds of clothes we wear and what types of houses we live in.

We depend on heat for life, for if the sun should cool, all life on Earth would disappear. With this in mind, we should learn all that we can about heat. The study of heat in physics is called thermodynamics.

Note: The HOT symbol (shown below) will remind you to be extra careful at certain times when you will be using heat in these experiments. Always remember to use pliers, tongs, an oven mitt, or a pot holder to handle anything that may be hot. Even minor burns can be painful.

1 — Make a Foil Lamp Shade

HOT!

Some of the experiments in this book use a lamp with a 100-watt bulb as a source of heat. To collect and direct the heat from the bulb toward the experiment, make a cap-shaded lamp shade out of aluminum foil. Take a small square of foil and round off the corners by folding or cutting. Place the foil on top of the cold (not lit) light bulb and shape it into a cap shape. Turn the edges of the foil up slightly, and you have a shade ready for your experiments with heat. Remember to watch for the HOT symbol (see above), and be careful.

18

Step on a Crack

Have you ever wondered why sidewalks are laid out in sections with spaces, or cracks, between them?

YOU WILL NEED:

empty can
large nail
hammer
lamp (100-watt bulb) with foil shade
kitchen timer
pliers or tongs

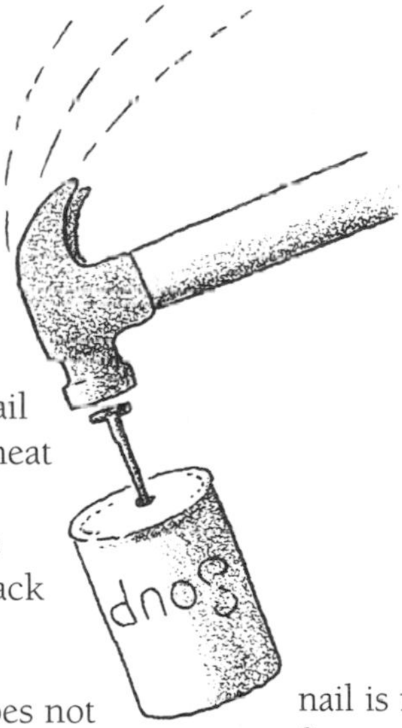

What to do: Hammer the nail into the bottom of the can. Work the nail in and out a couple of times to make sure that it slides through easily. Pull the nail out of the hole.

Turn on the lamp with the foil shade. Set the kitchen timer for two minutes. Now, using pliers or tongs, hold the nail over the lamp shade on the bulb and heat it until the timer bell rings. Be careful not to touch the hot bulb or foil shade with your hands. Try to put the nail back into the hole in the can.

What happens: The heated nail does not fit back into the hole.

Why: Heat from the light bulb excites the tiny, separate particles called molecules that make up the nail. These excited molecules move faster and spread out to take up more space. So the heated nail is now bigger than it was before and no longer fits in the hole.

Like the nail, a sidewalk's molecules also spread out on hot summer days. If there were no cracks between the sections of sidewalk, the heated molecules would have no room to expand and the concrete sidewalk would crack or break up.

19

Day and Night in a Can

Why do you suppose the people who design clothing use dark colors for winter coats but white or light colors for summer things?

What to do: Prepare for this experiment by painting one side of the inside of the can black. (Be careful of sharp can edges.) Leave the other half shiny.

When the paint is completely dry, take the cotton swab and put two dime-size blobs of petroleum jelly on the outside of the can, one in the center of the dark half and one on the other side. Push a penny down firmly into each blob so that it sticks. Make sure that one penny is stuck outside the dark half, and one outside the shiny half.

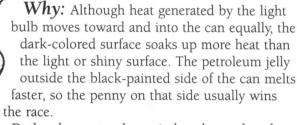

With the foil shade in position on the bulb, carefully balance the can, open side down, on top of the shade. Now, turn on the lamp.

What happens: The petroleum jelly melts and the pennies drop off, of course, but the penny outside the darkened half drops first.

Why: Although heat generated by the light bulb moves toward and into the can equally, the dark-colored surface soaks up more heat than the light or shiny surface. The petroleum jelly outside the black-painted side of the can melts faster, so the penny on that side usually wins the race.

Dark colors not only retain heat better, but they also do a better job of soaking up, or absorbing, the waves of heat that come to us in the light rays from the sun. So, in winter you want a dark coat to keep you warmer. Light-colored clothing reflects, or bounces, most of the heat-making light waves back into the atmosphere, so it keeps you cooler on hot summer days.

Decorate a Hat

How does heat change solid forms to liquids? Here's a chance not only to understand the process of melting, but to use it to make a fancy hat as well.

What to do: Before turning on the lamp, turn up the edge of the foil shade all the way around, giving it a nice big brim. Fit this hat-shape securely over the light bulb.

Turn on the lamp. Carefully, hold the tip of the birthday candle against the top of the foil hat.

What happens: After a few seconds, the candle begins to change into a liquid that quickly drips away from the wick.

Why: The heat from the light bulb excites the tiny particles, or molecules, of wax that make up the candle. As these molecules expand, or spread out, they begin to move about so wildly that they change into a liquid. This process is, of course, called melting, and the temperature at which a substance melts is called its melting point.

What next: Finish decorating the foil hat by letting the different-colored candles drip all over the hat and around the brim. When you are finished, turn off the lamp and let the hat cool before removing it from the bulb. Later, you can design a face on an apple or a potato and create "a someone" to wear the decorated hat.

Melt a Kiss

Our Earth gets its warmth from the sun's light. Fortunately, the Earth is constantly turning on its axis and is not made of chocolate.

What to do: Put a little water into the bag. Swirl it around to coat the inside of the bag and pour the rest out. Put the chocolate kiss into the bag. Then, carefully, hold the bag over the shaded light bulb. Do not let the bag touch the shade.

What happens: The chocolate kiss inside the bag begins to melt, but the bag doesn't get hot.

Why: The heat energy coming from the light waves is soaked up, or absorbed, by the film of water molecules inside the bag and by the chocolate kiss.

This heat energy, which cannot be seen but can be felt, moves in circular waves away from its source, like the expanding ripples a stone makes when it is thrown into calm water. It is this form of heat, called radiation, which allows the sun to heat our earth, and the lamp to melt the chocolate kiss.

Color Me Warm

Warmed air rises, cools off, and sinks down. This experiment uses water to give you a clear picture of how warmed air reacts.

YOU WILL NEED:

2 clear drinking glasses
hot tap water
very cold water
food coloring
a small measuring spoon

What to do: Fill one glass with hot water, and the other with icy-cold water. Measure some food coloring into each glass.

What happens: The food coloring quickly swirls around to mix with the hot water—but not so in the cold water.

Why: Because its tiny, separate particles, or molecules, are moving faster than the cold-water molecules, the hotter water at the bottom of the glass whirls around and up to the top, taking the food coloring with it. As the water at the top cools, warmer water takes its place, and now the cooler water sinks. This process, called convection, will continue until all the water is at the same temperature.

Because there is less motion in the cold water, the food coloring sinks to the bottom of the glass and stays in place longer.

Birds on a Wire

7

If you have ever grabbed a hot metal handle of a cooking pan, you have actually felt hundreds of speeding molecules striking your hand like tiny bullets. Unfortunately, such a "hands-on" experience usually results in a painful burn or blister.

What to do: Straighten out the paper clip to make a straight piece of wire. Clip the clothespin to one end of the wire as a handle. With the spoon, line up three separate, jelly-bean-size blobs of petroleum jelly on the wire. Try to space the blobs evenly, so that they look like birds sitting on a telephone wire.

Place the end of the waxed paper underneath the lamp's base. With the foil shade covering the bulb, turn on the lamp. Holding the clothespin, touch the far end of the wire to the bulb and hold it there. The "birds" need to be sitting on the wire over the waxed paper leading away from the bulb.

What happens: Beginning with the "bird" perched nearest the light bulb, one after the other begins to drop off the wire, until all three are gone.

Why: When one end of the wire is heated by the light bulb, the tiny, separate particles, or molecules, in that area of the wire zoom into motion. Soon these heated molecules begin to jostle the ones next to them, then those molecules bump others nearby, until the heat is passed all the way down the wire, melting each "bird" in turn.

This passing of heat from one excited, jostling molecule to another, like a handshake sent down a line or around a circle, is called conduction.

WHY IS THERE AIR?

Air alone has no color, taste, or smell. You can't see it, and you can put your hand right through it without feeling anything. However, air is more than just nothing at all. It is actually made up of many gases, mainly nitrogen and oxygen, which consist of tiny molecules that are far apart and move about quickly. This is why gases are thin and appear invisible.

About Air

Scientists estimate that one cubic inch (16.4 cubic centimeters) of air contains about 300 billion billion molecules! Even though the molecules are so tiny, there is still plenty of space between each one. Each air molecule has enough energy to zip through space at 11,000 miles (1600 kilometers) per hour.

The Collapsing Bottle

The following experiment will help your recycling efforts by giving you more room in the collecting bin.

YOU WILL NEED:
plastic 2-liter bottle with cap
very hot tap water

What to do: Pour hot water into the bottle until it is about half-full and swish it around for about a minute. Then pour the water out and, quickly, put the cap on and twist it tightly.

What happens: The sides of the bottle suddenly collapse inward!

Why: The hot water heats the air inside the bottle and, with the cap left off, it fills to the brim with warm air. When the hot water is poured out and the cap is replaced, the air inside of the bottle quickly starts to cool. Since cooler air takes up less space than the same amount of warmer air, there's now extra room in the bottle!

To fill that extra space, the sides of the bottle are pushed in by the force of the air pressure outside the bottle, which is constantly pressing in every direction.

The Wonderful Whistle-Stick

Can you turn a piece of wood into a whistle? Sure you can. It's a great experiment, and fun, too.

YOU WILL NEED:
wooden paint stirrer or small paddle
hammer
large-size nail
long piece of string

What to do: Use the hammer and nail to make a hole in the narrow end of the stirrer or paddle. Put one end of the string through the hole and tie a tight knot. Now, make two or three holes in the wider end of the wood. You can put the holes all in a row, or make up your own pattern.

To hear your whistle-stick, go outside or find a large open area where you can swing the stick without breaking anything. Hold tightly onto the loose end of the string and whirl the paddle around in front of you or over your head. Be careful NOT to do this experiment where people are passing by.

What happens: You hear an unusual whistling sound over and over again.

Why: As you whirl the paddle around, the air passes through the holes in it at a higher speed than the air going around the paddle. When this happens, the paddle whistles.

What next: Different numbers and sizes of holes make different whistle sounds. You might want to make several whistle-sticks—some with only a few small holes to catch the air and others with larger or a lot of holes. Then you can compare the whistle sounds that each one makes.

The Talking Coin

You may have heard somebody say that money talks, but until you do this experiment you have probably never actually seen it speak.

What to do: Put the quarter in the cup of water and place the empty bottle in the freezer for five minutes.

When the time is up, remove the bottle from the freezer and, immediately, cover the mouth of the bottle with the wet coin. (It is important to completely cover the bottle's mouth with the coin.)

What happens: The quarter becomes a tongue for the bottle and begins to chatter at you.

Why: When the bottle was put into the freezer, the air molecules inside of it cooled and moved closer together. Since the air in the bottle then took up less space, it left room for extra air to flow in—so it did.

When the bottle was removed from the freezer, however, the air molecules inside of it began to warm up and spread out again. It's a great example of, "There was enough room for everyone to sit comfortably in the car until we all put on coats and it was crowded." Suddenly there was no room for the extra air molecules.

It is that "extra air" that is being pushed out of the bottle as the air warms that makes the coin move up and down as if it were talking.

The Incredible Shrinking Face

11

Air has a magical quality about it, in that it can expand or shrink flexible material almost instantly.

What to do: Blow up the balloon until it is fully inflated; then hold it tightly in one hand so that no air leaks out. While holding the balloon, pick up a black or dark marker with your other hand. Draw a large face on the balloon, completely covering one side of it. Next, relax your grip on the balloon's neck and watch as you slowly let a constant stream of air escape.

What happens: Right before your eyes, the huge face that covered the whole side of the big balloon shrinks to a miniature drawing.

Why: As the air is allowed to escape, the balloon material that expanded as you blew into the balloon goes back to its original small size, taking the marker "face" with it. If your marker ink tends to smear, spray the drawing while the balloon is full of air with a clear gloss aerosol finish to keep it neat.

Launch Your Own Astronauts

In the same way that a hurricane can blow you off your feet, you can make a flying chamber for your own band of brave adventurers.

YOU WILL NEED:
Ping-Pong balls
blow dryer
permanent markers
(optional)

What to do: For fun, using the markers, make a face on each of the balls. You could even identify your astronauts by writing their names on the balls. Next, plug in the hair dryer, turn it to the high setting, and point it straight up.
Place one of your homemade astronauts in the dryer's airstream and let go.

What happens: The astronaut is launched toward the ceiling, but stops and bounces around in the airflow partway up.

Why: The airstream from the dryer pushes the astronaut upwards, against the force of gravity, until the upward and downward pushes are equal and the astronaut just floats.

The high pressure in the still air surrounding the airstream keeps the astronaut in the center of the visible flying chamber.

What next: Try letting two or more astronauts fly at the same time. You may be able to do this if the blow dryer's airstream is wide enough (or if you have an attachment called a diffuser that spreads out the airflow). If not, your astronauts will probably "bounce" off each other—into unknown galaxies.

13 The Trick Straw Race

This race is just for fun, but you might want to challenge someone you know is a good loser to compete.

What to do: Before the race, use the straight pin to punch 15 or 20 small holes in one end of the "trick" straw. Punch the holes where the colors change on the straw so that they will be harder to see. Place the straw, punctured end up, in your friend's drink and say, "Let's see who can drink it all first."

What happens: While your glass empties quickly, most of your friend's drink will remain in the glass.

Why: By sucking on the straw, you are lowering the air pressure inside of it, so the air pressure pressing down on your drink pushes it up the straw and into your mouth. In the "trick" straw, air rushes into the holes in the straw so that your friend can't lower the air pressure inside—at least not enough to win the race.

The Collapsing Tent 14

Everybody knows that moving air has more power than air that is not moving. Or does it? The following experiment will help you draw your own conclusions.

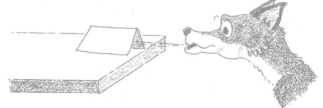

What to do: Fold the paper in half, creasing it with your finger to form a tent. Open the tent and place it near the edge of the table or a countertop, with one open side facing you. Get into position so that your mouth is level with the edge of the table, take a big breath and blow a steady stream of air through the tent.

What happens: The tent collapses, becoming a flat sheet again.

Why: When you blow through the tent, you are lowering the air pressure inside of it. This allows the higher air pressure above the tent to crush down and flatten it.

Make a Parachute

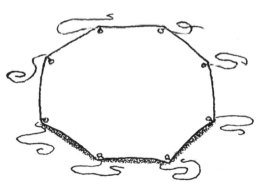

Race car-builders make their creations as streamlined as possible so that these machines cut through the air and attain the highest speeds. Parachute-makers, however, use yards and yards of billowing fabric so that their creations will grab as much air as possible on the way down.

What to do: Cut a large square piece from the front of the bag (without a seam) Trim off the corners to form an octagon, or eight-sided shape. With the nail, carefully punch a small hole near each angle of the plastic so that you have eight holes, spaced evenly, all the way around.

Tie one end of the pieces of yarn securely to each hole. Now, pull the other ends of the eight pieces of yarn together and tie them in a tight knot. Push the nail through a few of the knotted strands as a weight—this is your parachutist.

To test your parachute, stand on a sturdy chair or go outside in search of a breeze. Using both hands, hold the parachute out in front of you, high above your head, and release it.

What happens: The plastic parachute billows out and floats gently downward and away from you.

YOU WILL NEED:

lightweight plastic
grocery bag
scissors
nail
8 pieces of yarn

Why: It is a law of physics that the larger the surface area in contact with air, the harder it is for that object to travel through the air. So, the larger the parachute, the slower it moves—which is what you want if you are falling from a height!

But, the umbrella-like shape over a weight, like a truck parachuted out of a plane, also traps air beneath it. It is the air spilling off to one side of the parachute's top, or canopy, that makes it drift away from you.

What next: Make a very small hole in the middle of the canopy. This will make the parachute fall straighter. Now you can mark out a landing area and try to have your parachutist hit the target.

The Singing Balloon

YOU WILL NEED:

balloon
some music

Most balloons are content to just float around quietly. This mezzo-soprano is dying to let loose and sing.

What to do: Blow up the balloon, making it as full as possible. Pinch the neck of the balloon. Pull your hands apart gently to release a slow, steady stream of air from the balloon. Move your hands back and forth, stretching the balloon's neck to the music's beat.

What happens: A high-pitched squealing sound is heard. It changes tone as you pull and release the neck of the balloon.

Why: The molecules of air packed inside the balloon rub against the rubber molecules of the balloon's neck as they rush by on the way out. This causes the rubber in the balloon's neck to shake, or vibrate, and makes the squealing noise. Stretching the neck of the balloon makes it vibrate at different speeds to make different sounds.
For fun, why not form a Singing Balloon Band?

The Rising Notebook Trick

YOU WILL NEED:

school notebook
medium-size balloon
table or countertop

Even though you might think of air as a gentle, invisible "free spirit," it can be quite strong and powerful when pressured.

What to do: Place the balloon at the edge of the table or countertop with the mouth of the balloon sticking out toward you. Put the notebook on top of the balloon. Hold the balloon by the neck and blow into it.

What happens: The notebook rises.

Why: The high air pressure from your lungs causes the balloon to expand and lifts the notebook off the table. In repair garages, whole cars are lifted up in a similar way by air pressure.

Unfortunately, the air pressure in the balloon does not have a lifting effect on the grades of any homework in the notebook.

Air-Head Person

Even though you cannot actually see air, you can trap it inside something and see the shape that it makes. You can also bring that shape to life—sort of.

18

YOU WILL NEED:

latex balloon
square of heavy cardboard
thick nail
cellophane tape
scissors
permanent markers

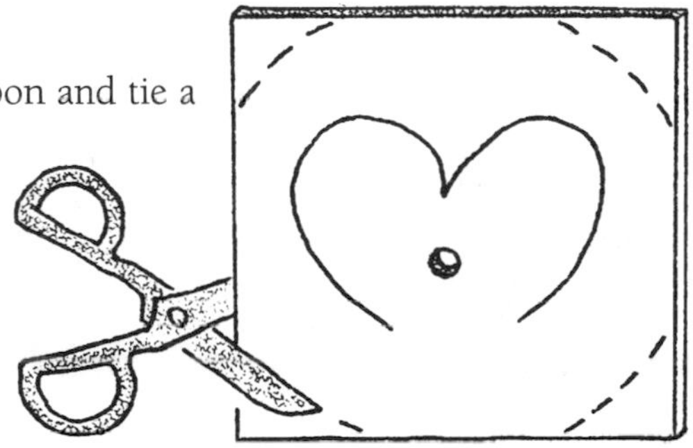

What to do: Blow up the balloon and tie a tight knot in the neck.

What happens: Your once-limp balloon has taken on a round, roly-poly shape.

Why: The air you blew into the balloon with the pressure of your lungs is now trapped in there. Crammed by the balloon into the smallest possible shape, it pushes equally against all sides of the balloon, making it round.

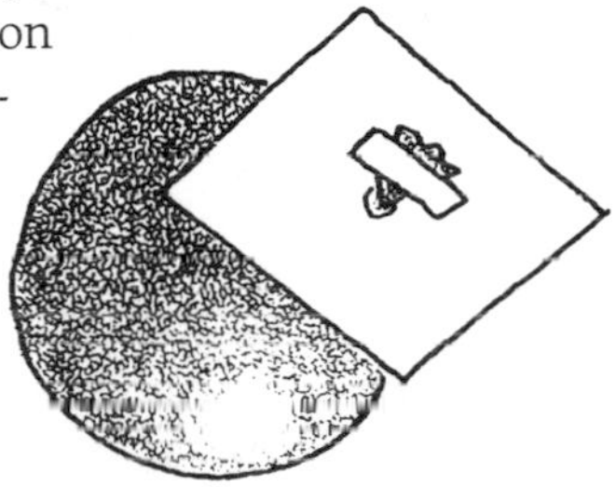

What next: Turn that roly-poly shape into an air-head person. Draw a large, rounded "W" on one side of the cardboard to make the feet. Cut around the edges of the cardboard, and then punch a hole in the center of it with the nail. Carefully poke the knotted end of the balloon through the hole in the cardboard feet. Pull the knot forward, toward the "toes," and tape the knot securely to the cardboard with some tape.

Your air-head person is now ready for a face (eyes, ears, mouth, nose, hair, glasses, mustache, or whatever you like), using the markers. And don't forget to print a name on its cardboard feet.

Decorate your room or make lots of air-heads for a birthday party, depending on how much air you have to spare.

Real String Soap in a Bottle

YOU WILL NEED:

plastic detergent bottle with cap

white string

scissors

a helper (optional)

By knowing a little about how air pressure works, you can make a great trick that is sure to surprise everyone.

What to do: Remove the cap from the detergent bottle. Using the scissors, bend the plastic strip inside the cap to one side, or remove it altogether. (If you have trouble doing this, ask someone to help you.) From the inside of the cap, poke one end of the string through the holes and out the top. Make sure that the string glides easily back and forth through the openings.

Then, tie a fat knot in each end of the string so that it cannot pull through the holes and will stay in place. Leaving only the fat knot outside, covering the cap opening, hide the rest of the string down inside the bottle. Now, replace the cap. To do the trick, point the bottle and give it a quick squeeze.

What happens: Watch it! A stream of white "string soap" squirts out!

Why: When the bottle is squeezed, air rushes out through the holes in the cap and the top, shooting the knot covering them into the air. Also, the air pressure inside the plastic bottle, when you squeeze it, is greater than the air pressure outside of it. This difference in pressure also helps to force the string out.

Underwater "Eggspert"

YOU WILL NEED:
fresh egg
deep cereal bowl
hot tap water
yellow food coloring
(optional)

You probably know that eggs have yolks, but did you know that they also contain air? This "eggsperiment" will show you how to prove it.

What to do: Carefully, place the egg in the bottom of the bowl and fill the bowl with hot tap water. Quickly add a little yellow food coloring. Watch the egg closely for several minutes.

What happens: Streams of tiny bubbles rise to the top of the water from the submerged egg.

Why: When the air inside the egg is heated by the hot water, the air molecules expand. Many of the now crowded air molecules push their way out of the egg through some of the almost 7,000 openings, or pores, in the egg's shell. These heated air molecules exit the egg, usually without cracking the shell, and rise to the water's surface as bubbles.

Acupuncture Balloon

YOU WILL NEED:
small latex balloon
adhesive or other strong, sticky tape
5 or 6 sharp straight pins
string

Acupuncture is an ancient Chinese medical procedure often used to relieve pain. You can practice acupuncture, without a medical license, on a balloon.

What to do: Blow up the balloon about three-quarters of the way. Knot the end and tie the piece of string around the neck to help hold the balloon. Cut off five or six pieces of the strong, sticky tape. Press the pieces as evenly as you can around the outside of the balloon. Make sure that each piece of tape is secured tightly to the balloon.

Now, one by one, carefully stick a straight pin through the middle of each piece of the tape and into the balloon, puncturing the balloon all over.

What happens: Nothing! The balloon doesn't burst!

Why: When the pins pass through the tape, the sticky adhesive on it forms a seal around each pin that prevents the air from escaping from the balloon when you push them in. And, as you may know, a balloon only "pops" when the air is under pressure, and it is suddenly allowed to escape.

"Boil, Boil, Magical Water"

Would you believe you can boil water without using a stove? Here's the key to this old, well-kept secret.

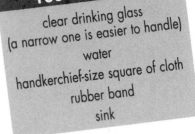

YOU WILL NEED:

clear drinking glass
(a narrow one is easier to handle)
water
handkerchief-size square of cloth
rubber band
sink

What to do: Fill the glass about half full of water. Lay the cloth evenly over the top of the glass and push the center of it down into the water. Then, put a rubber band tightly around the top to hold the cloth edges against the sides of the glass. Turn the glass upside down over the sink. Some of the water may dribble out, but most of it will stay inside the glass.

Hold the cloth tightly around the neck of the glass, between the rubber band and the covered opening, and push down hard on the upside-down bottom of the glass.

What happens: The water starts to boil! (It may take a couple of tries to get the hang of this, but don't give up.)

Why: Of course, the water isn't really boiling, because there is no heat source. Actually, it is the air that comes in through the cloth when the water is squeezed out (by pressing on the bottom of the glass and tightly pulling on the cloth) that causes the bubbles—and makes it look as if the water in the glass is boiling.

What next: Once you can control the bubbling, use this experiment as a trick lie detector. Ask friends some questions and tell them that the water will boil if they lie, but won't if they tell the truth.

Note: You can make this trick more mysterious by tinting the water in the glass with food coloring.

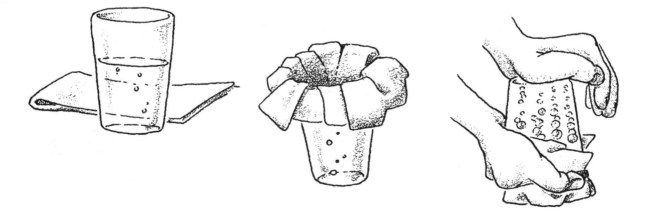

WATER, WATER, EVERYWHERE!

Water is the most common substance on Earth, covering more than 70% of its surface. Although it sometimes appears blue or green, water is a clear, colorless liquid. The thing about water that makes it different from most other liquids is that it is lighter as a solid (ice) than as a liquid.

About Water

Water is necessary to sustain life, making up most of an animal's blood, a plant's sap, and two-thirds of the human body.

Water is also a large part of our environment. It occurs as rain, sleet, snow, hail, frost, fog, dew, steam, humidity, and clouds. Not only are there lakes, rivers, oceans, and swamps that cover three-fourths of the Earth's surface, but water also accumulates in spaces between and within rock beneath the Earth's surface, supplying wells and springs and sustaining streams during periods of drought.

Water circulates constantly through our world, being used but never being used up. The glass of water that you drink today could contain the very same water molecules that a thirsty caveman enjoyed many thousands of years ago!

"I Was Here First!"

This experiment proves that two forms of matter cannot occupy the same place at the same time.

What to do: Fill the glass to about half-full of tap water. Next, put a piece of masking tape on the outside of the glass to mark the water level. Now, tilt the glass and carefully slide the marbles, one by one, down inside the glass to the bottom. Set the glass upright and check the water level.

What happens: The water level is higher than it was before.

Why: The water and the marbles are both examples of matter that cannot share space. When the

marbles are added to the glass, they are heavier than the water so they roll to the bottom of the glass and push the water there out of the way. The water level is, therefore, pushed up above the masking-tape marker.

Flowing Fountain

Blaise Pascal, a French physicist in the 1600s, discovered the scientific principle of how pressure affects liquids. Every time you enjoy watching water "dancing" from decorative fountains, you should thank Pascal.

What to do: Using the hammer and nail, punch eight holes evenly around the can, about two finger digits (1½ inches) up from the bottom rim.

Next, make a second row of holes, about one finger digit above the first one, except this time make

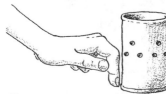

only four holes. Try to space them evenly around the can in a nice pattern.

Tear off two strips of freezer tape, each long enough to reach all the way around the can, and carefully cover each row of holes with the tape.

Fill the can with water, hold it over a sink basin, and rip off both tapes together. (You may need an extra helping hand here.)

What happens: The water flowing from the bottom holes squirts out just a little bit faster and farther than the water from the upper row of holes.

Why: The water in the lower part of the can is under more pressure, from the weight of the water above it, than the water higher up in the can.

Two Water Towers

Water towers come in all sizes, but does size make a difference to the water? Let's see.

What to do: Using the hammer and nail, make a hole about one finger digit (1/2 inch) up from the bottom rim of each can. Be sure to make the holes identical. Cover each hole completely with a small strip of freezer tape.

Fill each can to the brim with water. Set both cans on the edge of the sink, with the holes toward the basin. Rip off the tapes.

YOU WILL NEED:

2 cans
(one tall and thin; one short and bigger around)
hammer
nail (birthday-candle size)
freezer tape
water

What happens: The stream of water that flows out of the taller, thinner can is longer than the stream of water from the shorter can.

Why: It is the depth of the water that determines how fast the water flows out of the hole, and the deeper water is in the taller can. Shorter towers that are bigger around might hold as much or more water, but that water will come out slower and with less power. That is because the weight of the water pressing down, or water pressure, is less.

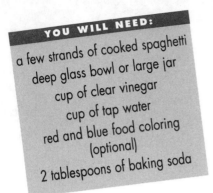

"I Think I'll Eat Worms"

When this experiment with bringing spaghetti to life is finished, you can amaze your friends even more by eating the "worms." They might taste a bit like pickles.

What to do: Tear the strands of cooked spaghetti into several worm-size pieces. In a bowl or jar, mix the cup of vinegar and the cup of water. Next, add three drops of red food coloring and three drops of blue food coloring to the mixture and stir to make the color purple.

Slowly add the two tablespoons of baking soda, then drop in the pieces of cooked spaghetti.

What happens: The purple "worms" seem to come to life! They swim back and forth, rising to the top of the water and then falling back to the bottom of the container.

Why: When vinegar and baking soda mix, they form tiny gas bubbles. These bubbles attach themselves to the small strands of spaghetti, raise these "worms" to the top, and then burst. The pieces then fall back to the bottom where, if more gas bubbles attach themselves, the purple "worms" will continue to swim up and down in the bowl.

The Power of Water

27

Turn on a faucet in your home until a stream of water trickles out. Then, put your hand directly under the faucet, and try to stop the water from coming out. You can't? This experiment will help you understand why you have to turn off the faucet to stop even the littlest stream of water.

YOU WILL NEED:

large-size can
hammer
nail
(birthday-candle size)
freezer tape
tap water
sink

What to do: With the hammer and a nail, punch three holes into one side of the can. Put one hole near the bottom of the can, just above the rim. Make the other two holes about a finger digit (1/2 inch) apart, going up the side of the can, above the first hole.

Cover all three of the holes with one long strip of freezer tape, then fill the can with tap water.

Place the can on the edge of a sink, with the holes positioned over the basin, and rip off the tape.

What happens:

The water stream from the lowest hole at the bottom of the can is the longest. The water stream from the middle hole is next longest, and the stream from the highest hole is the shortest.

Why: The water at the bottom of the can is under more water pressure than the water above it. The more pressure there is, the longer the stream of water.

Your faucet is like the long stream from the lowest hole. Some cities pump water into tall tanks, or towers. The pressure of the water from these tall containers forces water through long pipes beneath the ground and into people's homes. The water from the faucet has all that pressure behind it, that's why you can't stop it with just your finger or hand.

You didn't really think that all that water was right inside your wall, did you?

28 Ice Boat Float

What strange thing about water protects hundreds of millions of fish in lakes and rivers each winter? Here's how to find out.

What to do: Place the ice cube in the jar of water.

What happens: The ice cube floats like a boat.

Why: When water molecules freeze, they expand and spread out. This means that ice is not as heavy or dense as water. Because frozen water is lighter than regular water, it floats! This lucky law of nature causes water to freeze from the top down. When the layer of water on the surface turns to ice, it prevents the water below it, where the fish live and swim, from freezing, too. So, in winter, the fish's watery world is protected by a floating "sky" of ice.

29 The Floating Glass

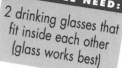

YOU WILL NEED:
2 drinking glasses that fit inside each other (glass works best)

Floating clouds, yes; but floating glasses?

What to do: In one drinking glass, pour in just enough water to cover the bottom. Then place the second glass inside the first.

What happens: The inside glass floats. (If this does not happen, add a little more water and try again.)

Why: The amount of water in the bottom of the first, outer glass is heavier than the weight of the inside glass.

It was Archimedes, a Greek mathematician who lived over 2,000 years ago (287–212 B.C.), who discovered that a floating object displaces, or pushes out of its way, an amount of liquid equal to its own volume.

Disappearing Salt

30

YOU WILL NEED:

tap water
clear drinking glass
drinking straw
box of salt
measuring cup

If you have ever gone swimming in the ocean, you have probably tasted salt in the water. No matter how hard you looked, though, you couldn't see it. Why not?

What to do: Fill the glass right to the brim with warm tap water. Measure a half-cup of salt and, very slowly, pour it into the full glass of water, while stirring gently with the straw.

What happens: If you pour carefully, you can add the entire half-cup of salt to the full glass of water without any of the water overflowing.

Why: The water does not spill over when the salt is added because no extra room is needed. The molecules of water have spaces between them. These spaces are filled nicely by the molecules of salt, just like pouring sand into a jar filled with marbles. (The sand finds its way into the spaces left by the marbles.) Such a neat arrangement between two substances is called a solution.

"Freeze Me and I'll Burst!"

31

Have you ever had the water pipes in your home burst because water froze inside them? The following experiment explains why this can happen.

YOU WILL NEED:

small jar
tap water
square of cardboard

What to do: Fill the jar to the brim with tap water. Cover the jar's top completely with the cardboard square. Now, carefully place the jar in the freezer and wait until the water freezes.

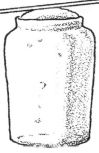

What happens: The frozen water lifts the cardboard square above the top of the jar.

Why: When the temperature of water drops below 32°F, or freezes, its molecules spread out and need more space—just like when water is heated (water is strange in this way). The freezing water molecules push up out of the jar looking for room to spread out.

If, instead of just laying a loose piece of cardboard on top, you had put a tight-fitting lid on the jar, what would have happened? The freezing water molecules would have expanded and broken the jar. This is what can happen to your water pipes in winter. To prevent their pipes from bursting, some people allow faucets to drip, drip, drip, on freezing winter nights.

32 ◆ 1 + 1 Does Not Always = 2

You might be a good math student, but you will have to be
a good physics student to figure out this experiment.

YOU WILL NEED:

large-size glass jar
masking tape
pen
cup of sugar
measuring cup
paper towel
drinking straw
warm water

What to do: Place a strip of masking
tape down the outside of the jar. Pour one
cup of warm water into the jar and mark
the level that it reaches on the tape. Then,
add a second cup of warm water and,
again, mark the water level on the tape.
Empty all of the water out of the jar and
dry the inside of it with a paper towel.
Now, pour one cup of warm water into the
jar. Follow that with one cup of sugar. Stir
this solution well with the straw
and then check the liquid level
on the masking-tape measuring
strip.

What happens: The liquid
level of one cup of water plus
one cup of sugar does not reach
the two-cup mark of the tape.

Why: If you caught the clue word,
solution, when you were instructed to
stir the sugar and water together, you
probably already know the answer.
The substances in a solution fit neatly
together, like puzzle parts. Instead of
taking up their own space, the grains of
sugar simply fill in the empty spaces
around the water molecules to make something
entirely new, a solution called sugar water… but
less of it than you thought you would have when you
added the sugar and water measurements.

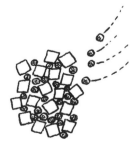

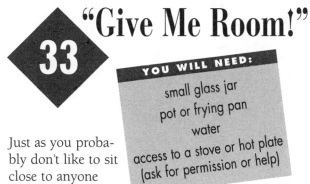

33 "Give Me Room!"

YOU WILL NEED:

small glass jar
pot or frying pan
water
access to a stove or hot plate
(ask for permission or help)

Just as you probably don't like to sit close to anyone when you are hot and sweaty, neither does a molecule of hot water.

What to do: Put some water into the bottom of the pot and place it on the stove or hot plate. Fill the jar right to the brim with water. Then, carefully, so you don't spill the water, place the jar in the middle of the pot. Turn the stove or hot plate on high heat and wait a few minutes as the water in the pot heats and begins to boil. Watch the water in the jar.

What happens: The water in the jar overflows into the pot.

Why: Like other liquids, water expands and needs more space when it is heated. As the water gets hot, the molecules in the jar start to bounce around rapidly, bumping against each other and looking for room to spread out, until they spill out over the top.

Warning: Turn off the stove or hot plate and let the water cool before removing the jar from the pot.

34 The Shrinking Molecule

When you are very cold, you sometimes huddle up, trying to make your body smaller and smaller to keep warm. What does a water molecule do when it's cold?

YOU WILL NEED:

jar
tap water
access to a freezer
kitchen timer or watch

What to do: Fill the jar to the brim with tap water. Place the jar uncovered in the freezer. Set the timer for 30 minutes. When the time is up, take the jar from the freezer.

What happens: The water level in the jar drops below the brim, even though none of the water has splashed out.

Why: As the water's temperature gets colder, to about 39°F, its molecules contract, or huddle closer together—maybe to keep warm. As a result of this "scrunching up," the molecules of cold water in the jar take up less space than they did before.

Shy Blue

Have you ever had a shy moment, such as at a family reunion, when you wanted to run and hide? If you have ever felt this way, then you can sympathize with Shy Blue.

YOU WILL NEED:
white plate
water
blue food coloring
rubbing alcohol
eyedropper or
drinking straw

What to do: Take some water and pour a small circle of it in the middle of the plate. Put three or four drops of food coloring into the water. Now, fill the eyedropper with alcohol and then squeeze it out, letting the drops fall against the circle of water. Do it again.

What happens: Shy blue trembles and shrinks back, away from the alcohol.

Why: Both the water and the rubbing alcohol have something called surface tension, a thin, invisible "skin" that holds them together. The surface tension of the water is stronger than the alcohol's, so it pulls its molecules away from the alcohol, trying to escape from its touch.

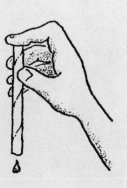

Make a "Dropper"

If you don't have an eyedropper (or medicine dropper) for use in some of these experiments, you can use a drinking straw. To do this, put the end of the straw into the liquid you need. Slowly and carefully, suck on the straw to pull a little of the liquid into it; then quickly put your finger over the top of the straw. Air pressure will hold the liquid inside. Next, move the straw into position and release your finger, and your "drops."

Square Bubbles from Square Holes?

Can it be done? Try the following experiment to see if you can blow a square soap bubble.

What to do: Bend the wire or pipe cleaner into a square shape with a handle. With your finger, mix some water with a few drops of dishwashing detergent in the saucer. Adding two or three drops of glycerin makes bubbles last longer. Next, dip the side of the square shape into the soapy solution. Be sure to completely cover the shape with the mixture. Lift the square form to your mouth and blow gently.

What happens: The bubble that emerges from the square form is not square, but round.

Why: The culprit is surface tension—that attraction of molecules for each other that forms a "skin" over them. In this case, the surface tension of the soapy water making up the bubble pulls it into a rounded shape, no matter what shape you use to make the bubble. The attraction of the molecules makes a sphere, or ball, because that's the shape that allows them to be closest together.

More Than Enough

Is a cup of water full when it's full? Can it be more than full? Seeing is believing.

What to do: On a table or countertop, set the cup in the saucer and fill it to the brim with tap water. Next, draw some tap water into the eyedropper. Add at least 20 drops of water, one after the other, to the full cup. Then bend over so that you are level with the cup and look at the water's surface from the side.

What happens: Without spilling, the water rises over the rim of the cup like a large bubble.

Why: When the water molecules across the surface are linked together with surface tension, they are strong enough to hold back the water so that it rises above the cup's rim without spilling. At some point, if more water drops are added, the mound of water in the cup will become so high and heavy that the surface molecules will lose their grip on each other and will tumble out of the cup and into the saucer. Ouch!

Water "Glue"

YOU WILL NEED:
faucet with running
water
large metal spoon

While water and flour mixed together make a paste that will hold paper together, water "glue" (without the flour) is really a trick your eyes play on you.

What to do: Hold the rounded part of the spoon (bottom side up) under the stream of water.

What happens: The water sticks to the spoon as if it were glued to it.

Why: The reduced air pressure under the water on the spoon's rounded bottom holds the flowing water against the spoon, rather than allowing it to splash away. But, it is the rapid movement of the running water, so fast that your eye can't following the speeding molecules, that makes it look as if the water were "glued" to the spoon.

What next: Turn the spoon over, right side up, and hold it under the stream of water from the faucet again. Does the water come unglued this time?

Stick Together, Stay Together

YOU WILL NEED:
foam plastic cup
pencil or nail
another cup or drinking glass
water
sink

You often use water to wash off your sticky hands, but have you ever thought that water itself might be sticky? Let's find out.

What to do: Using the pencil or nail, punch two small holes in the bottom of the foam cup. Make the holes as close together as possible without allowing them to touch. Next, fill the other cup with water, hold the cup with the holes up over the sink basin, and pour the cup of water into it. Now, very quickly, using your thumb and index finger, pinch together the two streams of water flowing out of the holes.

What happens: The two separate streams of water come together and form one stream. (You might have to refill the cup a couple of times until you get the pinch right.)

Why: Water molecules have such an attraction for each other that, when they come near, they grab on to one another and stick together. This sticking-together action is known as cohesion.

Fishing for "Clippies"

YOU WILL NEED:

6 paper clips
(colored ones make fishing more fun)
large bowl of water
facial tissue
pencil

With this experiment, you can fish at your kitchen table, on your back porch, or anywhere you choose.

What to do: Straighten one of the paper clips, shaping one end into a hook. Open and lay the facial tissue across the bowl of water. Next, quickly but gently place the remaining paper clips, one at a time, on top of the tissue. Then, tap around the edges of the tissue with a pencil until the paper sinks to the bottom of the bowl, leaving the "clippie fish" afloat.

Now that your homemade fishing pond is stocked, use the hook that you made to see how many clippies you can catch.

What to do: If you are careful, you hook all five clippie fish. If not, the clippies escape to the bottom of the bowl.

Why: Surface tension, that invisible skin that covers the water in the bowl, holds the paper-clip fish within reach of your hook. As long as you don't break that tension, you can keep fishing and end up with the "Catch of the Day."

Unfortunately, if you break the surface tension with your hook, the weight of the clips causes them to sink.

42 Water-Drop Art

YOU WILL NEED:

large piece of waxed paper
wooden toothpick
5 small cups of water
red, green, yellow, and blue
food coloring
eyedropper or drinking straw
paper towels (optional)

While you have probably only used water to clean up after an art lesson, the following experiment will show you how to create a picture using water as the main ingredient.

What to do: Put three or four drops of red coloring into one of four cups of water and do the same with the green, yellow, and blue coloring to make four cups of "water paints." Leave the fifth cup of water clear. Next, spread the waxed paper out on a flat surface. With the eye-dropper, put three or four drops of each color water paint on the waxed paper.

Remember to rinse the eyedropper in the cup of clear water first when you change colors. Continue by dipping one end of a toothpick in the cup of clear water and then putting it near, but not touching, a water drop.

What happens: The water drop moves toward the toothpick, gliding easily over the waxed paper, to help create a picture or design.

Why: The water drop rolls around on the waxed paper because the wax keeps it from soaking in. The water drop is drawn to the wet toothpick because of cohesion—the tendency of molecules that are alike to stick together.

What next: Continue creating your picture or design using water drops in each of the four colors.

When you are finished, you can save the pattern by laying a paper towel over it and letting the towel absorb it. If you don't want to save your work, you can let the different-colored drops touch each other—and watch as they gobble each other up.

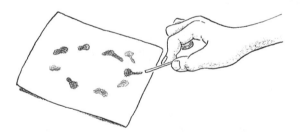

YOU WILL NEED:

eyedropper or
drinking straw
glass of water
rubbing alcohol
cooking oil
plastic or paper cup

43

Oil versus Water

44

Make a Waterwheel

YOU WILL NEED:

a plastic-foam or
plastic-coated plate
scissors
pencil
water faucet

Huge waterwheels are used in large rivers to generate, or produce, a certain kind of electricity called hydroelectric power. You can make a model of a waterwheel in your sink.

"Oil and water don't mix." After this experiment, next time you hear anyone say that, you'll know why.

What to do: Pull a few drops of alcohol into the eyedropper and then watch as you release them slowly just below the surface of the water in the glass.

Next, pour some cooking oil into the plastic or paper cup and refill the eye dropper with a few drops of cooking oil and add it to the water just as you did the alcohol.

What happens: The alcohol just disappears. The oil forms drops that float to the surface and stay there.

Why: Water and alcohol attract each other. On leaving the dropper, the molecules of alcohol rush to grab hold of the nearest water molecules, fitting together perfectly to form a solution.

Oil and water are the opposite. They push each other away. So the oil molecules pull together against the pressure of the surrounding water to form bubbles. Because water is heavier than oil, it presses down and the bubbles of oil are forced upward to float on the surface of the water.

What to do: Using the scissors, cut six 1-inch slits spaced evenly around the outside edge of the plate to form the waterwheel's blades. Bend these blades away from the plate to make them more efficient. Next, push a pencil through the center of the plate and work it back and forth a few times so that the pencil moves easily.

Now, turn on the water faucet so that a fast stream of water flows out. Hold the pencil so that one blade of the plate catches the water.

What happens: The waterwheel will begin to spin!

Why: The water tumbles out of the faucet, pushes against one blade of the plate, then another, and another, until the waterwheel is powered into motion. This motion can be used to generate more power. That is why electricity plants are built next to dams or fast-flowing rivers.

Deep-Bottle Diver

If you have ever played submarine in the bathtub, you will like the following experiment.

What to do: Fill the bottle to the top with water. Pull a little tap water up into the eyedropper and place it inside the bottle so that the dropper floats near the top. Replace the bottle cap. Now, press the sides of the bottle in and then release them.

What happens: When you press the sides of the bottle, the eyedropper "diver" sinks to the bottom. When you release the sides, the "diver" rises again.

Why: When the sides of the plastic bottle are pressed in, it increases the water pressure equally throughout the bottle and some additional water is forced into the eyedropper. This makes it "dive." The amount of water in the eyedropper can be controlled by changing the water pressure in the bottle: pressing = more pressure; not pressing = less pressure.

The Warm and Cold of It

46

When swimming in a lake, have you ever glided down deep beneath the smooth surface and found the water there to be suddenly colder? Here's why.

What to do: Fill each of the balloons with cold water, loop the end over and tie a tight knot to keep the water inside. (If your tap water is not very cold, put some in a pitcher and add ice to cool it before filling the balloons.) Now, fill one of the jars about halfway with warm water and the other one halfway with cold water. Place a water-filled balloon into each jar.

What happens: The balloon filled with cold water sinks to the bottom of the jar of warm water but floats in the jar of cold water.

Why: Cold water is heavier than warm water because the cold-water molecules are denser, that is, stick closer together. So the weight of the cold water in the balloon drags it down to the bottom of the jar of warm water. Where the balloon floats in the jar of cold water depends on the temperature difference of the water in the balloon and the jar.

Make a Purple People-Eater

Sometimes, on a dull, rainy day, it's fun to mix up a Purple People-Eater.

YOU WILL NEED:
red food coloring
blue food coloring
2/3 cup of tap water
mixing bowl
spoon
1 cup of cornstarch
2 marbles (optional)

What to do: Put three drops of red and three drops of blue food coloring in the water to make purple. Pour the cornstarch into a mixing bowl. Slowly add the water, stirring to mix well. Now, grab a handful of the mixture and form a ball by rolling it between your hands. Stop rolling and let the mixture rest on your outstretched palm.

What happens: While you are rolling the mixture between your hands, it feels dry. When you stop rolling, the ball suddenly turns into an ooze!

Why: As you have already learned, both salt and sugar dissolve in water to form solutions. Cornstarch, however, does not form a solution with water. Instead, the cornstarch particles are simply held together by the water, creating a mixture called a suspension. When you roll the mixture in your hands, it squeezes together on all sides and feels dry. But, when you stop rolling, the cornstarch particles in the mixture drift apart, creating an ooze.

What next: Press two marble "eyes" into your Purple People Eater, and you will have created a monster that any Dr. Frankenstein would be proud of.

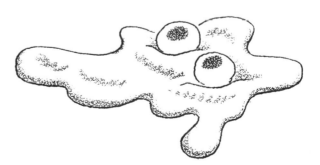

SEEING THE LIGHT

Like heat, sound, and electricity, light is a form of energy on which all life on Earth depends. Unlike sound, light can travel where there is not even any air, and it can do so at the fastest speed known—186,000 miles per second.

About Light

We see an object because light reflected from that object reaches our eyes. Over the centuries, people believed that light consisted of tiny particles. Others thought differently, although nearly everyone agreed that light traveled in straight lines. Today, scientists have learned that light sometimes acts like particles and sometimes like waves. Maybe you'll be the one to discover someday what light really is.

48

Sometimes Bigger Is Better

YOU WILL NEED:

food box or package
clear glass of water

Have you ever wondered what is in some of the food you eat? Many people do, but they don't read the ingredients listed on the side of the package because the print is so small it is hard to see. The following experiment will help you to read more about it.

What to do: Hold the food box up close to the glass and look through it at the ingredients list printed on the box.

What happens: The print on the package appears much larger and is easier to read.

Why: Because the drinking glass is curved, the light rays enter at an angle and are bent as they pass from the glass to the water. This is called refraction. The result is a homemade magnifying "glass."

49

Make Your Own Movie Screen

Have you ever wondered, at a movie theatre, how that narrow beam of light from the projection booth at the back could light up and fill a whole movie screen from so far away? Here's how.

YOU WILL NEED:

shoebox with a lid
ruler
pencil
small knife or scissors
flashlight
graph paper
(lined to make squares)
a helper

What to do: With the ruler and pencil, measure and mark out a small square in each end of the shoebox and carefully cut them out. Replace the lid of the box. Turn on the flashlight and aim the light through the square cutouts in the box while a friend or helper on the other side of the box "catches" the light on a piece of graph paper. Ask your friend first to stand close to the box, then step back one ruler length from the box, then another ruler length. Watch the light on the paper.

What happens: As your friend moves farther away from the shoebox, more and more of the squares on the graph paper are lit up, but the light's brightness begins to fade.

Why: Once the light beam passes through the holes in the shoebox, it begins to spread out. The light loses more and more of its brightness as the same amount of light from the flashlight spreads out to fill a larger area.

Also, once it reaches the paper, part of the light's energy is absorbed by the molecules in the graph paper. Other light rays bounce, or reflect, off the graph paper and scatter around the room. This is called diffusion. It is your eyes' ability to detect this reflected light which allows you to see.

The Reappearing Penny

This is a fun trick to play on your friends because your hands never touch the penny.

YOU WILL NEED:

small dish (not see-through)
table or countertop
tap water
1 penny
a helper

What to do: Put the penny in the empty dish and set it on a table or countertop. Next, while watching the penny, have your friend back away from the dish slowly until its edge just blocks the view of the penny. Tell your friend not to move, and you'll make the penny magically reappear. Then, slowly fill the dish with water.

What happens: Your friend will see the penny gradually come back into view.

Why: When you put water in the dish, it bends the light reflected from the penny around the edge of the dish to reach your friend's eye again.

---

51 Big Bold Letters

Big, bold, or fat print is easier to see than small, skinny print. Here's how to make small letters appear fatter.

YOU WILL NEED:

vegetable oil
page from a magazine (ask before you rip!)
eyedropper or drinking straw
tap water

What to do: Using your finger, place a dab of vegetable oil on a word on the magazine page. Gently, rub it into the paper. Now, using the eyedropper, put one drop of water on top of the oil-coated word.

What happens: When you read the word through the water drop, it looks bigger.

Why: The oil you rubbed in has coated or conditioned the paper so that the water does not soak in. As a result, the drop of water sits on top of the word and forms a lens. This lens changes the path of the light that reflects off the page and reaches your eyes and makes the word look fatter.

This same principle is used in making eyeglasses, except that it is glass, not water, that bends the light, causing it to reach our eyes at the correct angle to see better.

Amazing 3-Ring Light Show

When blue, red, and green paint are mixed together, they make black. When blue, red, and green light are mixed together… a surprising thing happens! Can you guess what?

What to do: Using the rubber bands, fasten a different-colored sheet over the head of each flashlight.
Now, place the three flashlights on a table or bench, or get one or two helpers or friends to help you, and aim the flashlights at the wall. The two outside flashlights should be turned slightly toward the middle one, which should be aimed straight ahead.
Then, turn on all three flashlights, moving the two outer ones so that the three circles of light on the wall overlap.

What happens: A rounded triangle of white light appears in the middle of the three overlapped colored circles.

Why: Light has within it all colors, which is why it sometimes makes something called a continuous spectrum, in other words, a rainbow.

By passing the white light through the red sheet, only red light comes out. The same thing happens with the other color sheets, so you get the three primary colors: red, green and blue. When all the colors come together again, in the middle of the lights, the mixture of all the three colors forms a rounded white triangle.

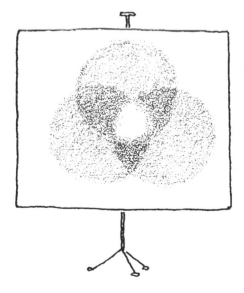

SOUNDS LIKE FUN

What you know as sound are vibrations that travel to the ear via a sound carrier. Because there is so much air, it is the most common carrier of sound, but it is also the slowest. Sound travels four times as fast in water as it does in air. Sound travels faster at high temperatures, but slower high in the atmosphere or on mountaintops where there are fewer air molecules to vibrate.

About Sound

Sound waves from vibrating objects are sent out in all directions. If you could see them, the waves might look like the circles, or ripples that spread out when a rock is thrown into a quiet pool of water. The object making the vibrations, or sound, would be in the center of the smallest circle.

Sound is measured by decibels. These measurements go from 1 (a sound that can barely be heard) to 130 or more. A sound that measures 120 decibels hurts most people's ears. Some sounds can be so high, or squeaky, in pitch that people can't hear them, but some animals can.

Deep "C", High "C"

Sound is made up of waves that move through the air much like the rippling circles that move across the surface when a rock is thrown into a quiet pond.

What to do: First, hold the opening of the large jar to your mouth and hum into it; then hum the same way into the smaller jar.

What happens: A deeper sound is heard when you hum into the large jar, and a higher sound when you hum into the small jar.

Why: The pitch of the sound depends on the height and diameter of the jar. Because there is more room in the large jar, your humming makes longer sound waves, so you hear a deeper, lower sound in that jar.

The sound waves in the smaller jar have less room, so they are shortened, and the frequency, or pitch, of the sound you hear is higher.

What next: Try some other empty jars. How do they sound?

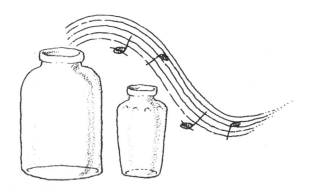

Catching Sound

The following experiment will show you how you can produce an echo, without leaving home in search of a canyon.

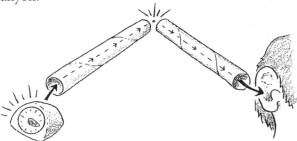

What to do: Place one end of each cardboard tube on a slant against a wall, so that they come to a point, or make at least a 45° angle.

Have your helper hold the ticking clock at the other, open end of his or her tube. Listen at the open end of your tube.

What happens: You can clearly hear the ticking sound of the clock through the cardboard tube.

Why: Normally, the sound waves sent out into the air by the ticking clock would scatter in all directions, becoming fainter the farther away from the clock they traveled.

By using the tubes, the sound waves of the clock's ticking are captured and directed down one tube. Then, if the tubes are held correctly, the sound waves bounce off the wall and shoot up through the second tube for you to hear—just like an echo.

Change places, now, so your helper is on the receiving end of the bouncing sound waves.

The Amazing Hum-o-comb

55

You don't need private lessons, sheet music, or even a teacher to learn how to play this musical instrument, and making it is a snap.

YOU WILL NEED:
tissue wrapping paper
pocket comb

What to do: Wrap the tissue paper around the comb, teeth side down. Now, hold the comb up against your lips and hum loudly.

What happens: Even though you aren't blowing on the tissue paper at all, you feel it vibrating. Your humming sounds different, too.

Why: The tissue paper vibrates, just like your vocal cords, because sound waves from your humming are hitting it. The vibrations of the tissue paper molecules add a whole new sound to your humming.

What next: Don't stop with one selection. Any song that you know can be played on a comb. Get several friends together and put on an Amazing Hum-o-comb concert.

56 Was It Ripped or Torn?

YOU WILL NEED:
old rag or piece of
fabric (ask before
you use it)

You snag your clothing on a nail or something at school. You can tell right away, without looking, if it was ripped or torn. How? Physics tells us, listen to the sound.

What to do: Hold the edge of the cloth in your two hands and pull evenly, tearing the cloth slowly. Now, grab the cloth and yank it apart suddenly, so that it rips in your hands.

What happens: When you pulled slowly, the tearing cloth made a lower sound than when you pulled suddenly.

Why: Each time a thread in the cloth is broken, the molecules in the air around it are set into motion. When the cloth is torn, the air molecules are not bumped around as fast and the sound, or pitch, is lower.

When the cloth is ripped, however, the air molecules are bounded around at a higher rate of speed, and a higher-pitched sound is heard.

Make Your Own Sound Studio

Do you like to sing in the shower? Usually your singing sounds better there than it does in the family room. How come?

YOU WILL NEED:

tape recorder with separate microphone

very large new or clean metal bucket

a helper

What to do: Hold the microphone and turn on the tape recorder. Sing any song that you like. Turn off the tape recorder.

Still holding the microphone, pick up and put the bucket over your head. Then, turn on the tape recorder again. (You might need a friend to help you here, with that bucket over your head!)

Now, sing the same song that you sang before. Remove the bucket and turn the recorder off when you are finished singing. Rewind and play through the tape.

What happens: Your song sounds richer in tone and louder in volume when you sing with your head in the bucket.

Why: The sound waves from your voice cause the molecules in the metal bucket and air inside it to vibrate and "build up" your normal voice, much like a professional sound studio does for recording artists. The same thing happens when you sing in the shower.

The Silence of Snow

Is it quieter outside after a snowfall? It's true that the snow does provide a soft carpet for your feet, but what about all the other noises?

What to do: Glue the cotton balls to the inside of one paper cup until it is completely covered with the cotton "snow." Then, blow the whistle inside the cup with no cotton stuffing and listen to the sound. Next, put the whistle inside the snow-covered paper cup and blow again.

What happens: The whistle's sound in the first cup is loud. Inside the "snow-filled" paper cup,

YOU WILL NEED:

2 paper clips
18 or 20 cotton balls
white glue
whistle

however, the whistle's shrill notes sound like a flute being played in a closet.

Why: Like snowflakes, cotton balls have hundreds of tiny spaces between them. Sound waves get trapped in these tiny spaces and are muffled, like in winter when you can't hear someone trying to talk to you through a heavy scarf or muffler.

Now, you also know why there is a law requiring all cars to have mufflers.

Cigar-Box Guitar

Years ago, many people made their own musical instruments. They loved music, but instruments were expensive and they had little money to buy them. Today, right now, you can do the same thing.

YOU WILL NEED:

cigar box (or similar box with rigid sides)

6 assorted rubber bands (including 1 very wide and 1

What to do: Open the lid of the cigar box and keep it open (or remove it altogether). Now, beginning with the widest rubber band, then to the next-to-the-widest, place them lengthwise around the cigar box. Try to space the rubber bands equally, about one finger-width apart.

When you have all six "guitar stings" in place, give each of them a pluck.

What happens: The wide rubber band has a low sound, the very narrow "string" has a high sound, and the sounds of the other rubber bands are somewhere in between.

Why: The wide rubber band has a low vibration rate and does not produce many sound waves.

The narrow rubber band, however, has a high vibration rate and produces a higher number of sound waves with a higher tone or pitch.

But that's not all. Pitch also depends on the degree of tightness, or tautness, of the "string." A wider but short rubber band that is pulled very tight might make a higher sound than a narrower rubber band that is put on more loosely.

What next: Listen to the sounds of each of your instrument's strings again. If needed, switch them around so that the sounds are in order, from the lowest to the highest. When you are ready, sing a tune and accompany yourself on your cigar-box guitar.

Dance, Sprinkles, Dance

60

YOU WILL NEED:

small, round oatmeal box, with top

sharp knife (ask for permission or help)

candy sprinkles

Does certain music make you want to dance like crazy? It's not wild—it's physics!

What to do: Cut an egg-size hole in the side of the oatmeal box, about 2 finger-digits (1½ inches) up from the bottom. Next, put a few sprinkles on the top of the box.

Now, put your mouth to the hole in the box and hum loudly. Begin with low notes and then move on up to the higher ones.

What happens: Somewhere, as you go up the scale of notes, the candy sprinkles will begin to dance!

Why: The molecules on the box top are set into motion when one certain note is reached. That particular note is called the box top's resonant frequency—a note that makes it all happen. When the box top vibrates, the sprinkles dance.

Other hummed notes will make the sprinkles move slightly, but only one really makes them jump!

Natural Vibrations

61

Do you know why soldiers deliberately walk out-of-step rather than march when crossing a bridge? Read on.

YOU WILL NEED:

2 small soda bottles (same kind)

a helper

What to do: Hold one of the small bottles to your ear and listen while your helper or friend blows across the mouth of the second bottle until it makes a clear sound.

What happens: The bottle that you are holding to your ear will vibrate "in sympathy," making a similar but weaker sound than your helper's bottle produced.

Why: Depending upon its size and shape, each object has its own natural rate of vibration. When two objects have the same vibration rate, like the two similar bottles, one can cause the other one to vibrate. When this happens, the two objects are said to be "in resonance."

The officers of soldiers approaching a bridge know that the bridge has a crumpling point related to its natural vibration rate. If the soldiers' even footsteps should happen to match the bridge's natural vibration rate, it could begin to swing and collapse! So soldiers are ordered to walk naturally as they cross the bridge.

62 Musical Nails

Visitors usually knock or ring the bell at your house door, but have no way to announce their arrival at a screened porch or patio door. A nail chime is the perfect welcoming sound.

YOU WILL NEED:
wire coat hanger
10 different-size nails
10 pieces of string

What to do: Tie a string to each nail. Tie the other end of each piece of string to the straight lower bar of the coat hanger. Hang the coat hanger on a door knob and open and close the door.

What happens: You hear a pleasant chiming sound as the nails jingle.

Why: When the door is opened and closed, the movement causes the nails to hit against each other and the door frame and vibrate. Each nail, depending on its size and what it is made of, makes a different note. All the nails vibrating together produce the chiming sound.

If the pieces of string were not attached to the coat hanger, and you just held them in your hand, the nails would not vibrate together or as long. Also, the sound from each nail would be much softer and quieter.

Make a Megaphone 63

Have you ever cupped your hands around your mouth when you wanted to yell a message to someone far away? You were on the right track.

What to do: Put the rubber band around the middle of the plastic jug to serve as your cutting guide. Then, carefully, force the sharp point of the scissors through the lower part of the jug, below the rubber band.

Following the edge of the rubber band, cut the jug apart. Discard the bottom half of the jug. Now, speak in a normal voice to someone across the room. Then, talk into the mouth of the megaphone that is aimed across the room.

YOU WILL NEED:
clean plastic milk jug or well-rinsed bleach container
large rubber band
heavy scissors or kitchen shears

What happens: Your voice is louder and can be heard farther when the megaphone is used.

Why: When you just speak, the sound waves ripple out in all directions, getting weaker the farther out they go.

The megaphone, on the other hand, aims all your sound waves in one direction, like a baseball hit to centerfield. Sound waves sent through a megaphone, therefore, lose less of their energy in transit and arrive with more volume.

What next: Create an original design for your megaphone, using markers, stickers, and cutouts. Decorate it with your school colors and your name. Don't forget to take it with you next time you go to the ballpark.

Dancing Cereal Puffs

While air molecules are usually invisible, in this experiment, disguised as cereal puffs, they dance and pass along the sound.

YOU WILL NEED:

10 pieces of puffed cereal

10 pieces of thread

coat hanger

rubber band

a helper (optional)

What to do: Tie a piece of thread around each piece of cereal. Tie the other ends of the threads onto the straight lower bar of the coat hanger. Hook the coat hanger onto a shelf or the back of a chair, or ask someone to hold it for you.

Then, holding one end of the rubber band in your clenched teeth, pull the other end of the band toward, but not touching, one of the middle pieces of puffed cereal. Pluck the stretched band like a banjo. Be careful not to let it snap out of your hand.

What happens: The middle cereal puff begins to move back and forth, touching its neighboring puffs on each side.

Why: The vibrations of the plucked rubber band stir the air molecules around and inside the middle piece of cereal. Like the invisible air molecules, the puff dances from side to side and passes along the vibrations to the other nearby puffs.

The cereal pieces will continue to swing until all the vibrations, or energy, from the plucked rubber band are gone.

If the rubber band is plucked harder a second time, more of the cereal pieces will move because the sound and vibrating air molecules will travel farther. None of the cereal puffs, however, will sway very far.

Wild Animal Calls

If you like to play jungle safari, here is a way to make your adventure sound more realistic.

What to do: Use the pencil to poke a hole in the middle of the bottom of the plastic cup. Push one end of the cotton string into and through the hole, then tie that end of the string tightly around the middle of the toothpick. Pull the string back through the cup so that the toothpick fits nicely in the bottom of the cup. (Break the ends off the toothpick, if necessary, to make it fit.)

Squeeze out any excess water from the paper towel (you don't want to get the string too wet). Then wrap the towel around the string near the cup. Now, squeezing the paper towel tightly around the string, pull down.

What happens:
A loud "screaking" sound is heard.

Why: The friction from pulling the paper towel down the string causes vibrations, which move along the string to the toothpick in the cup. From the toothpick, the vibrations travel on to the bottom and sides of the cup. Not only do these sound vibrations move farther, but they get louder because the cup also acts like a megaphone, sending the vibrations out into the surrounding air molecules.

What next: To make a variety of "animal" calls, try using different-size plastic cups. You can also experiment with different-texture strings for some really wild sounds.

A Matter of Gravity

Gravity is the pull that objects have on other objects around them. All objects have gravity, which means that they are always trying to pull other objects toward them. The larger an object, the stronger its pull. Because the Earth itself is the largest object in our world, the pull of its gravity is the strongest we can feel.

About Gravity

It was in 1687 that Isaac Newton discovered and proved the existence of a force called gravity. The story goes that one day Newton was sitting under an apple tree watching the moon moving in the sky when he was almost hit on the head by a falling apple. Many people before Newton had seen apples fall to the ground, but he not only saw it happen, he also wondered why... and figured it out.

When you throw a ball in the air, gravity pulls it down. When you sit on the sofa, gravity holds you down, and when you walk, gravity keeps your feet on the ground. Without gravity we would all float off into outer space.

Feel the Force

You can't see the force of gravity, but it is all around you. Want to prove it?

What to do: Place the low chair in front of you. Get ready, and jump onto the chair. Next, turn around, get ready, and jump down. Feel the difference?

Do it again. This time, when you jump down, close your eyes. Feel it this time?

What happens: It is a lot harder to jump up onto the chair than to jump down.

Why: Gravity is the force that pulls all objects down toward the middle of the Earth. When you jump up, you are jumping against the force of gravity, which is pulling you back. When you jump down, the force is with you. It is doing all of the work. You really only have to step off the chair seat.

67

Which Drops Faster?

Aristotle, a Greek philosopher (384–322 B.C.), once believed that the heavier an object was, the faster it would fall. Was he right?

What to do: Stand on the chair with the crumpled paper in one hand and the shoe in the other. Hold them out in front of you as high as you can and let them go at the same time.

What happens: The heavier shoe and the lighter ball of paper both hit the floor at the same time.

Why: Aristotle was wrong. (He was a philosopher, not a physics teacher.) An object's weight does not affect the speed at which it falls, which is a constant.

However, an object's shape does affect its speed. For example, if the paper had not been crumpled into a ball, the air hitting its under-surface as it fell would have slowed its rate of fall and the shoe would have hit the floor first.

Why not get another sheet of paper and try it?

Find the Center of Gravity

YOU WILL NEED:
any unbreakable object
table or countertop

Want to find an object's center of gravity? It may sound hard, but it's really very simple.

What to do: Slowly push the unbreakable object to the table's edge. Keep pushing, pushing, pushing until—

What happens: The object suddenly falls to the floor!

Why: When the object's center of gravity passes the table's edge, the object will fall to the floor. Try to balance the object on the table's edge. When you do, its center of gravity has been found.

Wacky Ball

YOU WILL NEED:
Ping-Pong ball
flat-headed straight pin
tabletop

If you have ever tried to play Ping-Pong with a ball that had a nick in it, then you have played Wacky ball.

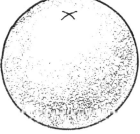

What to do: Press the pin firmly into any spot on the ball. Now, roll the ball across the tabletop.

What happens: The ball always stops rolling with the pin head touching the tabletop.

Why: Before the pin was pressed into the ball, all of its weight was concentrated in its middle, the point known as the center of gravity.

With the pin pushed into the side of the ball, its center of gravity is shifted from the middle to the side with the pin. Now, the ball will stop rolling only when the pin is at its lowest possible point, pulled there by the force of gravity. That ball's not as wacky as it seems.

Anti-Gravity Magic

70

YOU WILL NEED:
2 small clear-plastic bottles
bowl
blue food coloring
(or other dark color)
index card or piece
of cardboard
access to hot and cold
water faucets
funnel
helper

Everyone knows that water flows downwards. It has to because of gravity's pull. But here is a fun way to defy gravity and make water flow upwards…just this once.

What to do: About 30 minutes before you want to do the experiment, fill one of the bottles with cold tap water and put it in the refrigerator to make sure it's cold. When you are ready to start, turn on the hot water faucet and let the water run until it is very hot. Turn off the tap.

Put the funnel in the second small bottle, place it under the faucet, and carefully fill the bottle with hot tap water.

Set the bottle of hot water in a bowl on a table or counter top. Add three or four drops of food coloring to the hot water. Wait a few seconds until the coloring mixes with the water.

Now, remove the first bottle of cold water from the refrigerator and place the index card or cardboard over the top of it.

Next, holding the index card firmly against the bottle's mouth, with your helper's assistance quickly turn the bottle upside down and set the bottle of cold water on top of the bottle of hot colored water.

Match up the two bottle tops end-to-end, then ask your helper to hold the two bottles steady while you slide the index card out from in between.

What happens: The blue hot water flows upward into the cold-water bottle, seeming to defy gravity!

Why: Hot water is not as heavy as cold water and its molecules are more active, so it rises to the top of the cold water, taking the blue food coloring with it.

Gradually, the hot and cold waters will mix until the temperature is evenly warm throughout, and the blue food coloring will be distributed between both bottles.

Physics Mix

In earlier experiments, you have learned something about heat and air, water and light, sound and gravity.

About Physics

But there is still more, much more, to physics. There are laws of motion, natural rhythms, and strange forces that surround you and that you can learn to understand and use.

The experiments in this short section will just touch on these other areas of physics. Here you will discover the whirlpool in your home, the energy you create by brushing your hair, and the working pendulum. But when you finish these experiments, it is only a start. Physics has so much more for you to examine and study, to learn from and to marvel at. And it's all around you. All you have to do is look.

The Deep, Dark Hole

YOU WILL NEED:
mixing bowl
water
large spoon

Ever try to make a hole in water? It's easy.

What to do: Fill the mixing bowl half-full of water. Then, take the spoon and stir the water quickly until it is spinning around the bowl.

What happens: The water climbs the sides of the mixing bowl, leaving a "hole" in the middle.

Why: When you stir, the spinning water moves away from the center of the bowl because of the outward pull of centrifugal force and forms a whirlpool, or vortex.

The "hole" that forms at the bottom of the whirlpool is smaller than the one at the top because of water pressure. The weight of the water above prevents the water below it from spreading out too much.

A Gyroscope in Your Pocket

YOU WILL NEED:
large-size coin

Did you know that the reason you are able to stay up on a moving bicycle is because you are riding on two gyroscopes? Read on.

What to do: Try to balance the coin, make it stand up on end. Can you do it? Now, hold the coin straight up and "flick" it with your finger to make it spin.

What happens: Although the coin first fell over when you tried to balance it, the spinning coin balances on edge for a moment, until it slows down.

Why: As it turns, the coin becomes a simple gyroscope, or top. The spinning motion causes the coin to stand on its end. The coin's center of gravity now runs straight down through it from edge to edge, keeping the spinning coin in place and balanced.

What next: When you become an expert coin-spinner, try getting the coin to spin on smaller and narrower surfaces, like the end of a can or a glass, or on a book or a ruler.

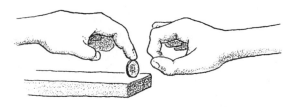

The Kissing Balloons

If kissing is frowned upon in your school, you'd better get permission for these two "kissing cousins" to visit your science class.

What to do: Blow up the balloons and tie a string to each one and hold them. Now, using the markers, carefully draw a "boy" face on one balloon and a "girl" face on the other.

When the marker ink is dry, hold the balloons and rub each face several times with the flannel or rayon cloth. Put the balloons face to face.

What happens: The balloons will begin to kiss. They will also kiss your hair and your sweater, if you let them.

Why: When the piece of flannel or rayon is rubbed across their faces, the friction, or rubbing, charges the balloons with static electricity. Made up of positive and negative electrical charges, which attract each other, it is very sticky stuff.

Unlike regular electricity that flows through

> **YOU WILL NEED:**
> 2 light-colored latex balloons
> 2 pieces of string
> piece of flannel or rayon cloth
> permanent markers

wires and is very dangerous, static electricity stays in one place. Although it can give you a scary "zap" sometimes, it is really harmless.

What next: Give the balloons a few more rubs, to make more static electricity, and see what other materials or things in your home the balloons will "kiss."

Want to see static electricity? Turn out the lights and do some experimenting in the dark.

Make a Balloon Rocket

A balloon rocket works the same way a real rocket does, except that it is powered by air instead of rocket fuel.

YOU WILL NEED:
balloon

What to do: Blow up the balloon as full as possible and hold the end tightly closed with your fingers. Now, let go.

What happens: Although it won't head for the moon, the balloon "rockets" around the room.

Why: When you blow up the balloon, the air pressure inside presses equally in all directions and makes the balloon large and round. Everything is so perfectly balanced that the balloon simply floats as you hold it tightly.

As soon as you let go of the balloon, the air inside rushes to get out. The perfect balance of air pressure is gone.

As the air goes in one direction, the balloon goes in the other. This action-reaction motion sends the balloon zooming forward, until all of the air is gone and the balloon falls to the ground.

You have just seen Sir Isaac Newton's third law of motion, "Every action has an equal and opposite reaction," in action.

The Magic Water Bucket

You can pour water out, but can you sling it out?

YOU WILL NEED:
small bucket
some rope
water

What to do: Fill the bucket half-full of water. Then tie one end of the rope to the middle of the bucket's handle. Lift the bucket off the ground with the rope and quickly start to sling the bucket around, turning and pulling on the rope until the bucket is swinging around you about waist-high.

What happens: The water stays in the bucket!

Why: As you turn, centrifugal force pulls the bucket, and the water in it, upward and outward as far as the rope will allow. Because the rope holds the bucket's opening toward you, the water is pressed against the bottom of the bucket, even against the force of gravity. Everything is great… until you try to stop! As soon as you slow down, centrifugal force becomes weak or is lost and gravity takes over. That's when, if you're not careful, the water will spill.

Pendulum Sand Painting

Sand painting is an art form. Using physics, you can create your own sand painting.

YOU WILL NEED:

coffee can with plastic lid
hammer
medium-size nail
string
light sand (the clean, store-bought kind works best)
piece of poster board
broom or mop handle
2 chairs
red sand and blue sand

What to do: Using the hammer and nail, punch a hole in the middle of the bottom of the can. Then, punch three holes equally spaced around the top edge of the can, just inside the rim.

Cut three short pieces of string, several inches long, and tie them to the can's rim through the holes. Gather the other ends of the strings together and knot them. Cut off a longer piece of string and tie it to this knot.

Set two chairs back to back, with a space between, and slide the broom handle through the chair's slats to hold it steady.

Then, tie the string with the can attached onto the middle of the broom handle. The bottom of the can should be just an inch or two above the floor.

Snap the plastic lid over the bottom of the can and fill the can with either red- or blue-tinted (and dry) sand.

Finally, sprinkle the poster board, giving it a thin layer of white sand, and position it underneath the coffee can. Pull the sand-filled coffee can slightly off to one side, remove the plastic lid to the sand can flow out, and release the can.

To adjust the pattern or give the can a little more "swing," give the string near the can a smooth, light push.

When one color is finished or you want to change colors, put the lid back on the can, put the second color in the can, remove the lid, and start the can swinging again.

What happens: As the sand streams from the can, it makes a series of arcs on the poster board, and a unique sand painting appears right before your eyes.

Why: What you have made with the coffee can is a small version of a pendulum, like Jean Bernard Léon Foucault hung in a church in 1851 to demonstrate the Earth's rotation. Allowed to swing continuously, a pendulum makes one complete circle of arcs every day.

Here, the swinging motion of the pendulum, back and forth and side to side, forms a physics-inspired pattern of curves, or ellipses, on the white sand.

It's Crystal Clear

Crystals are everywhere. Snow, sugar, salt, parts of rocks, and precious jewels are all crystals. Crystals are made up of atoms that join together in a certain different way.

About Crystals

In this part of the book, you'll make crystals from table and rock salt, bluing, sugar, washing soda, and alum. When you're finished, you can invite your friends over for a gem show and display all the crystals you've grown.

Your Diamond Ring?
Just Another Carbon Copy!

Diamonds are carbon crystals. Carbon is a material known as an element. Volcanoes were nature's chemists. The heat and pressure of volcanoes crystallized the carbon into diamonds. When lava reaches the surface of the earth, it cools and hardens and forms a rock called kimberlite. Diamonds are found in kimberlite. Tons of kimberlite have to be washed and crushed just to find one small diamond.

The diamond is the hardest substance found in the earth. An imperfect diamond, not good enough to be mounted on a ring, makes a perfect tool for cutting hard metals. Diamonds are so hard they can cut anything. (If you find something you think might be a diamond, test it by trying to cut with it. If it doesn't cut, it is probably only a piece of glass.)

Sparkling Soda

No, we're not using soda pop in this experiment, but washing soda. That's right! Although this soda is all washed up in this activity, it still sparkles!

YOU WILL NEED:
disposable cup half-filled with hot tap water
spoon
1/2 cup washing soda
magnifying hand lens

What to do: Pour the washing soda slowly into the water, stirring as you pour, until no more will dissolve. Set the cup aside and check the experiment often over the next few hours.

What happens: As the water cools and begins to evaporate, crystals form on the sides and bottom of the cup.

Why: When you dissolve the washing soda (solute) into the hot water (solvent) until no more can be dissolved, you put more solutes in the water than it can possibly hold when it is cool. When this saturated solution cools, the washing soda molecules hook up with each other and form crystals.

What next: Pour the washing soda crystals from the cup into a shallow disposable (frozen food) container. Place them in a warm, sunny place for 24 hours and let the water evaporate. (See "Astronomical White Asteroids.")

Astronomical White Asteroids

Asteroids are irregularly shaped, rocklike chunks in space. Like the planets, they revolve around the sun. Your washing soda, after it is chemically changed, will look very much like these rocklike chunks of space matter. The smallest and largest crystals can be compared to the largest and smallest asteroids, the smallest being less than one mile wide, the largest about 500 miles wide. Save these Sparkling Soda asteroid chunks for "The Gem Show," and use this information for your label.

Crazy Cave Icicles

79

You can make your own crystal rock formations (stalagmites and stalactites) to demonstrate how chemistry in a cave really works.

YOU WILL NEED:
hot tap water
2 one-pint jars
dishcloth
1 cup washing soda
small round dish
3 small pieces of
string

What to do: Fill the two jars almost to the top with hot tap water. Stir washing soda into each jar until no more will dissolve. Twist the dishcloth and tie the ends and the middle with the strings. Place the ends of the "rope" you have made into the two jars of water, making a bridge. Make certain that the "rope ends" touch the bottoms of the jars. Place the dish under the cloth bridge to collect the drips. Allow three to five days for icicles to form.

What happens: The water and soda solution travels up both sides of the dishcloth rope and drips from the middle. The drips turn into hard soda pillars with the two columns meeting in the middle. Something similar happens in caves.

However, the buildup of cave deposits takes hundreds of years, while yours take only a few days.

Why: The water travels through the dishcloth rope by filling up all the tiny air pockets in the cloth. This is known as capillary action and it is similar to a row of dominoes falling down. The washing soda is carried along the "rope" by the water, which drips down from the middle. The water evaporates and leaves behind the hardened soda pillar. When you stir the washing soda into the jars until no more can be dissolved, you saturate it. The cooled solution's molecules then crystallize, or harden.

Chemistry in a Cave

Most caves are made of limestone. Limestone is a rock that can be easily worn away by water. Over thousands of years, this solution of water and calcium bicarbonate has gradually carved out great rooms in huge pieces of rock. This same solution drips through cracks in cave ceilings. As the water evaporates in the air, carbon dioxide is given off and the solid mineral calcite is formed. This turns into the hard lime icicle deposits, known as stalactites, found hanging from cave dwellings. Stalagmites are similarly shaped rock formations that build up from the floor, because of the dripping, instead of from the ceiling.

The Diamond Mine

80

Alum is a type of mineral or chemical salt that puts the pucker into some pickles, making your mouth feel as if it wants to close up. It looks and feels very much like table salt (sodium chloride), but while table salt in a microscope looks like ice cubes, with flat sides, alum crystals have many angular sides, or facets. Try making your own clear alum crystals and you'll think you've discovered a diamond mine.

What to do: Slowly and carefully pour the alum into the cup of water, stirring as you pour, until no more will dissolve. You'll know when the solution is saturated because you'll hear the alum grains scratching on the bottom of the cup and you'll see some floating in the water. If you put your finger in the cup and touch the bottom, you'll be able to feel the undissolved crystals. Keep the solution in the cup overnight.

The next day, pour the water into the jar and tie one end of the nylon thread around a large piece of hardened alum crystal you'll find in the bottom or on the sides of the cup. (Be patient with this. If you've ever threaded a sewing needle, you'll understand what we mean. It's hard to tie the fine nylon thread around the small alum crystals.) Wind and tie the thread around the middle of a pencil and place the pencil over the jar mouth so that the alum dangles low in the water. Keep the jar in a protected place for several days and observe the crystals from time to time.

Note: Save the other alum crystals on the bottom of the paper cup and set them to dry on a paper towel. Place them on a dark piece of construction paper and study them with your hand lens. Save these shiny, many-sided alum crystals for "The Gem Show."

What happens: If you hold the thread up to the light and view the alum crystals, you'll see what appears to be many shiny brilliant gems.

Why: Again, the crystals are formed by dissolving enough solutes or solid substances (alum) in the solvent or water to make a saturated solution. Then the cooled solution causes the alum molecules on the string to build on one another. Crystals will continue to form on the crystal string until all of the solution evaporates.

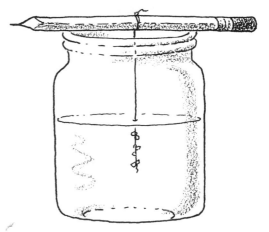

81

Blue Moon Rocks

You'll think you've stepped out on the moon when you grow this crystal garden. Make certain you cover your work area with newspapers so you won't have crystals growing everywhere!

What to do: Place a folded paper towel in the bottom of the tray. Crush the second paper towel and place it on top. In the disposable cup, mix all the ingredients together and slowly spoon the mixture over the paper. With the hand lens observe what happens.

What happens: Blue bubbly crystals instantly appear in the container. (For a full garden, it will have to set for at least 24 hours.)

Why: The salt solution with the bluing becomes saturated until no more can dissolve. As the water is soaked up by the paper towels and evaporates, the salt left behind forms new crystals around the powdery bluing.

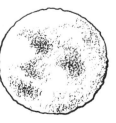

82

Rocky Mountains

Watch these beautiful rock salt crystals climb on the sides of a string and turn into sparkling mountains of diamondlike cubes. Follow the instructions as in "The Diamond Mine," but replace the alum with 1/2 cup of rock salt. Use a strong string dangling from a pencil to catch the growing crystals. Don't rush this one! Great mountains of crystals may take as long two to four weeks to grow.

About Crystals

Crystals can be grown from a string tied to a pencil and placed across a cup or glass, or scraped with a spoon from the sides and bottom of the container. Keep the crystal solutions in a warm, sunny window. The longer the crystal solution is left to evaporate, the larger the crystals will be.

Store your crystals in a dry place and be careful handling them. If your hands are wet or damp, it is best to use tweezers or a plastic spoon.

 # The Gem Show

Invite your friends over for a gem show. It's easy and it's lots of fun! Display your sugar, salt, alum, and washing soda crystals in a special way. Line lids of small boxes with dark paper or cloth and place your crystals in them. Place the lids on an outside table for "crystal viewing" on a sunny day. Use information from this book to make labels for your crystal trays. Supply plenty of magnifying hand lenses for viewing. You may even give a demonstration on how to make crystals with a saturated solution.

Also, you can separate your crystals and glue some onto rings for a special display. (Plain rings can be purchased at hobby stores or made with pipe cleaners.) Try adding a drop or two of food coloring to your solutions when you make crystals. You'll be able to make simulated or fake rubies, emeralds, or sapphires. You can add these to your rings, make crystal-designed holiday ornaments, or use them in other crafts. With a little imagination, the possibilities for exciting crystal-craft projects are endless.

 # Hi, Sugar!

With all your experience with saturated solutions, now make a saturated sugar collection. You can use a string on a pencil to catch your crystals or leave them in the bottom of a jar or cup and collect them later. Keep them for displaying in "The Gem Show."

Unlike salt crystals, which look like cubes, sugar crystals are long and have flat, slanted sides.

The Lab: CO$_2$ and You

In this chapter, you'll make a manometer, an exciting and great piece of chemistry equipment to put in your laboratory, a place where you, as chief chemist, will be doing your own research and studies. A manometer is easy and inexpensive to make and fun to use. With it you'll be able to test substances for carbon-dioxide (CO$_2$) gas.

But first, it's time to solve the mystery of the rising doughs and find out which contains the most CO$_2$ gas, a definitely air-raising experience!

Dynamite Dumplings

YOU WILL NEED:

small cup, for mixing

cup filled with very hot water

test substances:

1/2 tablespoon baking powder

1/2 tablespoon baking soda

1/2 tablespoon quick-rising dry yeast

flour

cool water

teaspoon

tablespoon

85

What substances added to flour and water produce the most carbon-dioxide (CO_2) gas? In this three-part experiment you'll make a water and flour dough three times, using a different combination of substances.

Each part of the experiment will be done separately, using the same equipment and ingredients, almost.

The only thing to change will be the substance to be tested: baking powder, baking soda, or quick-rising dry yeast. Before you start, make a hypothesis, or scientific guess, as to which substance contains the most carbon dioxide gas. Then do the tests and find out if you are right.

What to do: With a teaspoon, mix a full tablespoon of dry flour with the first test substance, the baking powder, in a cup or mug. Add a little bit of cool water, a drop at a time, and make a ball of dough. If the mixture becomes too wet, add more flour. Place the ball of dough in a tablespoon. Leave the spoon in a cool place while you fill another cup or mug with very hot water (from the tap, or warmed on the stove or in a microwave).

For about two minutes, hold the spoon with the dough over the hot water. Let the spoon touch the water, and a little of the hot water enter it. Set the ball of dough inside.

Now, repeat the experiment, but instead of the baking powder, use baking soda. Then do the experiment again with the third substance, the quick-rising yeast.

What happens: All the dough balls grow much larger.

Why: The baking powder contains bicarbonate of soda. When combined with flour, water, and heat, it produces a chemical change which produces carbon-dioxide gas. This is seen in the gas-bubble holes that appear in the dough and make it larger. The baking soda and the yeast doughs also produce chemical changes and CO_2 gas. The baking soda dough will probably grow less than the baking powder and yeast doughs, which may even double in size. Of the two, the yeast dough should grow slightly larger. Was your hypothesis corrected?

86 How to Make a Manometer

Your manometer is simply a plastic tube pushed down inside a glass bottle with the other end attached to a stick. You'll use it to test different substances for carbon-dioxide gas and have the fun of watching the colored water rise in the plastic tube, somewhat like a ther-mometer. You can even calibrate, or put lines on, your tube-stick with a marker pen to measure, and record, how much gas is in a substance. If the colored water shoots up the tube or even comes out of it, you'll know the test substance produces a lot of carbon dioxide gas.

What to do: Clean the bottle thor-oughly. Have someone make a large hole in the bottle lid with the nail and ham-mer. (It will have to be large enough to hold the tube.) Push about 4 inches of the 28 inches of tubing through the hole in the lid into the bottle. (Bend the tube back and forth to straighten it). Make a small clay rope and press it around the hole in the cap to make the bottle airtight. Now take the jar lid and press clay into the bottom of it; put a little more in the middle.

At this point, you may wish to draw some measurement lines on the stick with a marking

YOU WILL NEED:

- 16-ounce (473 ml) glass bottle with a screw-on top
- 28 inches (71 cm) of home aquarium air tubing
- small drinking glass half-filled with water
- food coloring (any color)
- wide-mouth jar lid
- large nail and hammer
- stick about 16 inches (40 cm) long
- rubber bands or twist ties
- medicine dropper
- modeling clay
- scissors

pen. Each line should be 1 cm from the next, starting from the middle of the stick to one end. Number the lines, starting with "1" in the mid-dle. This makes a nice scale and lets you know how much each sub-stance causes your manometer to register.

Now, push the stick into the clay stand so that it stands up. Bend the outside tubing to the bottom of the bottle and stand to form a lower loop and fasten the rest of the tubing to the stick with the rubber bands. The tube opening should be at the top of the stick. You are now ready to fill the lower loop with colored water.

Put a few drops of food coloring in the half-glass of water to color it. With the medicine dropper, drop one or two drops of colored water into the top of the tube on the stick. If the water separates in the tube, gently suck or blow on the straw to bring the water drops together. You now have a new piece of chemistry equipment to use in your lab experiments.

87 — The Care and Use of Your Manometer

1. Work on a kitchen counter, in case your manometer blows its top (loses liquid)!

2. Keep added colored water in a small, closed bottle, to replace any water lost during experiments or storage.

3. When taking the top off the manometer bottle to add solutions, place the tube with the lid on it into another similar empty bottle so that the colored water in the tube won't escape or break up.

4. So as not to twist the tube and loosen the seal, screw the bottle into the cap instead of the cap onto the bottle.

5. Store your manometer in a small box. Make certain the cap with the tube in it is screwed tightly on the bottle.

6. Drop only one or two drops of colored water into the top of the plastic tube on the stick. If the water breaks up, gently blow and suck into the plastic tube. The colored water should come back together.

7. To do tests, pour powders first, followed by liquids, into your manometer bottle and cap it immediately. Your experiments will not work if you mix the solutions in other containers and then pour them into the manometer bottle, or if you do not close the bottle quickly enough.

88 — CO_2 Uplift

YOU WILL NEED:

manometer
test substances:
1 tablespoon baking powder
1/2 cup vinegar
empty spare bottle
colored water
medicine dropper

How much will the colored water marker rise when certain substances are placed in the manometer? Whether you do these manometer experiments in one day or on several different days, it is very important to keep a scientific journal, or record book, and write down what happens in each and every experiment. Doing and recording these experimetns will make a real chemist out of you!

What to do: Set up your manometer on the kitchen counter or with newspaper under the container to catch any spills. Keep the bottle and stand close together so the tube makes a low loop between them. With the dropper, place one or two drops of colored water in the open tube attached to the stand. 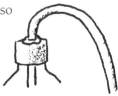 Only a few drops are needed! The water should drop down into the lower loop. If it does not do this, or if it breaks up, gently blow or suck on the tube to bring the liquid together and move it into place in the lower loop.

Now, measure one tablespoon of baking powder and 1/2 cup of vinegar. Take the cap off the manometer bottle and rest the tube in another bottle. Pour the baking powder into the bottom of the manometer bottle, followed by the vinegar (the liquid always goes in last). Quickly, screw the cap back on tightly and shake the bottle a little. Write down what happens and how far the solution makes the colored-water marker rises in the tube.

Wash out the manometer bottle thoroughly before going on to the next experiments, and remember to wash it again between experiments or you might invalidate, or spoil, your results.

Now test the next five combinations as you did the baking powder and vinegar experiment:

Test substances:
1 tablespoon baking soda and 1/2 cup vinegar
2 antacid seltzer tablets and 1/2 cup water
1/2 cup carbonated soft drink
1 tablespoon baking soda and juice of 1 lemon
1 tablespoon baking soda and 1/2 cup water

Note: For added experiment effects and results, try varying, or changing, the amounts of dry ingredients to liquids, and of different liquids to powders.

What happens:
The colored water in the manometer tube rises forcefully up the tube with much sputtering and bubbling, or it rises slightly but does not sputter, or it does not rise at all.

Why: There is obviously more CO_2 gas given off in some chemical reactions than in others. In the above experiments, both vinegar-and-baking-soda and vinegar-and-baking-powder produced the best results. Both mixtures drove the colored-water marker bubbling noisily up the tube.*

While there was definitely some CO_2 gas given off with the seltzer tablets, soda, and baking-soda-and-lemon solutions, the water marker did not move as much as it did with the powder and vinegar solutions. In these tests, there was little movement and no noticeable sound. But absolutely nothing happened with the baking-soda-and-water solutions, which released no CO_2 gas at all.

Note: If you did not get this reaction, do the experiments again. Be sure to put the powder in first, and to cap the bottle quickly before the CO_2 gas.

84

KITCHEN ALCHEMY

Most people don't think of cooking as chemistry, but when batters turn into cakes, cookies, and pancakes, and sugar crystallizes and turns into candy, it definitely is.

About Cooking and Chemical Reactions

In fact, most cooking does involve chemical change or reactions. If pizza stays in the oven too long, a black substance called carbon results. Carbon-dioxide gas, through yeast, makes bread rise, and salt causes water to leave pickles through a process called osmosis.

Don't be too surprised if these experiment-recipes become family favorites. Besides being great chemistry experiments and fun to make, they're fantastically delicious!

89 Spicy Infusion

Chemists often use the word infusion. Anything dissolved in hot water is called an infusion. Some people drink infusions every day in the form of coffee and tea. In this activity, you'll make your own infusions and you'll have the fun of drinking them, too!

What to do: Put one herb or spice in the strainer, and place it on top of a cup. Pour some water from the teakettle over it. Let the substance steep, or soak, for two to three minutes. Remove the strainer and clean it out under cold water. Now taste your infusion "tea" and describes its taste. Repeat these steps with the other herbs and spices.

What happens: The spices and herbs steep and dissolve in the water to color and flavor it.

Why: Some herbs and spicy substances are more soluble, or dissolve more easily, in hot water, than others. The chemical composition, or the way the molecules are arranged, has a lot to do with a substance's solubility. A tea may be sweet and pleasant, or bitter and sour. It may make your mouth pucker when you taste it, or may be so weak you can hardly taste it at all. What do you like or dislike about your infusions?

90 Give an Infusion Party

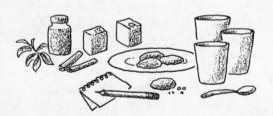

Invite some of your friends over on a wet and cold day for an infusion-test "tea" party. Provide a list of spices and herbs used but don't identify or name the samples. Have among your "teas" some made from such popular and favorite herbs and spices as nutmeg, anise seed, mint, fennel seed, allspice, cinnamon bark, and clove. Also, try thin slices of ginger root. Use sugar or honey for flavoring and supply small disposable plastic spoons and cups for sampling. Serve your infusion "teas" with some light, crispy cookies. Give each person a pencil and a small notepad and ask them to identify each infusion and its solubility, or how well-flavored it is. Have fun and enjoy!

Butter Me Up

You can make your own butter very easily. This experiment-recipe is made in small quantities to use immediately. (Get help with this one!) It may take about ten minutes for your cream to turn to butter but it's definitely worth it—you butter believe it!

What to do: Pour the cream into the chilled bowl. Mix on high until the cream forms yellow clumps. This will not happen right away; allow at least ten minutes. As you mix, a liquid separates from the clumps. Pour this liquid off into the measuring cup as you continue to mix.

What happens: The cream is turned into butter, and there's a good bit of liquid in the measuring cup.

Why: Cream is a combination of butterfat and water molecules. The butterfat floats throughout the water. This, again, is an example of a suspension, a solid suspended in a liquid. When you use the mixer on the cream, the molecules of butterfat collide and stick together, the clumps get larger, and you have butter, a solid substance. The water molecule part of the cream is the liquid you now have in the measuring cup. How much of the cup of cream was butterfat and how much water?

YOU WILL NEED:
1 cup cold heavy whipping cream
small bowl chilled in refrigerator
electric hand mixer
measuring cup

92 "Emulsional" about Mayonnaise

Don't cry over cracked eggs and when your egg whites get beaten up, send in the substitute! You're sure to get "egg-cited" about this tasty and delicious spread. Make mayonnaise in small quantities to use immediately. This serves two to four.

What to do: Place the egg substitute in the bowl. Add the mustard, lemon juice, and seasoning. Beat these with the spoon. Add the oil a little at a time, then beat. Add some more oil, and beat again. Do this until the mayonnaise gets stiff, then you can add the oil faster.

If the oil just seems to sit there (now you'll learn how emulsions act), simply add a touch more mustard and continue beating. The secret of making good mayonnaise is to keep on beating the ingredients. At the end, add a teaspoon of boiling water to keep your mayonnaise from separating.

What happens: From the separate ingredients, you have made mayonnaise, a mixture of liquids suspended or floating in one another, called an emulsion.

Why: In the case of mayonnaise, the mustard and boiling water are the emulsifying agents that keep the oil and the lemon juice from separating and keep the mixture emulsified. Without these agents, the mixture can and will separate.

YOU WILL NEED:
small mixing bowl
spoon for mixing
2 tablespoons egg substitute
1/2 teaspoon mustard
1 teaspoon lemon juice
salt and pepper to taste
1/2 cup cooking oil
1 teaspoon boiling water

Tarragon Mayonnaise Dressing
Add shredded leaves of fresh tarragon (an herb found in your supermarket's produce department) to your mayonnaise, and you have a delicious, light salad dressing. It's great on sliced tomatoes, too!

In a Pickle

Now make some simple delicious pickles you can eat tonight. You'll be using salt and vinegar, compounds that keep foods from spoiling.

What to do: Scrub the cucumber. Cut deep grooves down and around the length of it with the prongs of a fork. Slice the cucumber thinly, so you can almost see through the slices. Place the slices in a deep bowl and sprinkle the salt on top. Toss the slices thoroughly with a spoon to mix in the salt. Cover the slices with a small plate and place something heavy on top—a tin can will do. Let the cucumbers stand at room temperature for one hour.

Drain the slices and put them in the serving container. Mix the sugar and vinegar, and pour it over the cucumber slices. Chill thoroughly for two to three hours. Before serving, drain off the liquid and sprinkle with chopped dill, parsley, or tarragon. Enjoy!

What happens: The cucumbers turn into a simple version of crispy, crunchy pickle slices.

Why: The salt and vinegar combine to ferment the cucumber. The process, called osmosis, draws water out of the cucumbers to make pickles crisp and crunchy.

Fermentation

Salt keeps foods from spoiling. Pickles are usually made by placing vegetables, usually cucumbers, in salt water. The salty solution is called a brine. The salt draws out the juices and helps the good bacteria change, or ferment, the cucumbers into pickles while killing the bad bacteria. Chemists know that bacteria are everywhere, even in our bodies. Some cause disease, while others cause chemical changes in foods to make new foods, such as pickles.

YOU WILL NEED:
large unpeeled cucumber
1 tablespoon (15 ml) salt
1 tablespoon (15 ml) sugar
1/2 cup cider or white vinegar
small, covered serving container
1 tablespoon (15 ml) chopped dill, parsley, or tarragon (fresh or dried)
fork
knife
deep bowl
spoon
small plate and weight

Atoms Apple

Try rearranging the same apple atoms, and make a delicious warm dessert that serves four.

What to do: In the pot, cook the first three ingredients together for five minutes, then remove the lemon slice. Peel, core, and slice the apples, and add them to the sugar solution, a few at a time. Cook until soft, adding water as needed. To serve, move the apples to plates, pour the warm sugar syrup over the apples, and sprinkle with cinnamon.

What happens: The firm apples soften and make a delicious apple dessert.

Why: The lemon acid and sugar combine with a substance in the apples called pectin. This softens them into a jellylike mixture. The heated water helps break down the atoms of the apple or the structure of its molecules. Then it is chemically changed by "cooking," from a hard state to a soft one.

YOU WILL NEED:
large pot
1 1/2 cups water
1/2 cup sugar
lemon slice
6 small-medium apples
peeler and knife
use of stove (ask for permission or help)
cinnamon

95 Lemon Aide

Chemistry, as you can see, is everywhere in the kitchen. Like candy, syrups are supersaturated solutions of sugar and water, and the difference between the two is the degree of heat that chemically changes in substances. In this recipe-experiment, you'll make your very own lemon syrup for instant fresh lemonade.

What to do: Place the sugar and water in a pot. Boil the solution for five minutes; then let it cool and add the lemon juice. Pour the syrup through a strainer and into the container. For keeping, store in the refrigerator. You'll need 2 tablespoons of syrup to one glass of ice water for a great fresh lemonade. Enjoy!

What happens: The sugar, lemon, and water solution turns into a thick, lemony syrup.

Why: The heat causes the sugar and water to mix thoroughly, then it boils away some of the water molecules through stream, or water vapor. When the thickened sugar solution cools, it chemically reacts with the lemon juice, making the syrupy mixture.

Herb 96 Dressing: To Be or Not to Be?

Salad dressings don't know whether they are emulsions or not; let's make one and see why. (Makes about 1 cup).

What to do: Place all the above ingredients in the jar and shake well. Store in refrigerator, and shake before using.

What happens: When shaken, the vinegar and oil combine, but then they eventually separate.

Why: The vinegar, oil, and water are a temporary emulsion, or "colloid," of small molecular substances, which combine temporarily with other small molecular substances in a liquid. Salad dressing is not a true emulsion, as mayonnaise is, or it would not separate.

I Scream! 97

Endotherm another frozen treat by replacing the Cranberry Lemon Snow juices with 1 tablespoon instant vanilla pudding powder, 1/2 cup chilled evaporated milk, 1/2 cup low-fat milk, 1 tablespoon sugar, and 1/2 teaspoon vanilla extract. Mix the ingredients thoroughly before packing the open jar in ice. It's a delicious soft-serve vanilla ice cream!

Endothermic Frozen Treat: Cranberry-Lemon Snow

98

Can an endothermic change, or one where heat energy is used instead of produced, make a delicious frozen treat? Let's see what happens with fruit and lemon juice. You'll have the fun of doing this great chemistry experiment and eating it, too!

YOU WILL NEED:

small, clean jar

medium-size mixing bowl or container

sheets of paper towels or 2 small dishtowels (to fold and wrap around bowl)

spoon

1/2 cup cranberry or other fruit juice

1 tablespoon lemon juice

1/2 cup rock salt (available in spice section of supermarket)

6 cups crushed ice

What to do: Pour the fruit and lemon juice into the jar and shake. Place the open jar in the middle of the bowl. Carefully pour crushed ice around the jar up to the top. Sprinkle rock salt in and around the ice. Fold the paper towels or dishtowels lengthwise and wrap them around the bowl. Place a heavy object or two against the bowl to keep the towels in place. Be patient! It will take about two hours for your experiment to turn into an icy treat.

What happens: The juice turns into an icy slush.

Why: The salt on the ice draws the heat out of the juices in the jar and the temperature goes down below the freezing point.

Maple Snow Sugar

99

Early colonists in America made a special maple candy called "Jack Wax." Boiled maple syrup was poured onto the snow and hardened into a sugary maple treat. You can make your own Jack Wax in just a few minutes. (Involves hot, boiling syrup! Adult help is recommended!)

YOU WILL NEED:

1/2 cup maple syrup

1 microwave-safe container

medium bowl half-filled with crushed ice

spoon

fork

an adult helper

What happens: The hot syrup turns into strands of taffylike maple candy. With the fork, you can now pick out strands of taffylike maple sugar and roll it into hard bands. Enjoy them alone or as a morning treat with doughnuts, or with delicious sparkling apple cider pancakes in "Batter on the Moon."

What to do: Pour the syrup into the microwave-safe container. Cook on high power for five minutes. Very carefully (hot sugar can cause a bad burn), spoon the maple syrup over the crushed ice.

Why: The maple syrup, boiled to the hard-sugar stage, is chemically changed so that the individual sugar crystals link up and harden together to form a solid.

100 ▸ Batter on the Moon

No, they don't play baseball on the moon but you can make light, delicious, sparkling apple cider pancakes that are guaranteed to be out of this world! The chemically changed mixed batter, with its bubbles and holes, will remind you of craters on the moon. You won't strike out with this experiment if you keep your eyes on the batter. (Makes 16 four-inch pancakes.)

What to do: Pour each ingredient into the bowl and mix them together with the wire whisk or spoon. Do not overmix.

Pour the batter into the pouring-type measuring cup. Lightly grease the grill, pan, or electric fry pan (set at 350°F). When the grill or pan is hot, start the pancakes by pouring the batter. Pour enough to make four- or five-inch cakes onto the hot grill or pan. Let the pancakes cook on one side until bubbles appear and until the surface is somewhat dried out. Turn the pancakes over with the turner and cook until cakes lightly lift from pan.

What happens: As you mix the batter, bubbles appear in it. When you add heat, cooking the batter, it turns into light, delicious pancakes. Serve them with butter, syrup, and applesauce. Adding your "Maple Snow Sugar" candies would make this breakfast an even bigger hit.

Why: The apple juice in cider is carbonated, or creates carbonic acid. This happens when carbon dioxide is dissolved into the solution. The craters, or holes, in the pancake batter are created by the carbon-dioxide gas. This also makes the pancakes lighter and puffier. If you save leftover batter for later, the pancakes will be heavier and flatter, because the CO_2 gas bubbles will be less or gone. This is similar to when you put uncapped soda in the refrigerator and it loses its fizz.

101 ▸ I've Got a Crush on You

If your refrigerator does not have a crushed ice dispenser, ice cubes can be crushed in a special appliance, food processor, or blender, or by putting them in a towel and breaking them up with a hammer.

In an electric blender, place two cups of ice cubes into the blender container, along with one cup of water. Press the CHOP or high-speed button to blend. Turn off the blender occasionally and stir the ice with a rubber spatula or wooden spoon. This will distribute the cubes equally so that they can be crushed more evenly.

If needed, ask for help making crushed ice.

FOOD FOR THOUGHT

What makes us hungry? Why do salted potato chips make us thirsty? How does the temperature of food affect its taste? What does salt do in the pot—and in our bodies? Is it better to use honey than sugar? And more….

About Hunger and Food

Why do we cook? First of all, to make food digestible and safe. But we also cook for other reasons. We cook to make food tasty so that we will enjoy eating as we satisfy our hunger. But what makes us feel hungry?

Chemicals in the body—in our blood, our digestive hormones and our nervous system—all give us signals, sensations such as stomach movements. When these signals reach the brain, it recognizes them as a need for food.

Our sense of hunger and satisfaction is also influenced by other things. Sometimes we want and eat food when we don't need it. Maybe we eat because it's our favorite food, or because we are upset about something and think food will make us feel better. Or maybe we eat just because everybody else is eating. Sometimes, too, we refuse food even though we need it—perhaps because we are sick or worried or afraid we'll gain weight. Sometimes, we don't eat enough because we don't like the taste or smell or looks of a particular food.

Taste, Bud?

How your food tastes to you depends largely on your tongue. It has about 3,000 taste buds located on its surface. The sensation of taste arises from the activity of clusters of cells (the epitheli-ads) that are embedded in the small bumps (the papillae) on the tongue's upper surface.

Strangely, your nose, your sense of smell, plays a big part in tasting food. Without this important sense, as when you have a bad head cold, you cannot even recognize the flavor of foods you are eating; you just can't "taste" anything.

102 Tasting Through Your Nose

YOU WILL NEED:
small peeled potato
2 spoons
small grated apple
grater

The smell of a food is as important as its taste! In fact, its smell actually influences how it tastes! If you doubt it, try this experiment.

What to do: Grate part of a peeled potato and put it on a spoon. Grate an equal amount of a peeled apple and put it on a second spoon.

Close your eyes and mix up the spoons so that you're not sure which is which. Hold your nose and taste each of the foods.

What happens: You will have trouble telling which is which!

Why: The nose shares the airway (the pharynx) with the mouth. Therefore, we smell and taste food at the same time.

Only salty, sweet, bitter and sour are pure tastes. Other "tastes" are combinations of taste and odor. Without the help of your nose, you may not be able to tell what you are eating.

103 Some Like it Hot

YOU WILL NEED:
glass of cold water with
1/2 teaspoon of salt
glass of cold water with
1/2 teaspoon of sugar
glass of cold water with
the juice of half a lemon
a pot
food thermometer (optional)
use of the stove (ask for
permission or help)

Believe it or not, the temperature of food affects the taste!

What to do: Taste the cold salty water. Let it stand on the table for an hour or so until it is at room temperature. Taste it again. Then heat it slightly and taste again. Bring the salty water to a boil. Let it cool slightly and taste it again.

Repeat the process with the sugary water and finally with the lemonade.

What happens: The salty water tastes saltier at room temperature than at the other temperatures. The sugary water tastes sweetest and the lemonade most sour when they are just slightly warm.

Why: The temperature at which tastes are strongest ranges from 72° to 105°F (22° to 40°C). Salty and bitter tastes are stronger at the lower range, which is room temperature. Sweet and sour tastes are stronger at the upper part of the range.

If food is really hot or cold, it is hard to taste it. The receptor molecules on the tongue can't easily capture the food molecules. Ice cream makers, for instance, have to use twice as much sugar as they would if the ice cream were served at room temperature.

However, whatever the temperature, we are all much more sensitive to bitter tastes than any others.

Certain substances can make a taste stronger—or get rid of it altogether. The cynarin in artichokes, for instance, makes everything taste sweet. It blocks the other tastes. MSG (monosodium glutamate), used in some prepared foods and in Chinese restaurants, makes salty and bitter tastes stronger.

104 Wilting a Cucumber

YOU WILL NEED:
cucumber or lettuce
salt

Though our bodies need the two minerals (sodium and chloride) that salt provides, too much salt—and too much of the foods preserved by salt—can cause health problems. Salt is powerful! Let's look at its effect on a vegetable.

What to do: Cut off two or three slices of cucumber or tear off several leaves of lettuce. Salt them and let them stand.

What happens: They wilt!

Why: The salt draws the water out of the cells of the vegetable. The same thing happens to our body's cells if we eat too much salt and the amount of sodium in the fluid surrounding the cells is too high. The "wilted" cells don't function properly.

Salt is an essential part of blood and other body fluids. But when we eat too much of it, too much water and potassium are drawn from the body's cells. This may cause high blood pressure or kidney damage.

Too Many Potato Chips! 105

Here is one way the body keeps us from getting too high a concentration of salt.

YOU WILL NEED:
salt pretzel or several
potato chips

What to do: Eat a salt pretzel or three or four salted potato chips.

What happens: You will need to take a drink of water!

Why: You want extra water to dilute the extra salt you have eaten. Thirst keeps the body functioning by making sure it doesn't have too high a concentration of salt.

When there is too great a concentration of sodium and potassium in our body fluids, the hypothalamus (a part of the brain located near its base) triggers a feeling of thirst.

An increased concentration of sodium also can be caused when we perspire. You may have heard that you should eat salt when you're sweating, but that's a mistake. Your impulse—to drink water—is right.

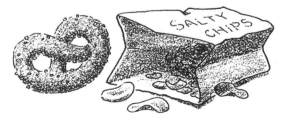

106 Too Salty!

Besides sprinkling on too much salt, what makes food taste too salty?

What to do: Add 2 tablespoons of salt to 2 cups of water. Stir and pour half into one pot and half into the other.

Boil the water in the first pot for 20 minutes. Boil the water in the second pot for 10 minutes. Let them cool and taste each one.

What happens: The first will taste much saltier than the second.

Why: After the boiling starts, the water turns into water vapor, an invisible gas, and escapes into the air (evaporates). Continued boiling does not raise the temperature. It just speeds up evaporation. The longer the salted water boils, the more water evaporates and the saltier the remaining water tastes.

Water, Water— Every Time

It was once believed that athletes and dancers should never drink water after working out. But today we know it's important for them to drink plenty of water before and after they perform—and even during the competition or game if it lasts long.

Not drinking enough water can cause an athlete to lose the race, miss the hoop, drop the catch. If their muscles don't have enough water, they feel weak and tired.

Although salt is lost along with sweat, the amount is less than the amount of salt in the blood. That means that we need to replace more water than salt when we sweat a lot. Doctors tell us that the safest way to replace lost sweat is with plain water.

What Pot?

Does it matter what size pot we cook in?

What to do: Pour a cup of water into each pot. Place both pots on the stove over medium heat.

What happens: The water in the short pot boils first!

Why: There is less atmosphere in the shallow pot. That means there is less air pressure keeping the molecules down and they have an easier time escaping into the air. The tall, narrow pot is under greater pressure from the air, its molecules have to work harder to escape into the air—and so its boiling point is about 1° higher.

Watch That Salt Shaker

Food tastes most salty at room temperature. When we season hot food such as potato salad that is going to be eaten cold, we can use less salt, knowing that it will taste saltier when we eat it. When we're salting cold food that is going to be reheated later, we can use a little more salt than our taste tells us—or better still, wait until after we heat it and salt it then.

Which Boils Faster— Salted or Plain Water?

What effect does salt have when you boil water?

What to do: Add two tablespoons of salt to one of the pots of cold water. Don't add anything to the other pot. Heat both pots on the stove. Which one starts to boil first?

What happens: The pot without the salt boils first!

Why: The point at which a substance changes from a liquid to a gas is called the boiling point. The more salt in water, the higher the temperature must be for the water to boil. Salt molecules turn to gas at much higher temperatures than water molecules.

So we add salt to cold water if we want our food to cook faster since it will be cooking at a higher temperature. Spaghetti and other pastas, for instance, cook well in vigorously boiling salted water. The difference in temperature between salted and unsalted water can be important when we're cooking sauces and custards that call for exact temperature or timing.

109 Poached Egg Physics

In which pot—the short, wide one or the tall, narrow one—can we poach an egg faster?

What to do: Pour 2 cups of cold water into each pot. Place the short pot on the stove over medium heat. After the water boils, carefully break open one of the eggs and slip it into the water. Set the timer at two minutes or count 120 seconds. (You do this by saying, "And 1, and 2, and 3," and so on up to 120.) Then quickly remove the egg with a slotted spoon.

Repeat the process with the egg in the tall pot, again allowing it to cook exactly two minutes.

What happens: The yolk of the egg in the tall pot gets harder than that of the egg in the short pot!

Why: Because the boiling point is higher (see "What Pot?") in the tall pot, the food cooks at a higher temperature than in the short, wide pot. Therefore, it takes a shorter time to cook.

Salt versus the Sweet Stuff 110

If someone pulled the labels off identical containers of sugar and salt, could you tell which was which? There are ways to tell besides tasting them.

What to do: Place the salt in one of the pans and the sugar in the other. Heat each for a few minutes over low heat.

What happens: Nothing happens to one. That one is salt. The other melts and gets brown. That one is sugar.

Why: All sugars are simple carbohydrates. They all contain carbon and hydrogen and oxygen. Heating sugar separates its molecules. At about 360°F (189°C), the sugar breaks down into water (the hydrogen and oxygen) and carbon. The carbon makes the sugar turn brown, or caramelizes it. Have you ever toasted marshmallows over an open fire? Then you've seen it happen.

Freezing Salt and Sugar

The Candy Trap

YOU WILL NEED:
1 tablespoon salt
2 cups food coloring (2 colors)
1 tablespoon sugar
water
ice cube tray with separators

Here's another way to tell whether a substance is salt or sugar!

What to do: Fill the cups halfway with water, and color each one with a few drops of a different food coloring. Dissolve the salt in one cup and the sugar in the other.

Pour the solutions into opposite ends of an ice cube tray with separators. Put the tray in the freezer for an hour or two.

What happens: The sugar cubes freeze. The salt cubes remain liquid.

Why: Plain water turns into ice at 32°F (0°C). Both sugar and salt lower the freezing point of the water. But sugar molecules are heavier than salt molecules. There are more salt molecules than sugar molecules in a tablespoon. So salt lowers the freezing point twice as much as sugar.

YOU WILL NEED:
1 medium-size apple
1 medium-size banana
Tootsie Rolls
pieces of chocolate

When we feel hungry, we often reach for a candy bar. But suppose we ate a piece of fruit instead?

What to do: For your afternoon snack, try a Tootsie Roll one day and an apple the next. On a third day, try chocolate. On the fourth, eat a banana.

What happens: They all taste great. But the candy leaves you hungry and wanting more. You may go on to eat three or more Tootsie Rolls and two or more ounces of chocolate. However, chances are that one apple or one banana will leave you feeling full.

Why: The sugar in candy is highly refined, and it gets digested very quickly. It doesn't stay in the stomach very long and so we stay hungry. Raisins, apples, bananas, pears, and melon contain sugar (fructose) in a form that we digest more slowly, and therefore they fuel the body more gradually.

It's possible to eat a whole pound (.45 kg) of apples before using up the amount of calories in three Tootsie Rolls! Three medium-sized bananas are equal in calories to two ounces (56 g) of chocolate.

The piece of fruit also supplies vitamins and minerals and fiber instead of just "empty" calories.

Salt and Ice Cream

When you make ice cream, you put milk or cream, sugar, flavoring and gelatin in a special container that sits in a cooling bath of ice-cold water. The water is kept liquid by adding enough salt to lower the temperature to below 27°F (-3°C). That's why salt is such an important ingredient in the making of ice cream.

The Cookie Test

Compare the taste and feel of different sugars and honey in these great cookies.

What to do: Preheat the oven to 350°F (175°C). Soften the margarine at room temperature before you start to mix it with the various sugars.

Using a food processor or a bowl with a wooden spoon, cream a half stick (4 tablespoons) of margarine with the white sugar. Add a half teaspoon of lemon juice. Gradually mix in a half cup of the flour. Continue mixing until the dough is smooth and beginning to form a ball.

Repeat the process with the brown sugar and then with the honey.

Drop rounded teaspoons of the dough onto cookie sheets about two inches (5 cm) apart. Press each cookie flat with the back of the spoon. Each batch makes about a dozen cookies. Bake 15 minutes or until the cookies are a light brown.

Let cool—and taste.

What happens: The cookies are equally sweet, but the tastes are different!

Why: Each sweetener comes from a different source.

White sugar—sucrose—is made either from a tall grass known as sugar cane or from the roots of sugar beets. When it is processed, impurities are removed; it is then refined, and made into the granulated, lump, or powdered form we buy in the supermarket.

Brown sugar also comes from sucrose, but it is made by coating sucrose crystals with molasses, the thick syrup left when water is boiled out of sucrose.

Honey, of course, is manufactured by bees. They make the sweet, sticky thick liquid from the nectar of flowers. Honey has 10 more calories per tablespoon than sugar, but because honey is sweeter than sugar, you need less. You used only half as much honey as sugar for your cookies.

Honey has small amounts of vitamins and minerals, but too little to offer much nutrition. Cookies made with honey, though, may stay moist longer because honey retains moisture longer while baking. It may even bring moisture from the air into the finished cookies. That's why candy made with honey tends to get sticky.

Green Broccoli
and Other Vegetables

How do plants eat and drink? When do turnips smell like rotten eggs? How can we make beans user-friendly? The answers to these questions—and much more.

About Vegetables

Vegetables are plants grown for the parts we can eat—root, stem, leaf, flower, seed, or fruit. Sometimes, though, a fruit is a vegetable and sometimes a vegetable is a fruit!

According to botanists, the scientists who study and classify plants, fruits are the part of the plant that contains the seeds. But whether we call a food a fruit or a vegetable seems to depend on its sweetness. Both cantaloupe and squash are in the same fruit family. But squash is not all that sweet and it is served as a vegetable.

Many vegetables are eaten raw. Lettuce and other greens, tomatoes, and cucumbers are among the most usual salad ingredients. Onions and peppers are often added. Cauliflower and broccoli are often eaten raw and dipped in a spicy or creamy sauce. However, many vegetables are easier to digest when they are cooked. Others, like potatoes and yams, can't be digested at all unless they are cooked.

The Vegetable Game

114

Botanists divide the vegetables we eat into the following groups: leaf, stem, root and tuber, flower and bud, seed and seed pod, fruit-vegetable, and fungi. A carrot, for instance, is a root, celery a stem. Potatoes are tubers, fleshy underground stems bearing a bud. Fungi are plants like mushrooms that live on other plants because they lack chlorophyll—the green coloring matter (see "How to Feed Celery"), and so cannot manufacture their own food.

How much do you know about veggies? See if you can identify the following vegetables according to the part of the plant we eat. (Answers on page 00).

a. Root
b. Tuber
c. Stem
d. Leaf
e. Flower
f. Seed
g. Fruit
h. Fungi

1. asparagus
2. beets
3. broccoli
4. Brussels
   sprouts
5. carrots
6. cauliflower
7. cabbage
8. celery
9. corn
10. cucumber
11. eggplant
12. kale
13. leek
14. lettuce
15. morels
16. mushrooms

17. okra
18. onion
19. parsnip
20. peas
21. pepper
22. potato
23. pumpkin
24. radish
25. spinach
26. squash
27. sweet
    potato
28. tomato
29. turnip
30. water
    chestnut
31. yam

YOU WILL NEED:
stalk of celery with its leaves
half a glass of water
1 teaspoon of red food coloring

115

How to Feed Celery

Plants feed us, but how do plants get fed?

What to do: Stand the stalk of celery in a half glass of water colored with a teaspoon of food coloring. Start it off in bright light and let it remain overnight.

What happens: The leaves turn reddish.

Why: The celery stalk is the stem of the celery plant. It absorbs water and minerals from the soil through its root hairs by means of osmosis. Osmosis is a process by which some liquids and gases pass through a membrane—a kind of skin. The water passes into nearby cells and is carried up through its center tubes to the plant's stem and leaves.

The chlorophyll in the leaves—their green coloring—turns the light of the sun into energy. This energy is used to combine some of the water from the soil with carbon dioxide from the air. The carbon and oxygen of the carbon dioxide react with the hydrogen and oxygen of the water to form carbohydrates.

This sugar and starch serve as food for the plant—and eventually for us. You can eat the celery now, or you can use it in the salad on page 00.

116 Storing Carrots

What's the best way to keep carrots, beets and other leafy root vegetables fresh and tasty?

What to do: Wrap one of the carrots with leaves in a plastic bag that has air holes punched in it. Wrap one carrot without leaves the same way. Store them both in the crisper of the refrigerator.

Wrap the other carrots in plain plastic bags without air holes and store them in the crisper, too.

Observe the carrots daily for a week. Taste each one of them.

What happens: The carrot that tastes and looks the best is the one without leaves wrapped in the plastic bag with holes in it.

Why: When the leaves are not removed from the carrots, the sap continues to flow from the root to the leaf, depriving the part we eat of some of its nutrition and flavor. In addition, the leafy tops wilt long before the sturdy roots and start to rot the carrot.

In the bag with holes in it, the air can circulate. This prevents a bitter-tasting compound called terpenoid from forming.

Carrots Hate Fruit!

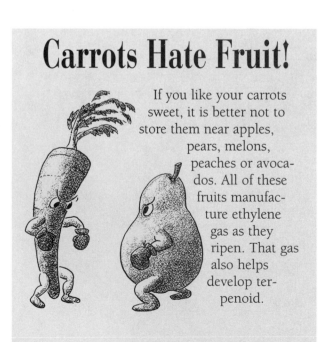

If you like your carrots sweet, it is better not to store them near apples, pears, melons, peaches or avocados. All of these fruits manufacture ethylene gas as they ripen. That gas also helps develop terpenoid.

Answers to the Vegetable Game

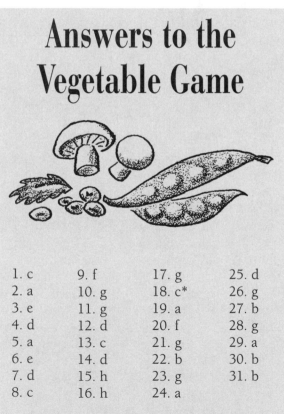

1. c	9. f	17. g	25. d
2. a	10. g	18. c*	26. g
3. e	11. g	19. a	27. b
4. d	12. d	20. f	28. g
5. a	13. c	21. g	29. a
6. e	14. d	22. b	30. b
7. d	15. h	23. g	31. b
8. c	16. h	24. a	

*bulb—a stem enclosed in fleshy leaves.

No Way to Treat a Lettuce

YOU WILL NEED:

2 lettuce leaves
2 bowls

People have been eating lettuce since ancient times. There are many kinds—Bibb, Boston, Iceberg, Romaine, Red-leaf, among others. Most of the time, we eat these leaves raw in salads, though we can cook them in a variety of ways—even into soup. But lettuce has to be treated right!

What to do: Tear one of the leaves into bite-size pieces and place them in a bowl. Leave the other leaf whole and place it in a bowl. Let both stand for an hour or so.

What happens: The torn lettuce turns limp, while the whole leaf stays crisp.

Why: The torn leaf exposes greater areas to the air, so more of the vegetable's water evaporates and escapes into the air. Tearing also releases an enzyme that destroys vitamin C. That's another reason why it's better not to tear lettuce until just before you serve it.

Salting lettuce in advance also makes it wilt. (See page 00.)

Helping Lettuce Last

To perk up limp lettuce, soak it in cold water. The lettuce absorbs the fresh water and the leaves become crisp again.

Lettuce turns yellow as it gets older because its green chlorophyll fades, allowing its yellow pigments to show through. Lettuce will last for a week in the refrigerator. Don't separate the leaves. Wrap the head of lettuce in damp paper towels and place it in a perforated bag. That way you provide the moisture and air it needs to stay fresh.

118 ◆ Taming an Onion

Cultivated since prehistoric times, the onion has a number of varieties. The most familiar are the yellow and red unions that are very strong and can make people cry if they try to slice them without knowing how to handle them.

What to do: Peel both onions. Slice one under water. Slice the other without the water.

What happens: Your eyes begin to tear when you slice an onion—but not when you do it under running water.

Why: When you cut an onion, you tear its cell walls and release a gas called propanethial-sulfur oxide that turns into sulfuric acid in the air. Sulfuric acid stings if it gets into your eyes. When you slice onions under running water, you dilute the gas before it can float up into the air.

Onion Talk

Some varieties of mild onions do not irritate your eyes—the Vidalia from Georgia, the Walla Walla from Washington, and the Maui from Hawaii. All of them have a higher sugar content because of the soil and climate in which they grow.

Believe it or not, onions may be good for your heart. A number of laboratory studies find that oils in onions appear to lower blood levels of the "bad" low-density lipoproteins (LDLs), which carry cholesterol into the bloodstream, and they raise the blood levels of the "good" high-density lipoproteins (HDLs), which carry cholesterol out of the body.

Chill It!

Another way to tame the onion is to chill it in the refrigerator for an hour or so before you slice it. The cold temperature slows the movement of the atoms in the gas so that they don't float up into the air so quickly.

Taking the Starch Out of a Potato!

119

What is starch? It's what people sometimes add when they wash shirts, and it is an ingredient in many medicines. But it's also an important food!

Plants make starch from sugar molecules in order to store food for the winter. Plants also use starch to feed seedlings or new sprouts. The starch is stored in the seeds of corn and wheat, in the stem in sorghum (a grain similar to Indian corn), and in the roots or tuber (underground stem) of yams and potatoes.

How do we know potatoes have starch?

YOU WILL NEED:

potato (peeled)
strainer or cheesecloth
aluminum foil
paper towel
1/2 teaspoon flour
grater
bowl
3 drops of tincture of iodine
1/2 teaspoon salt

What to do: Grate a tablespoon or two of potato into a bowl. Squeeze the potato mush through cheesecloth or a fine strainer onto a piece of aluminum foil. Pat the mush dry with a paper towel Then apply a drop of iodine to it.

Place the salt and the flour on the aluminum foil. Apply a drop of iodine to each.

What happens: The salt takes on the light brown tint of the iodine. The potato and the flour turn blue-black.

Why: The blue-black color tells us that starch is present. A chemical change takes place as the iodine combines with the starch. Starch is a carbohydrate, made up of carbon, hydrogen, and oxygen. In the supermarket, you may see packages labeled "potato starch." Inside is a white, powdery substance ground from potatoes by machines. Huge screens filter out the potato fiber, and the potato starch is then left to dry in large vats.

Potato starch is used to thicken sauces and gravy and to replace wheat flour in cakes, if you don't want to eat wheat.

Potato Race

120

You wouldn't want to eat starchy vegetables such as potatoes and yams unless you cooked them. You need heat to break the cell walls so the potatoes can be digested.

Water boils at 212°F (100°C). Your oven can reach temperatures up to 500°F. Which method of cooking is faster—boiling or baking?

YOU WILL NEED:

pot of boiling water
2 small potatoes of same size
use of the stove and oven (ask for permission or help)

What to do: Preheat the oven to 450°F (230°C).

Carefully scrub the skin of the two potatoes, but don't peel them. Place one potato on a spoon and lower it carefully into the pot of boiling water. Place the other in the center of your oven. Using a long fork, test each potato every 10 minutes until it yields to the fork.

What happens: The boiled potato cooks faster—even though your oven is set at more than twice the temperature of boiling water.

Why: In both the boiling and baking, molecules of gas or liquid circulate and transfer their heat to the food. But the molecules of bubbling water move more violently than the air currents of the oven. This is because water is much more dense than air (1000 to 1). It delivers heat more efficiently.

Tips on Saving Time and Vitamins

To cook a potato faster, always put it in a pre-heated oven or in boiling water. You can also make a potato bake faster by sticking two or three nails in it. They conduct the heat from the stove to the potato.

Some people wrap a potato in aluminum foil, believing it will bake faster. But foil actually slows down the transfer of heat from the oven. Also, because it keeps the moisture from evaporating, it keeps the potato's skin from getting crisp. Aluminum foil is useful, but only to keep the potato warm after it is cooked.

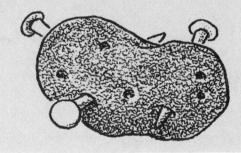

121 Milking a Potato

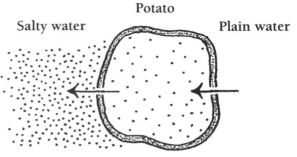

Potato
Salty water — Plain water

Arrow shows direction of liquid flow.

Plants draw water from the earth by osmosis. And food gets into our cells by osmosis. We talked a little about osmosis on page 00. What is it and what does it have to do with cooking?

YOU WILL NEED:

3 large raw potato cubes of the same size

3 glasses of water

ruler

salt

What to do: Put each cube into a glass of water. To glass #1, add a large handful of salt. To glass #2, add a pinch or two of salt. Leave glass #3 plain. After an hour, measure the potato cubes.

What happens: #1 will be smaller than it was; #2 will stay same size; #3 will be a little bigger.

Why: The more salt you add to the water, the stronger the mixture (the solution) becomes. The stronger the solution, the lower its concentration of water.

Osmosis is the flow of a liquid through a membrane (a thin wall). The liquid will always flow into a stronger solution—one where the concentration of liquid is lower.

In #1, the potato cube shrinks as the water in it moves from the weaker potato juice into the (stronger) heavily salted water. In #2, where the concentrations are equal, there is no movement. In #3, the potato juice is the stronger solution, so the water moves into its tissues and makes the cubes swell.

Making Soup

When you make soup, you want the juice to get out of vegetables and meat to flavor the liquid. That's why you add salt to the cooking pot. But when you are cooking meat or chicken as a main course, you want the juice to stay inside. Then you would start with plain water and add salt later, when the cooking is over. Cooking changes the wall of tissue so that osmosis can no longer take place. The liquid can't pass through.

Potato Soup

Why Do Some Vegetables Smell Bad?

It's easy to make your potato cubes into hot potato soup.

Bring the water to a boil, add a pinch of salt and pepper, and put in the potato pieces. In 20 or 25 minutes, when the potatoes are tender, put them in a bowl and mash them. Set aside 1 cup of the water in which the potatoes were boiled. Heat the milk until it just begins to bubble. Add the cup of potato water. Stir in the mashed potatoes and continue to heat the soup over low heat.

YOU WILL NEED:

potato cubes cut into quarters
2 cups of water
salt and pepper
1 cup of milk
2 teaspoons flour
2 teaspoons butter or margarine
3 or 4 tablespoons milk
2 tablespoons grated onion
1 or 2 teaspoons parsley or chives (optional)

In a separate saucepan, melt the butter or margarine. Blend it with the flour and then add the milk. Cook the mixture until it is smooth and bubbly. Then gradually add it to the pot of hot soup, stirring all the while. Add the grated onion. Cover the pot and cook over low heat about 10 minutes. Add salt and pepper to taste. Sprinkle with parsley or chives.

Some nutritious—and delicious—vegetables don't always get to our plates because of their unpleasant odor!

YOU WILL NEED:

small turnip
pot of boiling water
use of the stove (ask for permission or help)

What to do: Peel the turnip and cut it in half. Cut one half into cubes. Leave the other half whole. Place all the turnip pieces in the pot of boiling water. Test each half with a fork after 15 minutes or so, to find out if it is soft. Continue until both halves are firm but tender.

What happens: The cubed turnip cooks in less than a half hour. The other half needs more time and after a half hour it begins to smell bad.

Why: Turnips and rutabagas contain hydrogen sulfide, which smells like rotten eggs. When you cook these vegetables, you release this bad-smelling gas. The longer you cook it, the more smelly chemicals are produced and the worse the odor and the stronger the taste.

Shorter cooking time also means that you save more of the vitamins and minerals.

Other Smelly Veggies

Cabbage and cauliflower also contain smelly sulfur compounds. The longer you cook them, the worse they smell, but the better they taste! To lessen the smell, add a slice of bread to the cooking water. And keep a lid on the pot to stop the smelly molecules from floating off into the air.

Keeping of the Green

124 Green vegetables, such as broccoli, zucchini, spinach, green beans and peas, often come to the dinner table looking drab and unappetizing! Why?

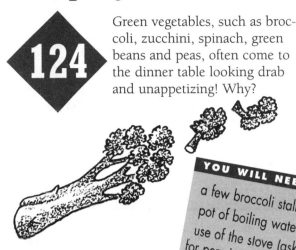

YOU WILL NEED:

a few broccoli stalks
pot of boiling water
use of the stove (ask for permission or help)

What to do: Cut off the stem and separate the broccoli flowers. Place the flowers in a pot of boiling water. After 30 seconds, scoop out half the broccoli. Let the rest continue to cook.

What happens: During the first 30 seconds, the broccoli turns a deep green. The broccoli left in the water loses color.

Why: The color intensifies because gases trapped in the spaces between cells suddenly expand and escape. Ordinarily, these air pockets dim the green color of the vegetable. But when heat collapses the air pockets, we can see the pigments much more clearly.

Longer cooking, however, results in a chemical change. The chlorophyll pigment that makes vegetables green reacts to acids. Water is naturally a little acid. When we heat broccoli or zucchini or spinach, its chlorophyll reacts with its own acids and the acids in the cooking water to form a new brown substance (pheophytin). That's what makes some cooked broccoli an ugly olive green.

125

YOU WILL NEED:

broccoli flowers or zucchini strips

pot of boiling water

1 teaspoon baking soda

use of the stove (ask for permission or help)

Looking Good but Feeling Rotten!

Restaurants sometimes add baking soda to a vegetable to make it look good or cook faster. Does it work?

What to do: Place the broccoli in the boiling water and add the baking soda.

What happens: The vegetable stays green, but after a short time it turns mushy.

Why: Baking soda is an alkali, the chemical opposite of an acid. When it is added to the water, it neutralizes some of the acids of the water and the vegetable. Because there are so few acids, the vegetable stays green—but the alkali dissolves its firm cell wall. The vegetable tissue rapidly becomes too soft.

Baking soda also destroys the vegetable's vitamins. It's a high price to pay for looking good!

126 Cold or Hot

We always start cooking green vegetables in boiling water. Why?

YOU WILL NEED:

broccoli or spinach

pot of cold water

pot of boiling water

use of the stove (ask for permission or help)

What to do: Place half of the broccoli or spinach in a pot half full of cold water. Place the other half in a pot half full of boiling water. Cook both until the vegetables are tender.

What happens: The vegetable in the cold water loses more color than that in the boiling water. Why: Plants contain enzymes, proteins that cause chemical reactions. They change the plant's color and also destroy its vitamins. The particular enzyme (chlorophyllase) involved here is more active between 150° and 170°F (66°-77°C) than at other temperatures, so less pigment is lost if the vegetables don't have to be heated through the 150°-170°F range. Water boils at 212°F (100°C). If the vegetable is put into boiling water, it avoids the lower range completely.

127 Keeping a Lid On

How can you preserve a vegetable's color better—
cooking it covered or uncovered?

YOU WILL NEED:
broccoli or zucchini
2 pots of boiling
water, one with a cover
use of the stove
(ask for permission
or help)

What to do: Cut off the stalk and separate the flowers of the broccoli or cut the zucchini into quarters.

Cook half the vegetable in a large quantity of boiling water in a covered pot for five to seven minutes.

Cook the other half in a large quantity of boiling water in a pot without a lid for five to seven minutes.

What happens: The broccoli in the uncovered pot retains its color. The broccoli in the covered pot does not.

Why: The color changes less in the uncovered pot because some of the plant's acids escape in steam during the first two minutes of boiling. When the pot is covered, the acids turn back into liquid, condense on the lid and fall down into the water.

The bad news is that, without the lid, you lose more vitamins into the air. And because it takes longer to cook without a lid, the nutrients have more time to be drawn out of the food.

128 There Must Be a Better Way!

In the last experiment, you saw that cooking a green vegetable in a large quantity of water with the lid off prevents it from discoloring. But cooking that way, more vitamins are lost. What's the solution?

YOU WILL NEED:
broccoli
steamer rack
(or colander)
pot with a cover
water
use of the stove (ask
for permission or help)

What to do: Separate the broccoli flowers and put them in the steamer rack. Place a half-cup of water in the pot and turn on the heat to medium high. When the water starts to boil, slip in the steamer rack with the broccoli, and cover the pot with a tight-fitting lid. Cook for seven to nine minutes.

What happens: The broccoli remains green.

Why: Steaming is less effective at conducting heat than water is. So the vegetable may take a few more minutes to soften than it would if boiled. But since it never comes into contact with the acids in the water, it doesn't lose its color or its vitamins.

129 Colorful Carrot

Unlike green and red vegetables, carrots do not lose their color when cooked in water!

What to do: Bring a cup of water to the boiling point. With a large spoon, lower the carrot slices into the pot of boiling water. Cook for 15 to 20 minutes.

What happens: The carrots remain orange, but you now can pierce them with a fork.

Why: Though they dissolve in fat, the coloring matter of carrots (carotenes) do not dissolve in water and are not affected by the normal heat of cooking. The carrots therefore stay orange.

Because heat dissolves some of the fiber (the hemicellulose) in the stiff carrot walls, cooked carrots are easier to digest and more nutritious than raw carrots. Cooked or raw, carrots are a good source of both vitamin A and the mineral potassium.

Strangely enough, eating huge amounts of carrots (two cups a day for several months) turns your skin yellow! Fortunately, when you stop eating so many carrots, it returns to its normal color.

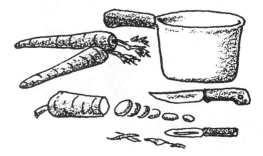

130 About Legumes

Legumes are foods such as beans, peas and lentils that come from the fruit or seeds of plants that have pods. We can eat them both fresh and dried. Kidney beans, for instance, are the dried seeds of green beans. But we call the green beans a vegetable and the kidney bean a legume!

Legumes are second in importance to grain as a source of food. They are valuable because they absorb nitrogen from the air. Nitrogen is the essential mineral of amino acids, the building blocks of the protein that helps grow and repair our body's tissues. So, in addition to fiber and essential minerals and vitamins, beans supply us with protein.

Among the thousands of beans that belong to the legume family, only 22 are grown in quantity for us to eat. These range from lima beans, split-peas and chick-peas to adzuki, used in Asian sweet dishes, and the soybeans from which soy sauce and tofu are made.

Though we call it a nut, the peanut is also a legume.

What kinds of legumes do you like to eat?

131 Culling

We cull beans to pick out small stones and other unwanted material. There is a quick, foolproof way to do it. Place the lentils or beans in a clear jar or bowl. Cover them with a half glass of water.

Most of the beans will stay at the bottom of the jar but the few defective ones will float up to the top—they are hollow and therefore lighter. You can lift them out with a slotted spoon.

132 Tough Cook, Tender Beans

Most legumes have a bland flavor. We season and flavor them to make them taste good. Mexicans add garlic and chili; Italians add garlic and oregano. The British add mustard and bay leaf. New Englanders make their famous baked beans dish with brown sugar and molasses.

Either tomatoes or lemon juice will make legumes tasty. And their vitamin C makes the iron in the beans easier to absorb. But not if our timing is off!

What to do: Cull the lentils (see above) and discard any that float to the top. Place three tablespoons in each pot and cover with water.

To pot #1, add the tomato sauce and lemon juice.

Don't add any juice or sauce to pot #2.

Simmer both pots on low heat. After 20 minutes test the lentils in both pots for softness using a fork. Retest every 10 minutes. Remove the pot from the heat when the lentils are tender but firm. Note how much time it takes them to cook.

What happens: The plain lentils take 30 to 40 minutes to soften. The lentils with the tomato sauce take much more time to soften.

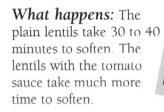

Why: When you add tomatoes or tomato sauce or lemon juice before the beans are soft, the acid of the fruit or vegetable reacts with the starch of the beans to toughen their seed coat. They do soften, but it takes them much longer. That's why acidic foods need to be added only after the beans are soft.

Adding molasses before the beans have softened also interferes with the softening process because molasses contains calcium.

Salt also reacts with the seed coating to form a barrier that keeps liquid from being absorbed and makes the skins tough. It too should be added only after the beans are cooked.

Lentil Snack

Dried lentils will swell up to two or three times their original size in the cooking. Add lemon juice to them or tomato sauce or vinegar and onions and serve your cooked lentils on crackers. They are even tastier served cold the next day.

Fabulous Soybeans

Soybeans are the only beans whose proteins are considered "complete." They contain all the amino acids that are essential for us to get through our food.

Soybeans are considered a perfect meat substitute and are ideal for vegetarian cooking. Tofu, a cheese-like curd made from soybeans, is a Japanese favorite that has become popular in the rest of the world. The secret of tofu is that it has no flavor of its own but takes on the taste and smell of the foods with which it is cooked. It can taste like eggs, cheese, chicken—even like chocolate pudding!

Sprouting Beans

133

The sprouts used in salads actually sprout from beans! You can easily sprout your own.

What to do: Cull the beans.

Soak 4 tablespoons of the beans overnight in warm water. Then drain them and divide them between two clean glasses. Put a layer of cheesecloth over the top of each of the glasses and tie it on with a string or rubber band.

Store the first glass in a warm, dark place like a cupboard. Store the second in the refrigerator.

Without soaking them, place the last two tablespoons of the beans in a third glass. Label it and store it in the cupboard.

Keep the sprouts moist in all three glasses by rinsing them twice a day with lukewarm water. Drain off the excess water through the cheesecloth to prevent rotting or molding.

Note what happens after four or five days.

What happens: The batch of soaked beans stored in a warm, dark place sprouts and yields four to six ounces (112–118 g) of sprouts!

The beans stored in the refrigerator and the unsoaked beans never sprout.

Why: During the overnight soaking, the hard outer shell splits, the starch in the beans absorbs the water and the beans swell. That permits the embryo within each bean to take in water. But in addition to moisture, seeds need warmth and darkness in order to grow.

Harvest your crop and use the sprouts raw in salads or on sandwiches, or stir-fry them with scallions, soy sauce and garlic.

FRUIT OF THE VINE AND OTHER PLACES

Who calls a tomato a fruit? Why not store bananas in the refrigerator? What does pineapple do to gelatin? Where does vinegar come from? Is one end of a fruit sweeter than the other? And more.

About Fruit

Botanists call tomatoes, eggplants, cucumbers, and pumpkins fruits because they are the part of the plant that has the seeds.

But as cooks—and eaters—we call them vegetables and save the term fruit for plants that are sweeter.

All fruits grow above ground. We harvest grapes, berries, and melons from vines and shrubs. From trees, we get apples and pears, citrus fruits, bananas, figs and dates, and cherries. The largest fruit to grow on a tree is the jackfruit, native to southeast Asia. It can weigh as much as 80 pounds!

Most fruits are eaten raw once they ripen. But many fruits are also cooked—stewed, poached, baked—as well as dried, canned, frozen, squeezed into juice, baked in pies, used to flavor other foods, and made into jams and jellies. Some, like plantains, quince, rhubarb and sour cherries, must be cooked.

134 Bite or Bake?

There are hundreds of varieties of apples to choose from. Which do you bite and which do you bake?

What to do: Core both apples and cut away a circle of peel at the top. Place them in a baking dish. Fill the center hole of the apples with sugar or raisins. Sprinkle with nutmeg. Add water to cover the bottom of the dish. Place it in a 400°F (200°C) oven for about an hour or until the apples are tender. Taste each one.

What happens: The Delicious apple is mushy and shapeless. The Rome is firm and tasty.

Why: The Delicious apple becomes mushy for two reasons. First, it lacks enough fiber (cellulose), the part of the cell wall that keeps it firm, to hold the peel intact. Second, the Delicious apple doesn't have enough acid to counterbalance the added sugar. The apple that is less sweet remains firmer and retains more fiber. Fiber is indigestible roughage that is good for us because it helps the intestines and bowels to work better to eliminate waste products.

Of course, a raw apple contains the most fiber!

> **YOU WILL NEED:**
> 1 Red or Golden Delicious apple
> 1 Rome, York Imperial, Stayman, Winesap or Jonathan apple
> 2 to 3 tablespoons sugar or raisins
> dash of nutmeg (optional)
> water
> baking dish
> use of the oven (ask for permission or help)

Bursting an Apple 135

Suppose you want a mushy apple!

What to do: Wash both apples, peel them and cut them in four sections. Cut away the core and slice each quarter into cubes. Cook the pieces in a small amount of water in a covered pot until they are tender. Add the cinnamon and nutmeg—or the lemon juice—and cook a few minutes longer.

What happens: You have applesauce.

Why: With the peel removed, the pectin—the cementing material between cells that stiffens the fruit—dissolves. The water inside the apple's cells swells, bursts the cell walls, and the fruit's flesh softens. An apple turns into applesauce.

> **YOU WILL NEED:**
> 2 apples
> water
> parer (optional)
> knife
> pot with cover
> 1/2 cup water
> 1 teaspoon lemon juice or
> dash of cinnamon and nutmeg
> use of stove (ask for permission or help)

Apple in the Cookie Jar

136

An apple in the bread box or cookie jar will affect our bread or cake!

What to do: Place one apple slice in a cookie jar with the slice of bread. Place the other in the cookie jar with the slice of cake. Don't open the jars for a day or so.

What happens: The bread gets stale—and the cake stays moist!

Why: Sugar dissolves in water. It will absorb water from the atmosphere, if given the chance. The more sugary food draws water molecules from the other food. The apple has more sugar than the bread, so the bread loses water to the apple. But the cake has more sugar than the apple, so the apple loses water to the cake.

137

One End Is Sweeter!

Did you know that different parts of the same fruit taste different?

What to do: Peel the orange. Cut one slice across the stem end and then one across the blossom end. Taste them.

What happens: The slice at the blossom end is sweeter.

Why: The blossom end develops more sugar because it is more exposed to the sun. For the same reason, fruits grown in the temperate zone are only 10 to 15% sugar, while those from the tropics, such as bananas, figs, and dates, range from 20 to 60% sugar.

Why Are Green Apples Sour?

What makes unripe apples sour? Malic acid. All apples have it, but as an apple ripens on the tree, the amount of malic acid declines and the apple becomes sweeter. Depending on the soil and climate in which they are grown, some varieties stay more tart than others. Some people prefer apples like Granny Smiths, which stay green, just because they are sour.

How to Ripen a Fruit

All too often, the fruit we buy is not quite ripe. What do we do with it?

YOU WILL NEED:

2 unripe peaches, nectarines or other fruit
brown paper bag
your refrigerator

What to do: Place one of the unripe fruits in the crisper of the refrigerator for a day or two. Place the other in the paper bag and close it securely. Put it somewhere out of the way—on top of the refrigerator, for instance. Let it stand for a day or two. Taste both.

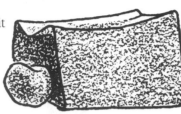

What happens: The fruit in the refrigerator softens—but it is not very tasty. The fruit in the paper bag softens—and sweetens!

Why: In the paper bag, you are trapping and concentrating the ethylene gas that comes from the fruit naturally. This gas speeds up the ripening process. In the refrigerator, the ethylene gas is shared with the other contents of the crisper.

Getting Juice from a Lemon

139

YOU WILL NEED:

2 lemons
knife

How do you get juice out of a lemon?

What to do: Cut the first lemon in half and squeeze out as much of the juice as you can.

Before you cut it, roll the other lemon on a hard surface like a countertop. Then squeeze out the juice.

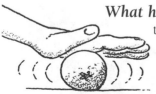

What happens: It is much easier to squeeze out the juice after you've rolled the lemon—and you wind up with much more juice!

Why: You break up the tissues of the fruit when you roll it on a hard surface, so the juice comes out more easily.

Lemon Ices

YOU WILL NEED:

freshly grated lemon peel
1/2 cup of lemon juice (1 or 2 lemons)
1 cup of sugar (or less to taste)
4 cups of water
ice cube tray without separators, or a metal baking pan
small paper cups

Use your lemon juice to make refreshing lemon ices. Grate the peel of one lemon into a small plate or jar.

Simmer the water and the sugar uncovered over medium heat about three minutes until the sugar dissolves. Let it cool and put it in the refrigerator for about an hour until it is cold.

Combine the cold sugar syrup, the grated lemon peel and the lemon juice, and pour it into an ice cube tray. Put the tray in the freezer for about 30 minutes—until ice crystals begin to form. Then stir the mixture well and return the tray to the freezer. Keep stirring every 30 minutes until the mixture is frozen through—about 2 to 2 1/2 hours.

Spoon it into small paper cups—and lick away!

Rescuing an Apple

How do you prevent a cut apple from turning brown?

What to do: Cut the apple into quarters. Let one of the quarters remain on the kitchen table. Place another in the refrigerator.

Sprinkle lemon juice on the other two quarters. Place one of these on the table and the other in the refrigerator.

What happens: The untreated apple on the table turns brown first. The apple with the lemon juice in the refrigerator stays fresh longest.

Why: When you cut into apple, you tear its cells, releasing an enzyme called polyphenoloxidase. The enzyme speeds up the process by which compounds in the apple (phenols) combine with oxygen from the air. This is what produces the brownish pigment that darkens the fruit and makes it taste bad.

The enzyme works more slowly at cold temperatures than at room temperatures. It works even more slowly in an acid like lemon juice, which completely inactivates it.

If you don't have any lemon juice around, you can use orange juice, but lemon juice is better because it contains more acid.

Not in the Refrigerator

Bananas are picked and shipped green, but green bananas are not digestible. You can ripen them in a few days—but is it true that you should never put bananas in the refrigerator?

What to do: Place one banana on the counter and one in the refrigerator

What happens: Within a few days the banana on the counter turns yellow and its flesh becomes soft and creamy. The one in the refrigerator blackens and its insides remain hard.

Why: Bananas release ethylene gas naturally to ripen the fruit. On the counter, the skin's green chlorophyll disappears and reveals yellow pigments (carotenes and flavones). Also, the starch of the banana changes to sugar and the pectin, which holds the cells of the banana firm, breaks down. And so the flesh softens and is easy to digest.

In the cold of the refrigerator, the tropical bananas suffer cell damage and the release of browning and other enzymes. The fruit doesn't ripen and the skin blackens instead of turning yellow.

Once a banana is ripe it is safe to store it in the refrigerator. The skin may darken but the fruit inside will remain tasty for several days.

142   Powerful Pineapple

YOU WILL NEED:

1 envelope of unflavored gelatin

1/2 cup of cold water

a few bits of raw pineapple (or frozen pineapple juice)

can of pineapple chunks

1 1/2 cups of boiling water

Gelatin is protein that comes from the connective tissue in the hoofs, bones, tendons, ligaments, and cartilage of animals. Vegetable gelatin, or agar, is made from seaweed. Gelatin dissolves in hot water and hardens with cold. We can put all kinds of fruit in it to make terrific desserts—but we're told on the package not to add raw pineapple. Why?

What to do: Stir gelatin in the cold water and let it stand one or two minutes. Then add the boiling water and stir until all the gelatin is dissolved. Pour into 2 cups or dessert dishes.

To one, add raw pineapple bits or frozen pineapple juice. To the other, add canned pineapple bits or canned juice. Put both in the refrigerator.

What happens: The gelatin with the canned pineapple becomes firm. The gelatin with the raw pineapple remains water.

Why: Pineapples, like figs and papayas, contain an enzyme that breaks proteins down into small fragments. If you put raw pineapple in gelatin for a dessert or fruit salad, this enzyme digests the gelatin molecules and prevents the gel from becoming solid. It remains liquid.

Cooking stops the enzyme from working. That's why you can add canned pineapple to the gelatin with no bad effects. Since it has been heated, it no longer contains the active enzyme.

Putting Pineapple to Work

Chefs sometimes simmer raw pineapple with a meat stew to help break down the protein of the meat and make it tender. A bonus is its sweet flavor.

143 Currying Flavor with a Lime

Sometimes "cooking" starts hours before you light the stove.

What to do: Mix the lime juice and olive oil. Add the herbs and spices and stir. Put one of the chicken breasts in a bowl and cover it with the marinade.

Season the other chicken breast with salt and pepper and, if you wish, herbs.

Refrigerate both chicken breasts for an hour or so. Broil each one. After 10 minutes, turn them over and continue to broil for another 5 to 10 minutes. Test them for tenderness and remove them from the oven when a fork goes in easily.

What happens: The marinated chicken breast cooks faster. The lime not only flavors the chicken but also cuts down on cooking time.

Why: In marinating, the essential ingredient is an acid such as lime or lemon or vinegar that softens the tissues.

In addition to tenderizing and adding flavor, marinades sometimes preserve color. If you are marinating foods more than an hour or two, it is safer to refrigerate them. Like cooked food, marinating food needs to be refrigerated to prevent the growth of dangerous bacteria.

144 How to Make Vinegar

Vinegar is often used to flavor salads and tenderize meats. Many vinegars are made from fruit or wine (which is made from fruit). You can use apples to make your vinegar.

What to do: Cut the apples into small pieces, place them in your blender or juicer, and press out the juice. Pour half the juice into one jar, and the other half into the other. Place one jar in the refrigerator. Place the other in a warm place. Compare the color and the odor over a period of a week.

What happens: Both change, but the juice in the warm place changes much faster—weeks faster! At first you see bubbles and smell alcohol. You may see a thick film forming on top. Then the liquid begins to smell sour.

Why: Chemical changes have taken place. Yeasts from the skins of the apple and from the air act on the sugars of the apple juice, producing carbon dioxide and alcohol ("hard" cider). Within the week, bacteria in the cider turn it into vinegar.

GRAIN: THE STAFF OF LIFE

What happens when you make toast? What puts the bubbles in the pancakes? Why is baking more expensive on a rainy day? What is yeast? And more…

About Grain

Grain, whole or ground into meal or flour, is the principal food of people and domestic animals. Even Goldilocks and the Three Bears ate cereal, though they called it porridge.

Cereals, breads, rolls, muffins, buns, bagels, pancakes, waffles, spaghetti, macaroni, rice, bulgur, kasha, cookies, crackers, cake—all are grain products. They are made from wheat, buckwheat, rice, rye, oats, maize, barley, and, in Africa and India and China, millet or sorghum. Less familiar grains include amaranth, which fed the Aztecs; quinoa, a staple food of the ancient Incas; and triticale, which modern scientists developed by crossing rye and wheat.

145 What is Toast?

Toast is defined in the dictionary as a slice of bread browned on both sides by heat. But what causes the bread to brown?

What to do: Place the pieces of bread in the toaster, in the electric broiler, or in the oven under the broiler. Let one stay in twice as long as the other.

What happens: One turns golden brown. The one kept in too long turns black.

Why: Too much heat releases the carbon of the starch and sugar. It is this carbon that makes the bread turn black.

Toasting is a chemical process that alters the structure of the surface sugars, starches, and proteins of the bread slice. The sugars become fiber. The amino acids that are the building blocks of the protein break down and lose some of their nutritional value. Toast, therefore, has more fiber and less protein than the bread from which it is made. Some nutritionists believe that when you eat toast instead of bread you are getting color and flavor at the expense of nutrition.

146 Science for Breakfast

Hot cereal feels good, especially on a cold morning. Does it matter whether you start it in cold or boiling water?

What to do: Stir 1/3 cup of the oatmeal into a pot with 1/2 cup of the water. Bring it to a boil, lower the heat, and simmer for five minutes, stirring occasionally. Cover the pot and remove it from the heat. Let the mixture stand.

In a second pot, bring the rest of the water to a boil. Add salt and pour in the other half of the oatmeal. Lower the heat and simmer for five minutes, stirring occasionally. Again, cover, remove from the heat and let the mixture stand for a few minutes.

Taste the first pot of oatmeal. Then taste the second.

What happens: Both are cooked and taste good. The oatmeal that started in the cold water is creamier than the oatmeal that started in boiling water.

Why: As you heat the grains, the starch granules absorb water molecules, swell and soften.

Then the nutrients inside are released and are more easily absorbed by the body.

When you start cooking the oatmeal in cold water, the granules have a longer time to absorb the water. The activity starts at 140°F (60°C), well below the 212°F (100°C) boiling point. The complex carbohydrates (amylose and amylopectin) that make up the starch change. They break up some of the bonds between the atoms of the same molecule and form new bonds between atoms of different molecules. The water molecules then get trapped in the starch granules, which become bulky and eventually break, releasing the nutrients inside.

Add milk and raisins or bananas or blueberries to the oatmeal and you have a terrific dish that also furnishes vitamins, minerals, and complete protein.

147 Why Not Eat Flour Raw?

Flour is the finely ground meal of wheat or other cereal grains. But we can't eat it raw.

What to do: Stir the sugar into one of the glasses of cold water. Stir the flour into the other glass of cold water.

What happens: The sugar disappears. The flour does not.

Why: The sugar dissolves in the water. The grains of flour are too big to dissolve. When you stir the flour and water together, you get a paste in which each grain is hanging suspended in the water.

When you chew your food—but before you swallow it—saliva works to help you digest it. Sugar molecules separate and mix with saliva immediately.

Flour, however, is suspended in the saliva, just as it is in the glass of water. The tough wall of plant cells around each grain of flour prevents the starch molecules from getting out. Nothing can get in unless the wall is broken—neither water needed to soften the starch nor the enzymes that would digest it. Heat breaks that wall. That's why flour needs to be cooked.

Popping Popcorn 148

Making popcorn gives you a good idea of how heat bursts the starch wall. Puffed cereals are made in a similar way.

What to do: Heat the pan on high heat for one or two minutes, and then pour in enough oil to cover the bottom of it. Lower the heat to medium. Add a few kernels and cover the pot. When you hear those kernels start to pop, add just enough popcorn to cover the bottom of the pot. Lower the heat. Put on the lid.

Shake the pot from time to time, but don't remove the lid while you can hear crackling sounds. When the sounds stop—within a minute or two—remove the pot from the stovetop and uncover it.

What happens: You have a mountain of popped corn!

Why: The moist and pulpy heart of the corn kernel is surrounded by a hard starch shell. When the kernel is heated, the moisture in the kernel turns to steam; the heart gets bigger—and the shell bursts. Grains of starch behave a lot like kernels of corn. When heat breaks the wall, the starch comes out and mixes with water. It is then in a form that we can digest.

All recipes that have flour as an ingredient— cake, biscuits, bread, gravies, sauces, puddings— must be cooked so that the starch in the flour can be released.

Buttered Popcorn

Many people eat popcorn exactly as it comes from the pot. But you may want to flavor it with a bit of melted butter or margarine and a pinch or two of salt.

Be sure to wait until after the kernels have popped to add the salt. Doing it beforehand makes the popcorn tough, just as adding salt before they cook toughens lentils and beans (see page 113).

149 Gluten: The Sticky Story

YOU WILL NEED:

2 tablespoons of warm water
4 tablespoons all-purpose flour
cold water
bowl
faucet with running water

In much of the world, flour is often made from wheat. There are two types of wheat—hard winter wheat and soft spring wheat. Soft wheat has more starch in it. It is made into soft, powdery cake flours and products that are meant to be tender and crumbly. Hard wheat, with more protein and less starch, is more gritty and coarse. It is better for bread baking because it forms a strong gluten. What is gluten?

What to do: Mix the flour and water. Roll it into a ball and soak the ball in cold water for 30 minutes. Gently fold and squeeze the dough under running water. Then knead the dough. The illustration shows how.

What happens: The dough becomes a sticky substance that stretches.

Why: All-purpose flour is a blend of both soft and hard flour. When you soak the dough in cold water, you wash away the starch, leaving the proteins. When you knead the dough, these proteins (gliadin and glutenin) interact to form an elastic substance—gluten. When the bread bakes, tiny bubbles of air get trapped inside the gluten. They make the dough rise a little. Without gluten, there would be no raised bread.

Only wheat produces the gluten that traps these air bubbles. That's why most bread and muffin recipes call for some wheat—even rye bread and corn muffins.

To form more bubbles within the gluten and get the dough to rise higher, bakers sometimes add other ingredients, such as yeast (see page 128) or baking soda or baking powder (see page 131).

Contents of Flour

	% Protein	% Starch
Cake flour	7.3	79.4
Semolina flour	12.3	73.5
All-purpose flour	10.5	76.1

Flour also contains 1% fat. The rest is moisture.

Whole wheat flour, graham flour, and cracked wheat all use the whole kernel—the bran (the hard, brown outer cover), the endosperm (the interior food for the germ) and the central germ (the part that sprouts). "White" flour has been refined—the brown bran and the germ have been removed.

Storing Bread

It's best to store bread in a breadbox at room temperature or in the freezer—but not in the refrigerator. Bread gets stale because the water from the interior flows to the crust where it is absorbed by the gluten (see page 125) and starch of the wheat. If bread is left uncovered, its water is lost in the air and the bread gets stale very fast. This happens fastest at temperatures like those of a refrigerator, just above freezing.

Because most of the water remains in the loaf, you can often "revive" stale bread by heating it. However, when bread becomes moldy, it is unsafe to eat.

Popovers: Gluten in Action

150

The way you mix batter or dough influences the amount of gluten that you develop and whether the baked goods will be spongy or flaky, coarse or fine, tender or tough.

YOU WILL NEED:
1 cup (112 g) flour
2 eggs
1 tablespoon (15 ml) cooking oil
1 cup (240 ml) milk
1/2 teaspoon salt (optional)
muffin tins
use of the oven (ask for permission or help)

What to do: Preheat oven to 450°F (232°C).

Beat the eggs, add the milk and gradually stir them into the flour to make a smooth batter. Beat the mixture thoroughly with an egg beater or in a mixer. The batter will be thin—like heavy cream.

Grease the muffin tins. Fill them half to two-thirds full. Bake at 450° (230°C) for 15 minutes. Then reduce the temperature to 350° (175°C) and bake for 20 minutes more. Don't open the oven door before the time is up.

What happens: The batter has baked into six to eight crisp, nearly hollow, delicious shells!

Why: When you started, you beat the dough hard to develop the gluten. In the oven, the combination of hot air and steam—formed from the large amount of liquid in the batter—causes the mixture to swell.

If you had opened the oven door, hot air would have escaped—and the popovers would have collapsed.

151 Hidden Sugar

Would it surprise you to find out that your body converts starch to sugar?

What to do: Place the cornstarch or the cracker on the tip of your tongue. Mix it with saliva and let it stay for a while.

What happens: At first, it doesn't taste sweet on the tip of your tongue. But when it mixes with saliva, it becomes quite sweet.

Why: A molecule of starch is composed of a chain of sugar molecules, which can be broken into separate links by enzymes, proteins that cause chemical reactions. The enzyme (ptyalin) in your saliva splits the starch into its sugar links. The links dissolve in your digestive juices and then move easily into your intestines, through the wall into the bloodstream, and then along the bloodstream to the cells.

152 Alice's Magic Pill

In Wonderland, Alice ate a little pill and grew and grew and grew. Do you suppose it was made of yeast?

What to do: Put the warm water in a cup. Test a drop of it on your wrist. It should not feel hot. Stir in the sugar and the yeast. Let it stand. Within 5 or 10 minutes, bubbles appear on the surface. While you are waiting, mix the flour and salt and 1/2 cup (180 ml) of water in one of the bowls. Divide the mixture in two, and put half into each bowl.

Add the bubbly yeast to the first bowl. Cover both bowls with wax paper or plastic wrap and let them stand in a warm place from 45 minutes to an hour.

What happens: The mixture with the yeast doubles in size. The other remains the same size.

Why: The yeast converts the flour into sugar molecules. It eats the sugar, digests it, and uses it for energy, producing carbon dioxide bubbles, which puff up the mixture.

153 The Sugar Eater

Yeast, a tiny colorless plant, has been used for thousands of years to put air into breads and cakes.

What to do: Pour 2/3 of a cup of warm water into each of the glasses. Number the glasses. Add the sugar to #1. Add the flour to #2. Don't add anything to #3. Next, add an equal amount of the yeast to each glass. Let them stand. Observe them after 10 minutes, 20 minutes, 30 minutes. Note the differences.

What happens: Glass #1 produces bubbles in the first 10 minutes. Glass #2 produces bubbles after 15 or 20 minutes or so. Glass #3 never bubbles.

Why: Yeast is a fungus. It feeds on sugar and breathes out carbon dioxide. In the glass with sugar, it eats quickly—and soon produces carbon dioxide, which makes bubbles. In the glass with the flour, it takes longer because the enzymes in the yeast have to turn part of the flour's starch into sugar before the yeast can digest it.

In the glass of plain water, the yeast has no sugar on which to feed and so does not produce carbon dioxide. Some sugar is required for yeast to feed on.

Too much sugar, however, slows the production of carbon dioxide or even stops activity completely.

Just Right

Some like it hot, some like it cold, but yeast likes it just right!

What to do: Dissolve the sugar and yeast in 2/3 cup (160 ml) of water that is warm to the touch. Let the mixture stand.

Mix the flour, salt, oil, and 5 ounces (150 ml) of water. When bubbles appear on the surface of the yeast mixture, add it to the flour and mix well with a wooden spoon, or in a mixer. Knead the dough on the chopping board for 5 to 10 minutes, following the illustrations.

Sprinkle on more flour if the dough gets too sticky to handle. Keep pushing against the ball of dough, pressing into it and turning it to knead it on all sides.

When the dough feels satiny, make it into a ball and divide it in three equal parts. Place each part in an oiled bowl covered with plastic wrap.

Number the samples. Place #1 in a warm place (without a draft). Place #2 in the warmest part of the refrigerator. Place #3 in a hot place—over a radiator or in a hot oven.

What happens: Within 45 minutes to an hour, the dough in a warm place doubles in size. The dough in the refrigerator eventually rises, too, but it takes much longer. The dough in the hot place does not rise at all.

1 **push it away** →

2 ← **pull it back**

3 **turn ball of dough**

4 **continue to knead and turn**

YOU WILL NEED:

2/3 cup (160 ml) of warm water
2 tablespoons of sugar
1 package of dry yeast
3 mixing bowls (or cereal dishes)
plastic chopping board
felt-tipped pen, paper, scotch tape
plastic wrap
3 1/2 cups (392 g) of flour
2 tablespoons (30 ml) of cooking oil (olive or corn oil)
5 ounces (150 ml) of water
pinch of salt
1 teaspoon of cooking oil (to oil bowls)
wooden spoon
use of the oven (ask for permission or help)

Why: Yeast requires a moist, warm temperature—above 50° and below 130°F (10°–54°C). Below 50°F (10°C), it is relatively inactive, and above 130°F (54°C), it dies of too much heat.

The Pizza Test

Yeast consists of tiny living cells that make carbon dioxide as they breathe. Its bubbles not only puff up bread and cakes but also pizza. With the dough from the last experiment, you can see just what a difference yeast makes!

YOU WILL NEED:

Dough #1 from the previous experiment

Dough #3 from the previous experiment

2 cookie tins or pie plates

small can of tomato sauce

pinch of oregano

rolling pin or glass

2 to 4 ounces (56–112 g) of cheese (mozzarella, Parmesan or cheddar)

1 to 2 teaspoons olive oil

What to do: On a lightly floured board, punch the raised dough with your fists. Knead it for a few minutes and stretch it out or roll it with a rolling pin or the side of a glass to a circle six to eight inches (15–20 cm) in diameter and ½-inch (.62 cm) thick. Leave the edges a little thicker so they make a rim.

Put the rolled-out dough on an oiled cookie sheet or a pie plate. Let it rise for another 15 minutes. Roll out the other piece of dough, the one that didn't rise because the yeast was killed. Knead it and then roll it out onto the same kind of circle.

Preheat the oven to 450°F (230°C).

Put a layer of cubed or grated cheese on each of the dough circles. Stir a pinch of marjoram or oregano into the tomato sauce. Then pour half of the tomato sauce into the center of each pizza and spread the sauce in circles toward the rim. Top each with another layer of cheese.

Place the pie plates near the bottom of the preheated oven. Bake each pizza for about 20 to 30 minutes or until its crust is brown.

Be sure to use a pot holder when you take the pizzas out of the oven. Let them stand for about five minutes before you cut them. Taste each one.

What happens: The pizza made from the raised dough puffs up even more and has a light, moist taste. The dough of the other "pizza" is unpizza-like—flatter, heavier, and not very tasty.

Why: The yeast in the raised dough is still active and continues its action during your kneading and for part of the time that the pizza is baking. The other dough bakes as though no yeast had been added.

156 About Baking Soda

Baking soda is sodium bicarbonate—sometimes called bicarbonate of soda. Some people use it for brushing their teeth, for absorbing refrigerator odors or as an antacid for indigestion! But we can also use baking soda to puff up bread and cake.

YOU WILL NEED:
2 teaspoons of baking soda
glass of orange juice or lemonade
glass of water

What to do: Add 1 teaspoon of baking soda to the glass of water. Add 1 teaspoon of baking soda to the orange juice.

What happens: Nothing happens in the glass of water. In the glass with the orange juice, you get bubbles. You have made orange soda!

Why: When you add an acid (orange juice) to the baking soda, you free the carbon dioxide of the baking soda—the bubbly gas.

Try adding baking soda to buttermilk, sour cream, yogurt, molasses, apple cider. They are all acidic and they will all bubble.

When baking soda is added to dough made with any of these or other acidic liquids, bubbles form and cause the dough to rise.

157 About Baking Powder

How is baking powder different from baking soda?

YOU WILL NEED:
2 glasses of water
1/2 teaspoon baking powder
1/2 teaspoon baking soda

What to do: Add the baking powder to one glass of water. Add the baking soda to the other.

What happens: The water with the baking powder bubbles. The water with baking soda does not.

Why: Baking soda is an alkali, the chemical opposite of an acid. When it combines with an acid, it forms carbon dioxide.

Baking powder is a combination of baking soda and an acid. When you add baking powder to water or milk, the alkali and the acid react with one another and produce carbon dioxide—the bubbles. There are three types of baking powder. Each one contains baking soda. In addition, they each contain an acid—either cream of tartar (tartrate baking powder), monocalcium phosphate (phosphate baking powder) or a combination of calcium acid phosphate and sodium aluminum sulfate (double-acting baking powder).

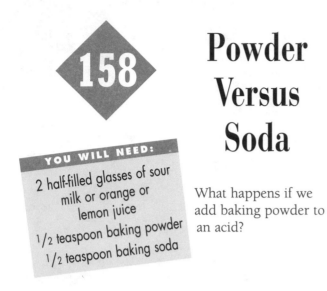

158 ◆ Powder Versus Soda

What happens if we add baking powder to an acid?

What to do: Add baking powder to one of the half-filled glasses of sour milk and baking soda to the other glass.

What happens: The sour milk with the baking powder does not bubble as much as the one with the baking soda.

Why: When you add baking powder to an acid, you are tampering with the balance of acid and alkali. You are adding more acid than alkali. The result is that you actually reduce the amount of carbon dioxide produced. Therefore, if you want to bake with sour milk or buttermilk instead of regular milk, you could do it by eliminating the extra acid. You would just replace each teaspoon of baking powder in the recipe with 1/2 teaspoon of baking soda.

Chemical Bubbles

It wasn't until the middle of the 1800s that people started using chemicals to put air into breads and cakes. Today, instead of yeast, we often use either baking soda or baking powder—sometimes both. It takes much less time to bake with them. Batters, such as those used for pancakes and certain cakes, contain much more liquid than doughs used for breads and other cakes made with yeast. These batters are so thin that slow-acting yeast can't trap enough air to make bubbles. That's why we use the modern chemicals.

159 Model Muffins

If you want light, fluffy muffins, take care to treat the batter right! See what happens if you don't!

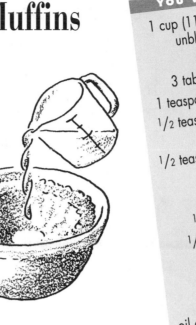

What to do: Grease the muffin pans. Using the smaller bowl, beat the egg with a spoon or a whisk. Then add the milk and oil.

In one of the large bowls, combine the flour, sugar, baking powder, cinnamon, and nutmeg. Make a hole in the center of the dry ingredients. Dump the liquid ingredients into the hole. Stir the mixture about 12 to 14 times, just enough to moisten the dry ingredients. The batter should be rough and lumpy.

Pour half of the batter into a second large bowl. Mix that batter until it is smooth.

Spoon a heaping tablespoon of the lumpy batter into one of the muffin cups so that it is two-thirds full. At the opposite end of the same muffin pan, do the same thing with the smooth batter. Repeat the process with the two other pans. Now you have three muffin pans, each with one muffin of smooth batter and one muffin of lumpy batter.

Turn on the oven to 400°F (205°C). Don't preheat it; instead, immediately put in one muffin pan. After 10 minutes, put in the second. In about 25 to 30 minutes, when the muffins are golden brown, remove them from the oven. (Use pot holders!)

Then put the third muffin pan into the hot oven and turn the heat up to 450°F (230°C). After 25 or 30 minutes, remove this pan from the oven.

Let them all cool and sample each muffin.

What happens: The muffins from the lumpy batter in the preheated oven—pan # 2—look and taste the best.

Why: For delicious muffins, you don't need to work hard! Overmixing develops the gluten and results in knobs or peaks on the top and long holes or tunnels inside the muffins.

It is also important to preheat the oven before you put the muffins in. If the oven is not hot enough, the muffins will be flat and heavy. That's because the baking soda isn't activated soon enough to cause the batter to rise.

However, if the oven is too hot, the carbon dioxide goes to work too soon, and the muffins will be poorly shaped and tough.

Weather and Cookies

Make the following cookies on two different days—one sunny and dry, the other rainy. The cookies will taste good on both days but…

What to do: Let the margarine stand at room temperature for 10 to 15 minutes. Then put it in a mixing bowl and add the sugar and vanilla extract. Cream the mixture well with a wooden spoon or in a food processor or electric mixer. Add the flour and continue mixing. When the dough is thoroughly mixed and smooth, remove it from the bowl and form a ball. If it is sticky, roll it in flour until it feels satiny. Wrap the dough in wax paper and refrigerate for an hour or more.

Preheat the oven to 325°F (165°C).

Cut the ball in half and roll out two logs, adding flour if the dough is sticky. Slice thin, as in the illustration, and place the circles a half-inch apart on an ungreased cookie sheet. Bake in center of the oven for 20 minutes or until the bottoms of the cookies are slightly brown.

What happens: On both the rainy day and the sunny day, you'll end up with 4 to 5 dozen great cookies. But it takes several more tablespoons of flour on the rainy day than it does on a dry, sunny day!

Why: On a rainy day, the dough soaks up water from the air, gets sticky and is harder to handle. You therefore have to use more flour than on a dry day.

What "Where" Has to Do with It

If you live in an area where the altitude is 500 feet or more above sea level (166 m), any dough with yeast or baking powder or soda will rise more quickly than it would at sea level. This is because the blanket of air (atmospheric pressure) is lighter. The carbon dioxide encounters less resistance from the surrounding air, and so it rises higher—with more force and more rapidly. This may make for tough, tasteless baked goods. The solution: Use less yeast or baking powder than you would at sea level. Some prepared commercial mixes solve the problem by directing you to add more flour at altitudes of 3,500 feet or more.

30 minutes!

60 minutes!

MAKING FOOD LAST

How do salt and sugar preserve food? How do you change a grape into a raisin? Why freeze herbs? What is cheese? And more about making food last.

About Preservation

To make foods last longer, we try to halt the growth of the bacteria, fungi, and molds that make it spoil. Sometimes we need to destroy destructive enzymes or prevent oxidation. Either of these processes changes the color, texture, taste, or nutritional value of a food.

We use many methods: drying, salting, smoking, pickling, canning, refrigerating, and freezing, among others.

For centuries, particularly in warm countries, people used salt to preserve many types of meat and vegetables. Beef still comes to the table as corned beef, cabbage as sauerkraut, cucumbers as pickles. Salt draws moisture from food by osmosis or absorption. This discourages the growth of bacteria. In dry curing (or corning), food is buried in salt. Other techniques involve soaking food in brine, a salt-and-water solution, or injecting salt into the food.

Smoking meat, poultry, and fish is also an age-old practice. The food is hung, usually in a special smokehouse, above hickory, apple, maple, or other aromatic wood chips burning at a low temperature—sometimes for days. The longer the smoking process, the stronger the flavor and the longer the food lasts.

When we talk about pickling, we usually think of pickled cucumbers. Cucumbers turn into pickles with the help of vinegars and other acids, spices such as dill, and salt and sugar. But other vegetables and fruit as well as fish and meats can also be preserved by pickling.

Canning dates back only to the early 1800s. It involves the rapid heating of sealed sterilized containers, glass or tin. Salt is often added and so is sugar. Like salt, sugar acts as a preservative, helping to keep mold from growing on such foods as jams and jellies.

In addition to these methods, commercial food manufacturers also add chemicals to extend the time food can remain on store shelves.

135

161 Hocus-Pocus— Raisins

A raisin starts life as a grape and a prune as a plum. What happens to these juicy fruits? See for yourself.

What to do: Wash the grapes in cold water and remove those that are bruised. Pull out the stems and place the cleaned grapes in a strainer. Dip them into a pot of boiling water so that the skins break. Spread the grapes on one of the drying trays so that they don't touch each other. Using the empty cans, prop the second tray over the first.

There are two methods you can use.
1. For four or five days, place the trays by a sunny window, turning them every hour, so that the fruit dries evenly.
2. Or place the trays on the middle rack of a pre-heated oven (140°F/60°C) and let them remain overnight.

When you think they may be dry, remove one or two of the grapes. Let them cool, and test them for moisture. If they still have water in them, let the fruit dry for another hour or so. Then test. If the grape is pliable and chewy, remove the rest from the drying tray.

What happens: You have raisins! Put them in a plastic bag and they will last for months and months.

Why: Drying as a means of preservation is thousands of years old. Normally fruit rots in a week or less at room temperature. Even in the refrigerator it will rot after a few weeks.

Fungi that start as spores—tiny seedlike cells—drop from the air and feed on the fruit's sugars and starches. When you dry out the grapes, you are taking away the moisture that the fungi need in order to grow. As long as the dried fruit can't take in moisture from the air, it will stay edible for many months.

About Herbs and Spices

For hundreds of years, herbs and spices were a symbol of wealth, valued because they preserved food or disguised its smell when it was spoiled. They also served as medicines.

Spices are the dried flavorings made from the buds, flowers, fruit, bark, and roots of fragrant tropical plants. Herbs are the leaves, stems, or flowers of aromatic succulents grown in temperate climates.
• Fresh herbs will keep for a week in the refrigerator. Wrap the stems in damp paper towels inside a plastic bag.
• Cut, crush, or mince the herbs just before you use them.

162   Freezing Herbs

Certain herbs, such as parsley, chervil, and chives are preserved better by freezing than by drying. The secret is to package them so that you keep air out and moisture in.

What to do: Wash the herbs in cold water and remove any leaves that are rotting. Drain and pat them dry with paper towels.

Strip the leafy herbs from their stems. Package the leaves in small plastic bags leaving 1/2 inch (1.25 cm) of headroom. You can use a drinking straw to remove as much air as possible. Or making sure that no water enters the bag, you can dip it in a pot of water. This pushes the plastic against the food, forcing out all the air.

Seal the bag tightly, using freezer tape if the bags are not self-sealing. Label each one with the name of the herb and the date, and place the bags in the freezer, preferably at 0°F (-18°C).

What happens: At that low temperature, herbs last up to a year and maintain flavor, color and nutrients. You can add them to soups, stews, sauces, salads, and other foods while they're still frozen.

Why: Enzymes, protein molecules that speed chemical reactions, harm foods by changing their color, texture, taste, and nutritional value. Like heating, freezing slows down active enzymes and delays the spoiling process.

You remove the air because air pockets between the food and the plastic bag collect moisture from the food, which results in frost and freezer burns. As ice crystals form, the water expands and ruptures cell membranes and walls.

Because food expands during freezing, you don't fill the bag completely. The bag or other container will split if it's too full for the contents to expand freely.

If the freezer temperature is higher than 0°F (-18°C), the herbs will not keep their flavor as long. Each 10°F (-12°C) above zero cuts the storage life in half!

You can substitute frozen herbs for fresh in recipes, but remember to use them while they're still frozen. If you let them thaw, microbes and enzymes have time to wilt and darken them.

- Buy dried herbs and spices in the smallest quantity possible—they lose flavor with age and exposure to air.
- Use less dried herb than fresh—1/3 to 1/2 teaspoon of dried to a tablespoon of fresh.
- Presoak dry herbs for a few minutes in lemon juice, soup stock or oil for more flavor.
- Add herbs the last 10 or 15 minutes of cooking.
- If you've added too much of an herb, add a raw potato to the cooking pot. It will take up some of the excess flavor and save your dish from being too spicy.
- Put a bay leaf in your flour canister to help protect against insects. Bay leaves are natural insect repellents.

163 To Freeze or Not to Freeze

Is freezing a good way to preserve any food?

lettuce leaves or green pepper or tomato
cloves of garlic
2 tablespoons (30 ml) of cottage cheese
3 plastic bags
labels and freezer tape
your freezer

What to do: Cull the vegetables, wash and pat them dry. Put them each in a plastic bag, whole or cut up, and remove the air as described on p. 137. Seal the bags, label them and place them in the freezer. Spoon the cottage cheese into a plastic bag. Remove the air, seal the bag, label it, and also place it in the freezer.

After two or three days, remove all the bags from the freezer and thaw the contents.

What happens: The foods are no longer appetizing. The lettuce and tomatoes have lost their crispness and become limp. The garlic has become stronger. The cottage cheese has separated and become grainy.

Why: When the water cools, it expands and turns to ice, damaging the cell walls of the foods. This loss of crispness is not so important if the food is to be cooked, but foods that we eat raw, like lettuce, tomatoes, and cottage cheese, definitely lose their appeal.

Salted foods also don't freeze as well as unsalted foods. This is because the salt lowers the freezing point and gives the enzymes more time to work.

Preserving a Pear

One great way to preserve fruit is to convert it into jam or jelly.

2 pears
1 teaspoon grated peel (zest) of lemon
1/2 small can of thawed frozen apple juice concentrate or
1 cup of apple juice
1/2 cup of water (optional)
1/2 teaspoon vanilla
1 teaspoon lemon juice
a pot
clean jar with lid
use of the stove (ask for permission or help)

In the past these have been made with heavy concentrations of sugar and pectin and stored in sterile jars. In fact, for commercial manufacturers to label a product "jam" or "preserve," the U.S. federal law requires that 65% of the final product be sugar. In Europe, there is a similar requirement for products labeled "conserve." A certain amount of sugar and acidity prevents the growth of dangerous microorganisms.

But now fruit spreads, sweetened with fruit juice concentrates instead of sugar, are being sold commercially. We can easily and safely make these in our kitchen to refrigerate for up to a month or two.

What to do: Peel the pears and remove the cores. Then cut the pears into cubes. Put the cubes in a bowl with the grated lemon peel and lemon juice.

Heat the thawed apple juice, water, and vanilla for 10 minutes or so. (It's okay to use canned or bottled apple juice, but if you do, don't add water.) Add the pears and lemon juice.

Bring the mixture to a boil. Then lower the heat and, stirring frequently, cook it for 30 to 40 minutes, or until it thickens. Place it in a clean jar and refrigerate.

What happens: You have pear jam that will keep for a month or two.

Why: The acid of the lemon juice and the sugar of the apple juice prevent the growth of dangerous microorganisms.

You can make chunky preserves by slicing your pears into eighths. Add grated lemon peel and lemon juice and cook in apple juice for 20 to 30 minutes, or until soft but not mushy.

165 Little Miss Muffet

Making cheese is one of our oldest ways of preserving milk. How is it done? Was Miss Muffet eating milk or cheese? And did her curds and whey come from a cow, a goat, a sheep, a mare, a camel, a llama, a reindeer or a buffalo? Milk and cheese can come from all these—and other animals!

You can make your own cottage cheese and observe the start of the process by which all cheeses are made.

What to do: Let the milk stand for two or three days at room temperature until it sours and starts to form chunks. Add a pinch of salt.

Using a rubber band or length of string, fasten a square of cheesecloth over a wide bowl. (Or line a strainer with a clean cloth—an old cotton handkerchief—and suspend the strainer on the lip of the bowl.)

Empty the sour chunks onto the cheesecloth Let them drip for two or three hours.

What happens: You have cottage cheese in the cheesecloth.

Why: Harmless bacteria act on the sugar in the milk to sour it and change the sugar into acid. The acid curdles the milk and separates it into a liquid (whey) and little solid chunks (curds). The curds contain a protein (casein), mineral salts, and the butterfat of the milk. Cottage cheese is a "fresh" cheese and lasts a relatively short time. Many other cheeses are cured—aged and ripened—by adding different molds and bacteria for varying periods of time. These give the cheeses their particular flavors and a longer life.

Why Swiss Cheese Has Holes
Carbon dioxide makes the holes in the Swiss cheese. It is released by bacteria that are added during the curing process.

Talking About Time

We use the word "time" to refer to the period when something happens or how long an event lasts.

About Time

People have measured time by the sun, by the moon, and by the stars. To measure time they have used oil and candles, water and sand, weights and pendulums, batteries and electric power stations, and the atoms of a metal called cesium.

In prehistoric times, people measured time by the seasons and night and day. Today physicists, studying particles of the atom, measure a picosecond, which is a trillionth of a second. Other scientists, including paleontologists, geologists, archeologists, and biologists, use "radioactive clocks" and "molecular clocks" to measure billions of years.

Astronomers, physicists, engineers, and statisticians, as well as blacksmiths and locksmiths, were all involved in the development of "the clock," which is the instrument for measuring time. Horologists, or clock-makers, based their inventions on the scientific theories of such scientists as Newton, Descartes, Galileo, Niels Bohr, and Einstein.

But it was natural phenomena—the spinning of the Earth on its axis and the rotation of the Earth around the sun—that provided the first means of measuring time.

YOU WILL NEED:

kitchen timer or
alarm clock
pencil
paper
a friend

Now and Then

166

We use words about time all the time. Play a game with a friend, or just challenge yourself, to see how many you can jot down in 10 minutes.

What to do: Set the timer or alarm clock for 10 minutes. Then list as many words and expressions about time as you can think of before the alarm goes off. "Then" and "before" are both examples, and so are such expressions as "in time" and "split second."

What happens: Check the list on page 143. Did you miss any? Are any of yours missing from the list?

Time to Wake Up

167

Scientists have discovered that the two sides of the human brain do different things. The left side of the brain has a strong sense of time; the right side has none. But when you tell yourself to wake up at a particular time, the right brain is the one that understands and wakes you.

See whether the two sides of your brain cooperate. Try waking at a particular time without an alarm clock—or someone else waking you.

168

The Time of Your Life

A "timeline" is a list of the dates of significant events in the order in which they occurred. You can make a timeline of your life, giving the dates of the important things that have happened to you.

YOU WILL NEED:

pencil and paper

What to do: Sit down and think about things that are important to you. Talk to your parents about dates that you aren't sure of. Make a list of all the things that occur to you—your birth date, when you first walked and talked, the time you entered kindergarten, when you learned to read, trips you went on, the date you first learned to ride a bike or to skate, the arrival of a sister or brother, a prize you won, a play you were in, when you met your best friend, your graduation from school.

Put them in order according to date and then make a timeline like the one on page 145. Liven it up with drawings if you wish. Later, you may want to revise your timeline because other things have become more important. And you may find it interesting to consult with your parents and your grandparents and make timelines of the events in their lives.

169

YOU WILL NEED:

watch with a
second hand
a helper
pencil
paper

How Long Is a Minute?

Do you know exactly how much time it takes before a minute has gone by? Have fun with a friend by seeing who can come closest to "timing" a minute!

What to do: Take turns. Your helper or friend holds the watch and gives a signal. You then put your hands on your lips and keep quiet until you think one minute is up. Then you shout "Time!" Your friend will record your time. Then you take over the timing while your friend keeps quiet for what seems like a minute and you record the time. Compare your time and your friend's.

What happens: You will find that a minute can be quite a long time!

Why: Time drags when you're concentrating on time passing. But try timing a minute when you are reading or drawing or playing a game and see how short a minute can seem.

Time Words and Expressions

(Answers to "Now and Then" on page 142)

after	earlier	infinite	now and then	synchronize
after a while	early	infrequent	o'clock	tempo
afternoon	eon	instantly	on time	temporal
all the time	epoch	intermittent	once in a while	temporary
already	equinox	interval	once upon a time	then
any time	evening	last month, last week,	overtime	this month,
as soon as	era	last year	past	week, year
at once	eternal	late	picosecond	timeless
before	eventually	later	perpetual	timely
biennial	final	latest	present	today
bimonthly	first	long ago	previously	tomorrow
biweekly	for a second, a	meanwhile	quicker	tonight
century	minute, an hour,	midnight	quickest	ultimate
chronology	a month, a season,	millennium	quickly	ultrashort
circadian	a year, a while	minute	rapidly	vernal
concurrent	forever	momentary	seasonal	week
contemporary	fortnight	month	second	when
constant	frequent	morning	sequence	while
continual	future	nanosecond	sequential	year
continuous	hitherto	never	slower	yearlong
daily	horology	next month, week, year	slowest	year-round
day	hour	night	slowly	yesterday
double time	immediate	nocturnal	sometimes	yesteryear
diurnal	in a flash	noon	split second	yet
during	in a minute	now	sudden	zero hour

143

TELLING TIME BY THE MOON

Some scientists, called archeoastronomists, combine the study of the stars and planets with the study of ancient civilizations. These scientists have studied 10,000 year-old bones found in Africa and Europe. They think grooves carved into them may be primitive calendars used to follow the cycles of the moon throughout the year.

Before our early ancestors became concerned with the hours of the day, they were involved with day and night, with the months and the seasons of the year. Peoples of many different cultures observed the phases of the moon and the movements of the sun and stars. They used them to keep time, so they would know when to plant and when to harvest.

The pyramids in Egypt and the Yucatan, as well as rock foundations like Stonehenge in England, all indicated those important times of the year and the religious holidays that celebrated those times and pacified their gods.

About Calendars

Calendars are orderly plans that fit days into months and months into years. As far back as 3000 B.C., Babylonians, who lived in what is now part of Iraq, and Egyptians devised lunar calendars. They were made up of 354 days with months based on the cycles of the moon. The Athenians had a similar calendar.

Later, because the floods came every 365 days, the Egyptians changed to a solar year, with a calendar of 12 months, each with 30 days. This left 5 extra days at the end of the year during which the people celebrated the birthdays of important gods.

The Romans originally had a lunar year of 355 days, but by the time of Julius Caesar, the Roman calendar was three months ahead of the sun's year. In 45 B.C., Caesar reformed the calendar, bringing it closer to the one we use today. He added almost three months to the year 46 B.C. and, like the Egyptians, devised a solar calendar of 365 days. He added an extra day every fourth year, our leap year. This calendar, called the Julian calendar, was used throughout the Middle Ages.

It wasn't until 500 years after the death of Jesus Christ that time was related to his birth. Many non-Christian societies use C.E. (Common Era) instead of A.D. (Anno Domini, the Year of Our Lord) and B.C.E. (Before the Common Era) instead of B.C. (before Christ). The Muslim Hijri calendar starts counting from A.H. (Anno Hegirae), the Year of the Emigration—the journey of Mohammed from Mecca to Medina.

Because the year was still too long by about 11 minutes, by the 16th century the Julian calendar was more than a week off. Eventually, Easter would coincide with the previous Christmas! So, in 1582, Pope Gregory XIII wiped out 10 days (October 5 became October 15), and decreed that no century year, like 1700, should be a leap year unless it was divisible by 400. That meant that three leap years would be omitted every four centuries. In addition, the calendar year was to begin on January 1 instead of March 21. September through December were to keep their original names—which meant sev-enth, eighth, ninth, and tenth months of the year—even though they were now the ninth to twelfth months of a year that began in January. This Gregorian calendar is the one we use today.

The Chinese calendar, devised about 2700 B.C., reckoned time with numbered months and years named for twelve different animals. It's still used for setting the dates of the festivals of the Harvest Moon and of the New Year (which is celebrated between January 20 and February 19 on the Gregorian calendar).

The Orthodox Eastern Church still uses the Julian calendar, so Greek Catholics celebrate Christmas a number of days after other Christians.

Calendar Timeline

4242 B.C.—Egyptian lunar calendar
3761 B.C.—Jewish lunar calendar
3300 B.C.—Possible date of first Mayan calendar
3100 B.C.—Egyptian solar calendar
3000 B.C.—Mesopotamian and Athenian lunar calendars
2680 B.C.—Egypt's Great Pyramids built
2637 B.C.—Chinese calendar invented by legendary Emperor Huangdi
1600 B.C.—Stonehenge erected in England
753 B.C.—Founding of Rome
600 B.C.—Zoroastrian calendar with year starting at vernal equinox—still used in Islamic Iran
46 B.C.—Julius Caesar revises Roman calendar
500—Dionysius Exiguus proposes using the term Anno Domini (A.D.), the Year of Our Lord

622—Hijri calendar
900s—Mayan calendar more exact than modern calendar
1077—Jalali calendar devised by Omar Khayyam of Persia
1100—Mayan pyramid built in the Yucatan
1582—Gregorian calendar
1752—Great Britain and colonies abandon Julian calendar
1844—Badi' calendar of the Baha'i faith
1873—Buddhists in Japan adopt Gregorian calendar
1917—USSR adopts Gregorian calendar
1957—India adopts Gregorian calendar

Moon Time

171 To know when to plant their seeds, and to fix the dates of religious holidays, many ancient peoples devised calendars based on the moon. One of the first words for moon meant "the measure of time." The word "month" comes from the moon—moonth.

What happens: You will observe the various phases of the moon from the full moon to the half moon to a crescent sliver to the new moon when no part is lit.

You can use a lamp and an ordinary tennis ball to see what causes the various phases of the moon.

What to do: Place the lighted lamp on a table in a darkened room. Hold the ball in your hand at arm's length with your back to the light. Raise the ball high enough to allow the light to strike the ball. Note the part of the ball lighted by the lamp. This represents the full moon.

Turn around slowly from right to left, keeping the ball in front of you and above your head. Observe the change in shape of the lighted part of the ball as you make one complete turn. Stop at each one-eighth turn and draw the shape of the ball (the moon) that is lit up.

Why: Every day the moon rises and sets about 50 minutes later than the day before, taking about four weeks to go around the Earth. During that time the moon waxes from new moon to full moon and then wanes to new moon again. The same half of the moon always faces the Earth as the moon goes around it. Half of the moon is lighted by the sun and half is in darkness. Actually you see a little more than half because the Earth's gravity causes the moon to librate, to vibrate, as it rotates. At new moon the half facing the Earth is dark because the

moon is between the Earth and the sun. Of course, you often see the moon in its various phases in the night sky. But you can also see the crescent moon and the half moon during the day because they rise before nightfall.

172 Different Drummers

Some societies set up their calendars to start with the year of their rulers, with the founding of a city, or with an important event in their religion. The Greeks measured time by referring to the Olympiads, the first of which was held in 776 B.C.

Even today, the Hopi Indians express time in their language by what happens "when the corn matures" or "when a sheep grows up." Off New Guinea, the Trobriand Islanders date events by saying they occurred "during the childhood of X" or "in the year of the marriage of Y."

Do you ever measure time by thinking about events in your life?

String Calendar

YOU WILL NEED:
large sheet of heavy paper
paper punch or scissors
long piece of string

The string calendar, a way of recording the passing of days in a lunar month, comes from Sumatra, an Indonesian island in the Indian Ocean. You can make one for yourself by threading string through each of thirty holes in a sheet of heavy paper. It may be easier to use a printed calendar to keep track of the days of the month, but your own string calendar can amuse your friends.

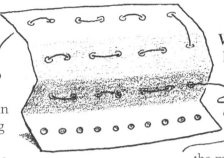

What to do: Fold your paper lengthwise in half and then in half again. Punch seven evenly spaced holes in each of the first three-quarters of the page. In the last quarter, punch 10 holes, as in the illustration. On the first of the month, knot your string and thread it through the first hole. The next day, thread the string through the second hole. Do the same every day of the month. When you want to know what day of the month it is, just count the number of holes you've covered.

Perpetual Calendar

You can find out the day of the week on which you were born. Indeed, you can find the day of the week of any date from 1920 to 2019.

YOU WILL NEED:
the charts on
page 148
your birth date

What to do: First check the Years chart for the letter next to the year of your birth. Next, on the Months chart look for your letter and find which number falls under the month in which you were born. Then, on the Days chart, use the number you just found and go down to the date on which you were born.

What happens: If you were born on July 19, 1986, for example, your letter is "B", your number is "1", and you were born on a Friday.

Amaze your friends and tell them the day of the week on which they were born. You can also find out about your parents or a historical figure, as long as you know their birth dates.

YEARS

1920 K	1940 H	1960 L	1980 I	2000 M
1921 F	1941 C	1961 G	1981 D	2001 A
1922 G	1942 D	1962 A	1982 E	2002 B
1923 A	1943 E	1963 B	1983 F	2003 C
1924 I	1944 M	1964 J	1984 N	2004 K
1925 D	1945 A	1965 E	1985 B	2005 F
1926 K	1946 B	1966 F	1986 C	2006 G
1927 F	1947 C	1967 G	1987 D	2007 A
1928 N	1948 K	1968 H	1988 L	2008 I
1929 B	1949 F	1969 C	1989 G	2009 D
1930 C	1950 G	1970 D	1990 A	2010 E
1931 D	1951 A	1971 E	1991 B	2011 F
1932 L	1952 I	1972 M	1992 J	2012 N
1933 G	1953 D	1973 A	1993 E	2013 B
1934 A	1954 E	1974 B	1994 F	2014 C
1935 B	1955 F	1975 C	1995 G	2015 D
1936 J	1956 N	1976 K	1996 H	2016 L
1937 E	1957 B	1977 F	1997 C	2017 G
1938 F	1958 C	1978 G	1998 D	2018 A
1939 G	1959 D	1979 A	1999 E	2019 B

MONTHS

	J	F	M	A	M	J	J	A	S	O	N	D
A	1	4	4	7	2	5	7	3	6	1	4	6
B	2	5	5	1	3	6	1	4	7	2	5	7
C	3	6	6	2	4	7	2	5	1	3	6	1
D	4	7	7	3	5	1	3	6	2	4	7	2
E	5	1	1	4	6	2	4	7	3	5	1	3
F	6	2	2	5	7	3	5	1	4	6	2	4
G	7	3	3	6	1	4	6	2	5	7	3	5
H	1	4	5	1	3	6	1	4	7	2	5	7
I	2	5	6	2	4	7	2	5	1	3	6	1
J	3	6	7	3	5	1	3	6	2	4	7	2
K	4	7	1	4	6	2	4	7	3	5	1	3
L	5	1	2	5	7	3	5	1	4	6	2	4
M	6	2	3	6	1	4	6	2	5	7	3	5
N	7	3	4	7	2	5	7	3	6	1	4	6

DAYS

	1	2	3	4	5	6	7
Monday	1						
Tuesday	2	1					
Wednesday	3	2	1				
Thursday	4	3	2	1			
Friday	5	4	3	2	1		
Saturday	6	5	4	3	2	1	
Sunday	7	6	5	4	3	2	1
Monday	8	7	6	5	4	3	2
Tuesday	9	8	7	6	5	4	3
Wednesday	10	9	8	7	6	5	4
Thursday	11	10	9	8	7	6	5
Friday	12	11	10	9	8	7	6
Saturday	13	12	11	10	9	8	7
Sunday	14	13	12	11	10	9	8
Monday	15	14	13	12	11	10	9
Tuesday	16	15	14	13	12	11	10
Wednesday	17	16	15	14	13	12	11
Thursday	18	17	16	15	14	13	12
Friday	19	18	17	16	15	14	13
Saturday	20	19	18	17	16	15	14
Sunday	21	20	19	18	17	16	15
Monday	22	21	20	19	18	17	16
Tuesday	23	22	21	20	19	18	17
Wednesday	24	23	22	21	20	19	18
Thursday	25	24	23	22	21	20	19
Friday	26	25	24	23	22	21	20
Saturday	27	26	25	24	23	22	21
Sunday	28	27	26	25	24	23	22
Monday	29	28	27	26	25	24	23
Tuesday	30	29	28	27	26	25	24
Wednesday	31	30	29	28	27	26	25
Thursday		31	30	29	28	27	26
Friday			31	30	29	28	27
Saturday				31	30	29	28
Sunday					31	30	29
Monday						31	30
Tuesday							31

175 The Wobbly Week

The week has not always consisted of seven days, except among the Jews. The Greeks had three 10-day weeks in a month; the Romans had an eight-day week. After the French Revolution, the French tried a 10-day week. That experiment lasted 10 years, until 1806. In 1929, the Soviet Union tested a shifting four-day work week with the fifth day a day of rest, but it, too, was abandoned after only two years.

- Sunday is named for the sun and Monday for the moon. The other days of the week are named for various ancient gods: Four days of the week are named for Norse gods and one for a Roman god:
- Tuesday for Tiv (the ancient German name for Mars)
- Wednesday for Woden (Mercury)
- Thursday for Thor (Jupiter)
- Friday for Frigga (Venus)
- Saturday for the Roman god Saturn, the father of Jupiter

Do you think you would like a 10-day work week? A four-day week? Why?

Telling Time
by the Sun

Our ancestors were mostly concerned with sunrise, noon, and sunset. For those, they watched the sun, or the shadows cast by trees or rocks or the distant hills.

For at least 10 and perhaps as long as 20 centuries, measuring the shadow cast by the sun was an important method of telling time. The sundial is mentioned in the Bible in an incident scholars say took place in 741 B.C.

In *Chaucer's Canterbury Tales,* written about 1400, the Parson estimates the time on the basis of his height and the length of his shadow. Characters in several of Shakespeare's plays use sundials.

Sundial Timeline

1500 B.C.—Fragment of earliest known sundial
(now in a Berlin museum)

900s B.C.—Egyptians make T-shaped shadow
timetellers with hoursmarked along their length

600s B.C.—Greek philosopher and astronomer
Anaximander of Miletus introduces sundial into
Greece

600-300 B.C.—An instrument is devised that
doesn't have to be turned in the afternoon

200s B.C.—Chaldean astronomer Berossus
describes the first hemispheric sundial

200 B.C.—Sundial commonplace in Rome

100—Sundial with gnomon (the arm on a sundial)
tilted at an angle according to latitude

1528—Portable sundial with 10 faces, each at a
different latitude

Where Does My Shadow Go?

Our ancestors told the time by the shadows made
by the sun. But why do we sometimes see a shadow and at other times "there's none of him at all?"

What to do: In a darkened room, place the lighted flashlight on the floor about five feet from a
light-colored wall. Stand behind the flashlight. Do
you cast a shadow? Now stand between the flashlight and the wall. Then move closer to the wall.

What happens: You don't cast a shadow when
you stand behind the light. You cast a big shadow
when you are near the light and far from the wall.
As you move farther from the light, the shadow
becomes smaller.

Why: You cast a shadow by blocking the rays of
light. As you move away from the source of light,
your shadow becomes smaller because you cut off
fewer rays of light. Any object that won't permit
light to shine through creates a shadow, an area of
lessened light.

Why Am I Sometimes Very Tall?

This simple experiment shows how the length of a shadow changes when the source of light changes position.

What to do: Put the spool of thread on the sheet of paper. Stand one of the pencils in the spool. Darken the room and hold the flashlight at different angles above the pencil. On the paper, using the other pencil, record the length of each shadow.

What happens: When the flashlight is high and directly above the pencil, the shadow is short. When the light is low and at a slant, the shadow is long.

Why: When the light is low and at a slant, the shadow is long because few rays of light pass through. This shows us why the shadows at the North Pole are longer than those at the equator. The sun hits the Earth directly at the equator and indirectly at the Poles.

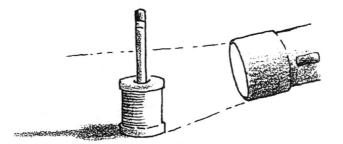

Shadow Watch

At what time of day is the shadow the shortest? You can find out by watching the shadow cast by the sun in the same way our distant ancestors did!

YOU WILL NEED:

tree

chalk or stones

pencil

paper

clock

tape measure

What to do: Find a nearby tree that is in sunlight much of the day. Using either small stones or chalk, mark off the shadow it casts right after you get up in the morning. Measure the shadow's length. Then do the same thing at noon or, if your area is on Daylight Savings Time, an hour later. Finally, mark the shadow cast late in the afternoon toward sunset and measure it.

What happens: The shadow is shortest at noon. The shadows cast in the early morning and late afternoon are both much longer.

Why: The sun is highest in the sky at noon and, therefore, casts the shortest shadow. However, your clock and the sun may have a difference of opinion about when it is noon. (See page 156 to find out why.)

180 Shadow Timepiece

YOU WILL NEED:

2 empty milk cartons

index card or piece of cardboard

tape

small compass

large piece of paper

marker

The earliest device for telling time, a crude forerunner of the more accurate sundial, was the Egyptian shadow clock. It dates from between the 10th and the 8th centuries B.C. and was made of stone. You can make your own from materials you have around the house.

What to do: Place one of the milk cartons on its side. Tape the index card, or a piece of cardboard, 1 inch from the top of the short flat end of the carton. Hold the second carton perpendicular to the first and attach it to the free end of the index card, as in the illustration.

In the morning, go outdoors and place the timeteller level on the piece of paper with the upper carton pointing east. In the afternoon, turn the timeteller around so that it points west. Check your watch clock every hour and mark where the shadow falls on the paper.

What happens: The shadow shortens as it gets to be lunchtime and lengthens again toward dinner time. And the distances from one hour to the next differ! The shadows are farther apart from one another early and late in the day and closer during the middle of the day.

Why: Only at the equator will the spaces allotted to hours be exactly equal because the sunlight hits the Earth directly. Unlike the day and the year, which are dictated by the revolution of Earth on its axis and around the sun, the hour is a division devised by people. The day runs from midnight to midnight, but it could be divided—and has been— into twenty parts or six parts or three parts instead of into 24 hours. Early Egyptians didn't talk about 2 or 3 o'clock. They agreed to meet when the shadow was, for instance, four steps long.

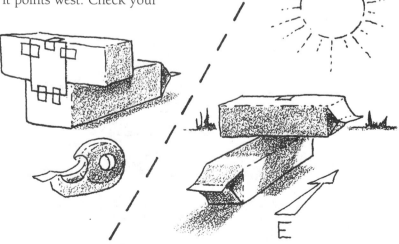

What's the Angle?

YOU WILL NEED:

atlas

2 pieces of heavy cardboard, approximately 6 x 8 inches (15 x 20 cm)

protractor

marker or pencil

scissors

stick, about 4 inches (10 cm) long

paste

watch

In about the first century, it was discovered that a slanting object cast a shadow that kept more accurate time than an object that stood straight up. This was especially true if the object, known as the gnomon, slanted at the same angle as the latitude of the place where it was being used. In that case, its direction was the same at any hour of the day, regardless of the season of the year. The term "gnomon" comes from the Greek word which means "know," and the gnomon was so named because it "knew" the time.

What to do: In an atlas, look up the latitude of your town—that is its distance north or south of the equator. Subtract it from 90°. (For example, 90° minus 50° equals 40°.) Using the protractor, mark that angle on one of the pieces of cardboard. Cut two wedge shapes with that angle; see illustration A.

On the second piece of cardboard, draw a line parallel to and 1 inch (2.5 cm) away from the long edge, as in illustration B.

Paste the 4-inch (10 cm) stick at right angles to the cardboard through the center of the line. With the protractor, divide the space above the line into 12 angles of 15° each. Label the middle line 12 and the bottom lines 6. Then fill in the other numbers, as in illustration C.

Paste the pieces of cardboard to the wedges so the boards touch at one edge and the hour lines of the upper board point away from the free edge. See illustration D.

Set the sundial level. Place the edge where the two boards meet so that they run east and west. A simple way of orienting the sundial is to set it up at noon and indicate where the shadow falls. Check the sundial each hour, marking the spot where the shadow falls with a marker or pencil.

What happens: The shadow of the stick will point to the time.

Why: You have set up the sundial so that the gnomon is in the same direction as the earth's axis and the upper board is parallel to the ground at the North Pole. But it will not always agree with your watch.

Why the Difference? L.A.T., local apparent time, is time measured by the actual movement of Earth and the sun. It differs from season to season and from place to place. It is the time measured by the sundial. L.M.T., local mean time, measures the average speed at which the sun rotates and Earth spins in its orbit. Our clocks and watches show local mean time.

182 Hand Dial

YOU WILL NEED:

pencil
your two hands
sunny day

A. M. ←W   P. M. E→

A 16th-century German woodcut shows a unique portable dial that requires no special equipment to tell time. If you know the latitude of your area, you can tell the time without a watch or sundial. Actually, you can be a human timepiece.

What to do: Look up the latitude of your area in an atlas. Using your left hand in the morning and your right hand in the afternoon, hold the pencil with your thumb. Tilt the pencil at an angle approximately equal to the angle of latitude of your area, as in the illustration below. Hold your left hand straight up toward the west. Hold your right hand straight up toward the east.

What happens: The shadow on your hands indicates the time!

Why: You have made the pencil into a gnomon and angled it parallel to the Earth's axis, as in the last experiment. But remember, your hand sundial may not agree with your clock.

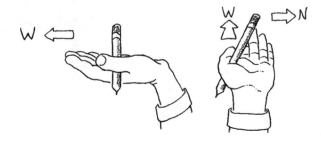

Noon Marks 183

Instead of noting time by the position of a shadow, you can note it from the position of a small beam of light. It is easy, but it takes patience—and two seasons.

YOU WILL NEED:

window that faces
south
hole punch
piece of black paper
masking tape
pencil

What to do: Punch a hole about 3 inches (2 cm) in diameter in the center of a piece of black paper. Tape the paper to one pane of a window that faces south. With a dot of masking tape, mark the spot on the floor where a sunbeam hits at noon on a winter's day. Then mark it again at noon on a summer's day. Connect the two spots on the floor.

What happens: Whenever the sunbeam crosses the line, it will be the local apparent noon, the time the sun (not your watch) says it is noon. Sun time and your watch will only agree on April 16, June 14, September 2, and December 25.

Why: Days measured by the sun differ in length. There are two reasons: First, the Earth moves faster when it is closer to the sun and, second, the Earth's path around the sun is an ellipse rather than a circle.

Time Zones

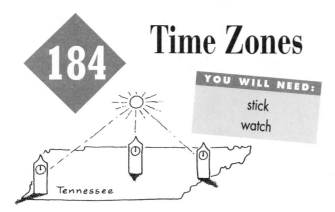

Tennessee

YOU WILL NEED:
stick
watch

The difference between sun time and clock time depends on where in a time zone you are located. You can see this for yourself with the shadow time-piece. See page 154 for an explanation of time zones.

What to do: Place the stick straight up in the ground. When its shadow is shortest, check your watch.

What happens: If you live in the eastern edge of your time zone, the sun at noon is earlier than the clock reading. If you live in the western edge of your time zone, the sun at noon is later than the clock reading. If you are on Daylight Savings Time, you need to take that into account; your watch will read before or after 1 o'clock.

Why: The geographical region in which the same time is used is large. It is only in the middle of the region that the sun will be highest in the sky at noon on our watches.

Noon Holes

Noon marks can still be seen in Europe's ancient cathedrals. In the Duomo in Milan, a church dating back to 1380, for example, there is a sun hole on one wall near the ceiling and signs of the Zodiac indicating the months on the marble floor. Posted on a bulletin board is a daily schedule of times the sun will shine on each month's symbol.

The Fickle Hour

We now divide the day into 24 equal parts, or hours, throughout the year, but it was not always like that. The Egyptians, for example, divided daylight into twelve parts and the darkness into twelve parts, except during the summer when days were longer, they lengthened the daylight divisions.

The Babylonians did the same thing, but they divided the day into 12 hours instead of 24. They had two systems. One of them began at midnight and divided the day into six parts, each with 60 subdivisions. The other measured the start of day from sunset and split it into twelve divisions with thirty subdivisions.

Early Hebrews divided the day into six parts, three light and three dark. While the Chinese adopted an equal hour system by the 4th century B.C., Europeans changed the length of hours according to the seasons until the 14th century. The Japanese continued to have variable hours until 1868.

CLOUDY DAY AND NIGHT TIMETELLERS

Sundials, of course, were of no use on cloudy days and at night. People used many kinds of household materials to measure time on those days and at night. They tied knots in ropes to mark the hours, and burned measured quantities of oil, incense, and specially prepared candles.

Cloudy Day Timeline

185

1400 B.C.—Egyptians and Mesopotamians
   produce glass
1450 B.C.—Egyptians devise water clock
700 B.C.—Assyrians acquire water clock
38 B.C.—Plato adds alarm to water clock
200s B.C.—Hourglass invented in Alexandria
250 B.C.—Alexandrian engineer Ctesibius adds
   gears connected to a pointer on a drum
   indicating time
150 B.C.—Pliny writes that the water clock
   replaced the sundial as the official timepiece
50—Athens acquires water solar clock
725—Buddhist monk T-Xing and Chinese engineer
   Liang-Zen build a water clock with an escape
   vent used to power various astronomical devices
875—Calibrated candles mark the passage of time

Candle Timekeeper

186

Religious candles are reminders of the candle timekeepers which date back to the 9th century. It's not difficult to make a candle timekeeper, but be sure to get an adult to help you.

YOU WILL NEED:

5 bolts or paper clips
5 two-inch (5-cm) lengths of heavy thread
2 tall, straight not tapered, white candles
pencil
paper
ruler
2 candle holders
2 china or metal plates
matches
clock

What to do: Attach a bolt or clip to one end of each 2-inch (5-cm) length of heavy thread. Measure the candles. Write down the results. Then insert one of the candles in a holder and place it on the plate. Light the candle in the holder and let it burn for 10 minutes. Then blow out the flame.

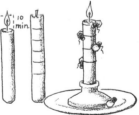

Measure the candle again and figure out how much of the candle burned in 10 minutes. Loop one of the lengths of string around the second candle at the 10-minute mark and secure it with a knot. Mark off the rest of the first candle in 10-minute segments. Measure it each time and wrap a length of string, with a bolt or clip attached, at the proper spot on the second candle. Depending on the size of your candle, you may be able to use more or less than five lengths of string.

Insert the second candle in a candle holder, place it on a plate, and light the wick. Check your watch every time you hear the clang of the bolt or clip.

What happens: Every 10 minutes, you will be alerted by an "alarm" as the thread burns off and the bolt or clip hits the plate.

187 By a Nose!

Add to eyes, ears, and touch the sense of smell in the service of time-telling! In the early 14th century the Chinese developed an incense clock. They placed aromatic powders in grooves carved into a hardwood disk and lit it. It burned for about 12 hours. Each hour was recognized by its particular scent.

What scents do you associate with various times of day?

188 Water Clock

One of the most ingenious of cloudy day time-keepers was the water clock, the clepsydra. It originated in Egypt and Babylon and came into use about a thousand years after the sundial.

The Egyptians made a small hole in a large clay bowl, which was wide at the top and narrow at the bottom and was marked with horizontal lines on the inside, one for each hour. They filled the bowl with water and as it leaked out they could tell how much time had passed by looking at the lines and the water left in the pot. You can make your own clepsydra with a plastic container.

What to do: Use your marker to make four lines equally distant from one another around the inside of the container. Then using the nail, punch a small hole in the bottom of the container. Cover the hole with a piece of tape. Fill the plastic container with water. Place the container over a large pot (or in the sink), uncover the hole, and see how long it takes the carton to empty. Write down your findings.

Fill the container again. This time note how long it takes to get to each of the lines you've drawn, as well as how long it takes for the container to empty.

What happens: It takes the same amount of time to empty during the two trials, but the time to move from one line to the next differs.

Why: The water pressure lessens as the water escapes, and so the water runs out more slowly than when the container is full.

What next: Now do the same experiment using plastic containers of different sizes and shapes. See if it makes a difference using hot water or ice-cold water from the refrigerator.

189 Having It Both Ways

YOU WILL NEED:
2 heavy paper cups
nail
yardstick
masking tape
large pot or bowl
water faucet
marker
watch

A more accurate water clock has water flowing in and out of containers at the same time.

What to do: Punch a small hole in the bottom of the paper cups. Hold the yardstick up and tape the cups to it, as in the illustration below. Tape the yardstick to the side of a large pot or bowl with the cups facing inward so that they are over the pot.

Cover the hole in the top cup with a piece of tape. Fill the cup with water. Then place it under a slow-running faucet as you uncover the hole.

Every five minutes, use tape or a marker to indicate the water line in the bottom cup and the water line in the pot or bowl.

What happens: The water flows out at a regular rate and the marks are equally distant from one another.

Why: Because the amount of water that flows in comes from a cup that is always kept full, the water pressure remains the same and therefore the water flows out at the same rate.

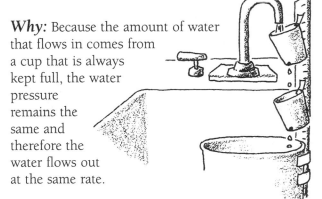

Not Quite Perfect

Unlike the candle or rope clocks, the water clock could be used over and over. But there were problems. Although it didn't need the sun to show how much time had passed, it was not really an all-weather timeteller. When it was very cold, the water would freeze; when it was very hot the water would evaporate too quickly. And when it was dirty, whether from human or natural causes, the water ran out more slowly.

190 A Knotty Problem

For many years, it was the practice at sea to throw overboard a thin rope weighted at one end with a piece of wood and knotted at regular intervals. A seaman would hold the rope as it was dragged through the water and feel how many knots passed through his hands during the time it took for a timed sandglass to empty. In this way, he estimated the speed or "knots" at which the ship was moving. Nautical speed is still measured in knots.

Hourglass Timekeepers

191

Hourglass timers were once used for serious jobs. They timed sermons, speeches, and court presentations. Four-hour models were used aboard ship to measure watches right up to the late 18th century, when accurate ship chronometers were invented. Today the most common task of the hourglass is to time boiled eggs. But the advantages of the hourglass over the water clock is that the hourglass is portable, there is no sloshing water—and weather does not affect it.

YOU WILL NEED:

2 small clear jars
heavy paper or cardboard
scissors
nail or hole punch
sand or salt
masking tape
clock or watch

What to do: Cut a circle out of heavy paper or cardboard to fit the mouths of the jars. Punch a small hole in the center of the circle with a nail or a hole punch. Place a few ounces of sand or salt in one of the jars and cover it with the disk. Tape the second jar to the first, mouth to mouth. Make sure they are taped securely. Turn the jars upside down. and time how long it takes for the top jar to empty.

Now make the hole larger and change the amount of sand or salt. How long does it now take for the top jar to empty?

What happens: By making the hole larger or smaller, or changing the amount of sand or salt, you can change the time it takes to empty the top jar.

Why: Gravity forces the sand to drop at a steady rate. You can use your "minute glass" over and over and time longer periods—if you just keep track of how many times you turn it over. You may even find it useful.

192 Invent Your Own Clock

Timetellers have ranged from natural phenomena to manmade devices, from primitive to sophisticated, from simple to complex. The writer Albert Camus tells of an old man who thought a watch a silly gadget and an unnecessary expense. He devised his own "clock" designed to indicate the only times he was interested in. He worked out the times for meals with two saucepans, one of which was always filled with peas when he woke in the morning. He filled the other, pea by pea, at a constant, carefully regulated speed. Every 15 pots of peas it was feeding time!

Fifth graders at the Fieldston School in Riverdale, New York, invented their own timers. One made a fizzy alarm clock using vinegar dripping into baking soda; another timed how long it took heat to blow up a balloon.

Can you devise a "clock" from items around the house or activities you do often?

TELLING TIME BY THE STARS

While the ancient Egyptians built sundials to keep track of daylight hours, during the night they measured the movement of the stars across certain portions of the sky.

They associated their goddess Isis, "the lady of all the elements, the beginning of all time" with the brightest star in the night sky, Sirius. They built temples facing the point on the eastern horizon where Sirius first appeared before sunrise. Ancient Egyptian astronomers, tracking Sirius for their calendar, started a new year at the first new moon following this appearance of Sirius—and all awaited the annual floods that irrigated the land.

In the Northern Hemisphere, a February evening is a good time to look for Sirius to the side and a little below the group of stars known as Orion the Hunter. Face south at about 9 p.m. Orion is high in the winter sky but not visible in northern skies during the summer. Using the line of Orion's belt as a guide, look southeast for the Dog Star.

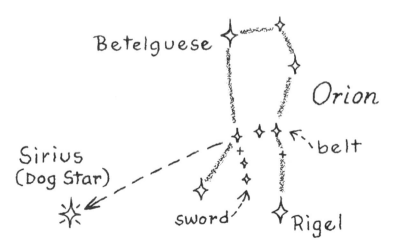

193 Star Timeline

3000 B.C.—Earliest Babylonian astronomical records

300 B.C.—Chinese astronomers chart position of stars

280 B.C.—Aristarchus suggests Earth orbits the sun

140—Ptolemy contends that planets orbit Earth, a theory accepted for fifteen hundred years

500—The astrolabe, developed in ancient Greece, is used for reckoning time and measuring the position of heavenly bodies. Later, mariners began to use it in navigation

1543—Nicholas Copernicus, a Polish priest, publishes theory that the sun is the center of the universe. Idea banned as challenging the Bible

1608—Hans Lippershey of the Netherlands invents first telescope

1609—Galileo Galilei confirms Copernicus's theory, but is eventually forced to recant

1620s—German mathematician Johannes Kepler proves planets move around the sun

1668—Isaac Newton invents a reflector telescope with a curved mirror replacing one lens

1739—Sextant is invented by Thomas Godfrey and John Hadley

194 Cereal Box Planetarium

You can make your own "planetarium" by creating a model of a cluster of stars you will see in the sky.

What to do: Make a circle of tracing paper to fit the bottom of the box. Then trace the illustration of the Big Dipper, the North Star, and Cassiopeia shown below onto the thin piece of paper. Glue the paper to the bottom of the box. With the nail punch holes through the box at each star.

Take your planetarium into a dark room and stand facing one of the walls. At the open end of the box tilt a flashlight so that it shines against the side. Turn the box slowly.

What happens: You get an enlarged image on the wall. When you turn the box, you will see the various positions of the stars as they seem to revolve.

Why: The Earth rotates on its axis, so the constellations appear to circle around the North Star, which remains at the same place in the sky. Therefore, you see these constellations in all positions—on their sides or even upside down. The "W" shape of Cassiopeia becomes an "M" depending on when it appears above the North Star.

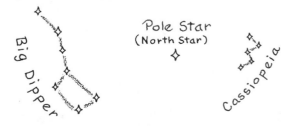

The Sky as Compass

If you are ever lost in a forest at night, you can use the sky to find your way. Face the North Star, which is the brightest star in the northern sky, and you are facing north. Look 180° across the sky to the horizon. That is south. East is 90° to the right and west is 90° to the left.

On a clear night, ask an adult to help you practice finding the North Star.

Star Map

Draw a star map of the constellations that circle around the North Star and use it to note the changes in the sky from hour to hour.

YOU WILL NEED:
circle of cardboard
flashlight
red cellophane and tape

What to do: To make your star map, copy the illustration below onto your circle of cardboard. Then tape the cellophane over your flashlight. (The red covering will prevent it from being too bright for you to see the stars.)

At 9 o'clock on a dry moonless night, take your star map and the flashlight outdoors. Turn the chart so that the month in which you are observing is on the top. Hold the chart above your head and look for the same pattern in the sky.

On another night, go out at 7 o'clock or at 10 o'clock and match the star map with the sky.

What happens: At 7 o'clock you have to turn the chart one month clockwise to match the sky. At 10 o'clock you have to turn it a half-month counterclockwise.

Why: The North Star remains at approximately the same place in the sky—far, far away, but directly above the North Pole. This is because the Earth's axis points to it throughout the year. All the other stars and constellations, however, seem to wander around the North Star once a day, moving counterclockwise. As the Earth rotates, it looks as if the entire sky is rotating, although the stars do not change position relative to each other. Since one turn of the Earth takes only 23 hours and 56 minutes, a star seems to rise and set about four minutes earlier than the day before. This adds up to two hours (30 x 4 = 120 minutes) in a month and, of course, one hour in half a month.

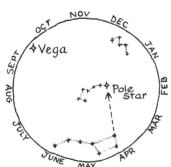

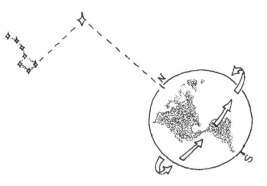

Some Timetelling Stars

A constellation is a group of stars that long ago people named for heroes and gods and animals that they thought the patterns looked like. There are 88 constellations. We still use many of these names in Latin and in the English translation. And we still use the stars as a calendar and a direction finder.

The equator is the only place from which all 88 constellations can be seen during the course of a year. In other latitudes, you can see perhaps 60 at different times, and about 24 at any one time.

In the United States, Canada, the United Kingdom, and Europe, you can see the constellation of Leo, the Lion, with the bright star Regulus high up in the sky in the middle of April at about 9 p.m.

In August, as it gets dark, high in the southeast section of the sky you will see three bright stars—the Summer Triangle. Directly overhead are Vega, in the constellation Lyra, the Harp; Deneb of the constellation Cygnus, the Swan; and Altair of the constellation Aquila, the Eagle.

In the evening skies of October, just below the W-shaped constellation Cassiopeia, you will find four bright stars arranged in a square making up the body of an upside-down horse with wings, the constellation Pegasus, the flying horse.

In the Southern Hemisphere, the Southern Cross (the Crux) is the easiest constellation to recognize. You can see it in the evening skies of Miami and the Florida Keys in May and June, but its four stars are always visible below the equator. Looking south, observers in Australia, southern Africa, and South America can see the Crux just below the two bright stars Alpha and Beta Centauri. Some think it looks more like a kite than a cross.

Get a book from the library about stars and constellations and on a clear night, ask an adult to help you practice finding constellations in the sky.

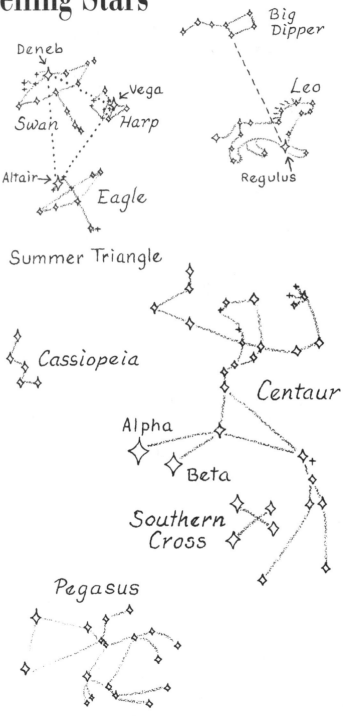

YOU WILL NEED:

compass (optional)
ruler
3 pieces of cardboard
scissors
marker
sheet of paper
glue
tape
hole punch or nail
fastener

198 ◆ Star Time

Stars tell us the time and direction on land, on sea, and in the air. You can have fun estimating the time by observing certain stars.

What to do: Mark out circles on two of the pieces of cardboard. Make one circle about 8 inches (20 cm) in diameter. Make the other 1 inch (2.5 cm) smaller with four 3-inch (7.5 cm) triangles sticking out as in illustration C. Cut out the two disks.

On the larger cardboard disk draw two ½-inch (1.3 cm) circles around the outer rim. Mark the outer circle with the months of the year. Mark the inner circle with the days of the month.

From the sheet of paper, cut out an oval 3½ inches (9.5 cm) deep and 4 inches (10 cm) wide. On the oval copy the sky map in illustration B.

Hold the larger disk so September is on top. Paste the sky map to the inner circle above the days of March.

On the smaller disk, 1 inch (2.5 cm) from the bottom, mark out an oval, also 3½ inches (9.5 cm) deep and 4 inches (10 cm) wide. Cut the oval section out.

Around the edge of the smaller disk draw a clock face like the one in illustration C. Notice that the numbers, like the stars, go in the opposite direction from an ordinary clock and cover twenty-four hours instead of twelve. Place the smaller disk on top of the larger disk so you can see the map through the "window" of the smaller disk.

Tape the tips of the triangles of the smaller disk

to the corners of the third cardboard. Punch a hole through the center of all three pieces if cardboard. Fit the fastener through the three center holes.

On a clear, preferably moonless, night, pick a spot where street lights, houses, and trees don't obstruct your view. Face north and look for the Big Dipper and Cassiopeia. Two pointer stars of the Big Dipper point to a fairly bright star, the North Star—also known as the Pole Star or Polaris—which is halfway between the Big Dipper and Cassiopeia. At a latitude of 40° (New York, Denver, Salt Lake City), it is almost halfway up in the sky. The farther north (London's latitude is 50°) you are, the higher up the North Star will be; the farther south (New Orleans is 30°), the lower it will be.

Rotate your Star Timeteller until it looks like the sky.

Draw an imaginary line from the North Star, one of the bright stars of Cassiopeia.

For each week after September 21 subtract a half hour, for each week earlier add a half hour. If you are on Daylight Savings Time, add an hour.

What happens: The imaginary line acts as the star clock's hour hand. With a little simple arithmetic, you can find the approximate time.

Why: You add and subtract depending on when you observe the stars because the solar day is longer than the star day. The star clock runs too fast. As we have seen, it gains four minutes every day. In a week it gains about a half hour (7 x 4 = 28 minutes); in a month it gains about two hours (30 x 4 = 120 minutes). Since the earth is rotating counterclockwise, it will be earlier when you observe after September 21, so you subtract. And it will be later before September 21, so you add.

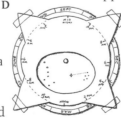

A

B

C

D

MECHANICAL CLOCKS

A kind of mechanical timeteller existed in the late 13th or early 14th century. Housed on a high bell tower, it used a heavy falling weight tied to a rope that was wound around a huge revolving drum. It had no dials and, at first, no means of striking, but it could indicate important times by means of a moving figure called a jack. It alerted the keeper of the clock, usually a monk, to sound a bell.

About Mechanical Clocks

The word clock comes from the Latin word *clocca,* which means bell. Up until this time, any instrument that measured time was known as an horologium, an hour-teller.

Huge public clocks, which struck the hours, but did not have a face with hands, appeared in Italian towns starting in the fourteenth century. Many of these—and some still exist—used a variety of jacks for entertainment.

Clocks made for royalty were even more elaborate. France's Louis XIV had a clock with models of several kings of Europe, who bowed to him before striking the hour with canes.

The cuckoo clock, with its carved wooden bird that pops out to "sing" the time, first appeared in Germany in 1730.

199 Mechanical Clock Timeline

1320—weight-driven mechanical clocks used

1350—public clocks in European towns

1510—portable spring-driven clocks invented

1583—Galileo Galilei of Rome shows that a pendulum swings at a constant rate

1656—Christian Huygens designs a pendulum clock

1660—Huygens and Robert Hooke invent the spiral hairspring (see page 171)

1668—Boston has the first town clock in Colonial America

1675—grandfather clocks available

1676—minute hands and crystal covers added to watches

1725—Nicholas Faceis of Basel, Switzerland adds jeweled bearings to reduce friction

1730—cuckoo clocks made in Germany's Black Forest

1773—Englishman John Harrison invents a seagoing chronometer

1803—Eli Terry of Connecticut begins clock mass production

1824—"time ball" standardizes timekeeping in some towns

1875—stem-wound watches replace watches with keys

1884—standardized time zones established

Yo-Yo Clock

200

If you think about how a yo-yo spins when you unwind its cord, you'll have an idea of how the earliest mechanical clocks worked. The energy of falling weights suspended from a drum were their source of power.

What to do: Tie one end of the cord to the washer or heavy button. Tie the other end around the spool and wind it up.

Turn the spool so that the weight hangs down, as in the illustration. Then rewind the spool. Again turn the spool so that the weight hangs down, but this time keep tapping the edge of the spool quickly with your finger.

What happens: When the weight falls, the cord unwinds and the spool turns quickly. But when you tap the spool, your finger acts as a brake. The taps stop the spool and the weight falls in small jerks with a slow and steady regular rhythm.

Why: The falling weight supplied the energy to turn the spool while the tapping finger regulated it. Early clocks worked in the same way by means of a device called an escapement. The escapement made sure the weight fell slowly and steadily and prevented the drum from rotating too fast and using up all the energy of the weight too quickly.

These early clocks, installed in bell towers, weighed hundreds of pounds and fell distances of more than 30 feet (9 m), but were highly inaccurate.

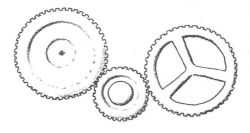

Get in Gear

YOU WILL NEED:

3 metal bottle caps
hammer and nail or
a punch
block of wood
3 thin nails
an adult helper

Gears are wheels with notches or teeth. Small gears are called pinions. Wheels with 20 or more teeth are called gears. Large gears that have an even greater number of teeth are called cogs.

The first clocks had a gear at each end of a spindle, the axle of the spool. The gear on the back of the spool axle meshed with a series of gears that regulated the unwinding of the cord. The other gear on the spool—the one on the front of the spool axis—controlled a moving figure (called a jack), which beat on bells to sound the hours. Later this front gear turned a hand that showed the hour on a round dial.

It's not difficult to make your own gears, but you had better ask an adult for some help with this project.

What to do: Be sure the caps are not bent. Ask an adult to help you punch a hole through the center of each cap.

Sundials Versus Mechanical Clocks

Early mechanical clocks were inaccurate and, therefore, sundials were used to regulate them until the advent of electrical clocks in the late 19th century!

Place the caps on the block of wood close enough to one another so that they touch. Tack them down loosely with thin nails so that they turn easily.

Turn one of the caps with your finger and notice what happens to the others. Turn one of the caps in the opposite direction. Turn them slowly, then quickly.

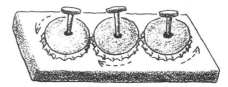

What happens: When you turn one cap, all three turn. But each gear turns in the opposite direction from the one next to it.

Why: The ridges of each cap act like the teeth of a gear and interlock, or mesh, with the ridges of the cap next to it. In addition to changing direction, gears change force or speed. Speed increases when a small gear is turned by a large one and force increases when a large gear is turned by a small one.

The set of gears of a clock changes slow turning into fast turning. It connects the axle to several wheels. As the axle turns, the wheels turn at different speeds. The regulator, called the escapement, controls the turning of the fastest of the wheels. Two of the slower wheels turn the hands on the face of the clock.

The main features of all clocks are: a device that swings at a regular rate; something that keeps the motion going by feeding energy to the swinging device; and a means of counting and indicating the swings.

Why Clocks Count to Twelve

Do you know how hard it is to count the chimes when a clock strikes 12? Well, imagine what it would be like to have to count 24 chimes! That's what people had to do years ago when more and more clocks were striking the hour in village squares all over Europe. That's why, in the early 15th century, a double 12-hour system took the place of the 24-hour system in many countries.

This system of dividing the day into two sets of 12 equal hours starting at midnight originated in southern Germany, scholars claim, where the sale of locally made mechanical clocks was thriving.

Most military organizations and some parts of Europe, however, still use a 24-hour system starting at midnight. For example, 12:59 a.m. is 0059; 1:00 a.m. is 0100; 12 noon is 1200; 12:59 p.m. is 1259; 1:00 p.m. is 1300; 10:59 p.m. is 2259. When you convert from a 12-hour clock to a 24-hour clock, the minutes are unchanged, but you add 12 from 1:00 p.m. on. To convert from a 24-hour clock to a 12 hour system you just subtract 12 hours between 1300 and 2359 and add p.m.

Try some conversions on your own.

Military Time

Portable Timekeepers

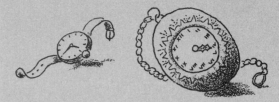

In 1510, Peter Henlein, a locksmith in Nuremberg, Germany, substituted small coiled springs for the huge weights in clocks and made the first table timekeepers that could be carried around. They were known as "Nuremberg Eggs" because of their oval shape. They were small enough to wear on a belt or on a chain around the neck, but they were not accurate enough to have a minute hand.

In 1660, Robert Hooke attached a small balance wheel to the mainspring, and a short, stiff hog's hair bristle to control the oscillations—the movements back and forth. Later, a fine steel wire was used instead of a bristle, but it continued to be known as the hairspring—and still is!

The watch now had a mainspring, the source of energy; an escapement and balance unit, which controlled the release of energy; and two gear trains, one transmitting the energy and another controlling the movement of the hands. It also had a mechanism for winding the clock and a frame or case to protect it.

When a mechanical watch is wound, the springs are coiled tightly around the central shaft, which is held by a gear attached to a bar with projecting levers. As the housing turns around the shaft, the spring gradually unwinds. The gear attached to the housing drives other gears that move the hands of the watch.

Jewels as Cushions

203

YOU WILL NEED:

2 different-sized jars
lidstape
pencil
marbles

Sometime between the end of the 17th century and the beginning of the 18th century, Swiss watchmakers began to use chips of sapphires and rubies to ease the friction between various parts so they moved more smoothly and didn't wear out as fast. A 17-jeweled watch has seventeen of these jeweled bearings, although now the "jewels" are probably synthetic. You can see the effect of the jeweled ball bearings by using a handful of marbles.

What to do: Turn both lids so the insides are upward. Tape the smaller lid to a table. Tape the pencil to the inside of the large jar lid. Then place the large lid on top of the small one and, using the pencil as lever, spin it. Note what happens. Now fill the small lid with marbles and then spin the large lid on it. Note what happens.

What happens: In the first experiment the top lid moves with difficulty. When you put the marbles in the top lid it spins easily.

Why: When two things move in contact with one another, they resist moving. No two surfaces are completely smooth. The bumps of one surface catch on the bumps of the other. The resistance that results when the surfaces rub against each other is known as friction.

The amount of friction depends on the kinds of surfaces as well as the force pressing them together. The rougher the surfaces, the greater the friction. Too much friction produces heat and wears away parts. The smooth, round marbles reduce the amount of friction. The contact between the moving parts and the marbles is very slight, and so the friction is very low. This is the reason that the tiny, hard gems in a watch reduce wear at the principal points of friction—the delicate axles around which the various wheels revolve. The more jeweled bearings in a watch, the longer it lasts.

About the Word "Watch"

Where did the use of the word watch for a timekeeper come from? Some sources say it originated during the Middle Ages, when the man who kept the night watch proclaimed "All's well!" and also announced the time. Others say it came about because people were at last able to see the time instead of merely hearing it announced by chimes or bells. Still others claim the word came from sailors who called their duty-period—and still do—a watch.

Early watches were wound by a key inserted in a small hole under the back case. It wasn't until late in the 19th century that watches were wound by a stem. In self-winding watches, the mainspring was tightened automatically by a weight on a rotor, a revolving part that responded to the slightest arm movements of the wearer.

Pendulum Clocks

In 1656, Christian Huygens van Zulicham, a Dutch scientist, invented the first pendulum clock. Based on the principle established by Galileo's experiments in 1583, the new clock was driven by a single weight—the bob—suspended on a long rope. Because pendulum clocks were housed in tall wooden cases designed to hide the unattractive weights, they were known as tall clocks. Later these clocks became known as grandfather clocks.

What to do: Tie a weight to the longest string and suspend it from the clothes hanger so it hangs freely. Pull the string slightly to one side and let it swing. Count the number of swings it makes in 60 seconds. Then pull the string farther over to one side and let it swing again, counting the number of swings in 60 seconds. Add additional weights and try swinging the string. Again count the number of swings made in 60 seconds. Write down your results.

Do the same thing with **strings of different** lengths: 10 inches, 20 inches, and finally 39 inches. In each case, note how many times the weight moves back and forth in 60 seconds and jot down the results.

What happens: When the string is 39 inches long, the weight moves back and forth 60 times in one minute.

Why: A pendulum takes the same length of time to make every swing no matter how far it travels or how heavy the weight at the end of it. But the longer the pendulum, the longer the time it takes to complete its swing; the shorter the pendulum the more quickly it travels back and forth. Since it takes one second for a length of string measuring 39 inches to swing back and forth, time can be measured with accuracy.

Seconds

When pendulum clocks became more accurate, first minute hands and, eventually, second hands were added to clock faces. Robert Hooke, an English physicist, was the first one to use the word "second" for one-sixtieth of a minute. Since there are 60 minutes in an hour, Hooke divided a minute into 60 parts, too. He called each part a second because he was dividing by sixty a second time.

205 ◆ Railroad Timetable

Barely more than one hundred years ago every local community kept its own "official" time, calling it noon when the sun was overhead. The time was announced to the people by a town clock, by a falling time ball in the center of town, or by a factory whistle. But when railroad travel became common, this was very confusing! The country needed a uniform schedule that everyone could follow. This brought about the uniform system of time zones that we have today. It met with much opposition, however, from many people who resented being "dictated to" by the railroads.

At a meeting on October 11, 1883, four time zones were established for the United States—Eastern, Central, Mountain, and Pacific—based on the 15° of longitude that the sun travels in one hour.

The next year, by general international agreement, the entire world was divided into time zones—24 of them. Greenwich Mean Time, which had become the standard for all of the United Kingdom, was selected as the starting point from which international time zones and degrees of longitude were measured. Each zone was one hour earlier than the one immediately to the east.

The United States and its territories now have eight standard time zones including Atlantic Time for Puerto Rico and the Virgin Islands (one hour later than Eastern Standard), and Alaska, Hawaii-Aleutian, and Samoan Standard (one, two, and three hours earlier respectively than Pacific Time). Canada's five time zones range from Atlantic time to Pacific-Yukon. Newfoundland is a half-hour later than Atlantic time.

Australia and other large land masses are also divided into time zones based primarily on longitude. Australia's three time zones range from Australian Western Standard Time in the city of Perth, to Australian Central Standard Time in the North Territory and North Australia, to Australian Eastern Standard Time in Queensland, Victoria, and New South Wales, with Lord Howe Island a half hour later. China has resisted zoning—all of that vast land uses Beijing Time, which coincides with that of Western Australia, eight hours later than London. South Africa Standard Time is two hours later than London, and at noon in London it is midnight in New Zealand.

Which time zone do you live in?

206 ◆ Daylight Savings Time

Daylight Savings Time, also known as Summer Time, is a system of putting clocks ahead an hour in the late spring and summer to extend daylight hours during the time people are awake. It was first suggested—perhaps as a joke—by Benjamin Franklin in 1784, but not until the 20th century was the idea put into effect.

During World War I, Germany, the United States, Great Britain, and Australia all adopted summer daylight savings time to conserve fuel by decreasing the use of artificial light. During World War II both the United States and Great Britain used it all year—advancing clocks one hour during the winter and two during the summer.

Summer time observance was formally adopted as United States government policy in 1966, but even now it is not used in Indiana and Arizona. All of Canada observes Daylight Savings Time during the summer, but only some parts of Australia move clocks forward during their summer months starting the last Sunday in October.

Have you ever noticed that the days seem longer in the summertime? That's Daylight Savings Time!

207 International Date Line

Do you know what the International Date Line is all about? Let's take a trip around the world and find out.

What to do: Fold the paper in thirds lengthwise, as in illustration A. Then fold it in half three times and number the strips, as in illustration B.

Unfold the paper and fill in the times and the names of the locales, as in illustration C. Then cut the paper along the fold lines into three lengthwise strips.

Tape the strips to one another, matching the numbers so that 5 follows 4 and -5 follows -4. Tape

C

midnight	1 a.m.	2 a.m.	3 a.m.	4 a.m.	5 a.m.	6 a.m.	7 a.m.
Wellington, Fiji, Wake Island	Samoa	Hawaii, Aleutians	Anchorage, Yukon	Los Angeles, Victoria	Denver	Chicago, Winnipeg	New York, Toronto
-12	-11	-10	-9	-8	-7	-6	-5
8 a.m.	9 a.m.	10 a.m.	11 a.m.	Noon	1 p.m.	2 p.m.	3 p.m.
Puerto Rico, Halifax	Buenos Aires	Mid-Atlantic	Cape Verde	London	Berlin	Athens	Moscow
-4	-3	-2	-1	0	+1	+2	+3
4 p.m.	5 p.m.	6 p.m.	7 p.m.	8 p.m.	9 p.m.	10 p.m.	11 p.m.
Abu Dhabi, Muscat	Karachi, Bombay	Tashkent, Calcutta	Jakarta, Bangkok	Beijing	Tokyo	Sydney	Solomon Islands
+4	+5	+6	+7	+8	+9	+10	+11

the ends (+12 and -12) to one another. Each of the numbers represents a time zone one hour later or one hour earlier than Greenwich Mean Time in England.

Let us assume it is noon on Tuesday and your two coins are going on a trip around the globe. They both start in London, but one travels east to Berlin and one goes west toward New York. Their planes meet one another on a remote Pacific island, west of Eniwetok (a coral island in the Marshalls) and east of Fiji.

The one traveling eastward sets its clock ahead for each 15° of longitude to gain 12 hours. The one traveling westward sets its clock back one hour for each 15° so that it loses 12 hours.

What happens: The two clocks differ by 24 hours in one calendar day.

The problem was solved by international agreement. At the International Date Line—at 180° of longitude, located in the Pacific Ocean—travelers are required to change the date. The one traveling east moves the calendar back a day; the one traveling west moves ahead a day.

The 180° meridian runs mostly through the open Pacific. But the date line zigzags to avoid a time change in populated areas—in the north to take the eastern tip of Siberia into the Siberian time system, to include a number of islands in the Hawaii-Aleutian time zone, and, farther south, to tie British-owned islands into the New Zealand time system.

International Date Line

SUPER CLOCKS

Although mechanical clocks and watches are still sold, more accurate and less expensive clocks and watches have been available for more than 50 years. These are the electric and electronic timetellers. And, of course, for true accuracy, there is now the atomic clock, but this is neither inexpensive nor available for our night tables or wrists—yet.

208 Super Clock Timeline

1800—Alessandro Volta makes the first chemical battery

1821—Michael Faraday uses a magnet to convert a wire carrying current to mechanical energy

1830—Joseph Henry builds the first practical electric motor

1840—Alexander Bain patents an electric clock

1881—Pierre Curie discovers piezoelectric oscillation

1894—Reliable master-clock system developed

1913—Niels Bohr and Ernest T. Rutherford develop theory of structure of the atom

1918—U.S. reliable AC current running at 60 cycles per second

1927—U.K. reliable AC current running at 50 cycles per second

1929—Warren Marrison invents quartz crystal clock

1949—Harold Lyons of the U.S. National Bureau of Standards constructs first atomic clock using ammonia molecules

1955—Dr. Essen and J.V.L. Parry in National Physical Lab in London develop atomic clock using cesium atom

1957—Electric wristwatches-battery replaces the spring

1958—First integrated circuit (microchip)

1959—Miniature tuning fork replaces the balance wheel

1965—Transistorized battery clocks

1960s—LED (Light Emitting Diode)

1969—First all-electronic watch with digital display

1967—Frequency of vibrations of cesium atom is designated definition of a second

1970s—LCD (Liquid Crystal Display)

209 Electric Clocks

You don't have to wind an electric clock. The spring, the pendulum, and the escapement have been replaced by a motor, which is powered by the electricity from an electrical outlet or a battery.

The first patent for an electric clock was filed as early as 1840 by Alexander Bain, a Scotsman living in London. In 1894, Frank Hope-Jones and George Boswell built a reliable electric master-clock system that had a pendulum powered by an electric battery. The system was used to power networks of clocks in railway stations and factories.

But despite these inventions, you still couldn't plug a clock into an electrical outlet until 1918 in the United States and nine years later in Great Britain. Before that, and in some places for years afterward, homes and offices were wired only for direct current (DC), which has a steady flow in one direction. This couldn't be used for clocks because clocks need current that flows in a circuit at regular intervals. That wasn't practical until a reliable alternating current (AC) was introduced. Then clock-makers were able to equip a clock with an electric motor with a rotor, a revolving part that spun at the same frequency as current from electricity-generating power stations (50 or 60 cycles a second).

Gears reduced the high speed to the slow turning needed by the hands of the clock.

Take a survey of the clocks in your house. How many are powered by electricity?

210 Make an Electric Motor

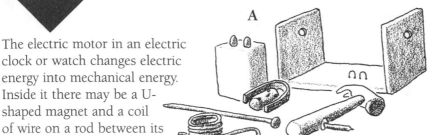

The electric motor in an electric clock or watch changes electric energy into mechanical energy. Inside it there may be a U-shaped magnet and a coil of wire on a rod between its poles. The electric current flows through the coil, which becomes magnetic. The forces of the coil and the magnet then push and pull on each other. This makes the coil spin around and turn a shaft. You can make a simple electric motor and see how it works, but you will need an adult to assist you.

What to do: Use the hammer and sharp nail to punch a hole approximately 1 inch (2.5 cm) from the top of each of the smaller pieces of wood. Make sure the knitting needle moves freely in the plywood holes. Then glue one of the smaller pieces of wood to each side of the larger piece, as in illustration A. Push two paper clips into the center of the base.

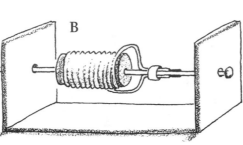

Choose a cork that is small enough to fit easily between the poles of your magnet.

Cut off two 4-inch (10 cm) strips of wire to serve as lead-in wires. Scrape the ends. Leaving an inch or two free at each end, wind the rest of the wire around the cork 30 times. Then scrape the insulation from the two free ends of the coiled wire.

Insert the knitting needle through the first ply-wood hole, through the cork and then through the second plywood hole. Secure it with a small lump or tape. See illustration B.

Tape the coiled wire to opposite sides of the knitting needle just above the bared ends.

Connect one end of the lead-in wires to the posts of the battery. Thread the two lead-in wires through the brads and then stretch them up so they make contact with the bared ends of the wire coil. See illustration C.

Finally, hold the magnet around the coil so the coil can turn without touching the magnet. Start the motor by moving the cork with your finger.

What happens: As long as you hold the magnet around the coil, the motor will move by itself.

Why: The magnet converts electrical energy into mechanical energy. It causes the wire that carries the current to move, along with anything attached to it.

Charged!

You can demonstrate what goes on in a watch.

YOU WILL NEED:

small compass
(or a needle, a
magnet, a thin slice of
cork, a shallow dish
filled with water)
2 pieces of wire
a battery

What to do: If you don't have a compass, you can make one by magnetizing a needle. Stroke the needle about 50 times in one direction with either pole of the magnet. Then float the piece of cork in the dish of water and carefully center the needle on it. Attach the wires to the two battery terminals and make contact with the needle or the compass.

What happens: The compass needle moves.

Why: When electrons flow through a wire they produce a magnetic field around it. This changes electrical energy into mechanical energy. The coil in a watch concentrates this magnetic field and so enables it to convert electric energy into mechanical energy

Coin Battery

You can make a small battery of your own. Just empty your pockets of your coins.

YOU WILL NEED:

vinegar
small bowl19 one-inch
by one-inch (2.5 cm
by 2.5 cm) strips of
paper toweling
10 copper coins
10 metal coins—any
metal except copper

What to do: Pour the vinegar into the bowl. Soak the paper strips in the vinegar. Make a pile of the coins, alternating copper and the other metal. Separate each kind with one of the vinegar-soaked paper strips. Moisten one fingertip on each hand and hold the pile of coins between those fingers.

What happens: You get a slight electric shock.

Why: The vinegar, an acid, conducts the electricity created by the separated metals of the two coins. It is a wet cell, a kind of battery.

A battery is usually made up of two metals (a zinc container and a carbon rod) separated by absorbent paper soaked in a strong acid. A chemical reaction between the two metals produces a current of electrons between the two poles, and the chemical energy is converted into electrical energy. The battery is a storehouse of energy that wears out when the chemicals it contains are used up.

 # Quartz Crystal Clocks

The invention of Dr. Warren A. Marrison, the quartz crystal clock dates back to 1929. Electric current makes the quartz vibrate, like a violin string, at a number of frequencies depending on its thickness and the electrical power applied. This is called the piezoelectric effect.

In contrast to the balance wheel, which swings back and forth a few times a second, the crystal molecules swing back and forth at least 32,768 times a second, turning the electric current off and on each time. In an area of less than a half inch (1 cm), the modern quartz crystal watch has a crystal the size of a match head, a tiny battery the size of a fingernail, and a microchip, which is an integrated circuit containing hundreds of thousands of transistors and resistors that conduct and control the amount of current flowing through.

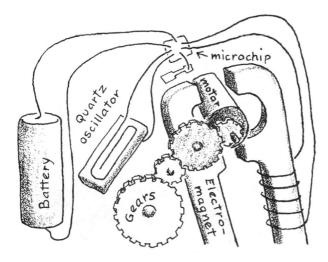

The Piezoelectric Effect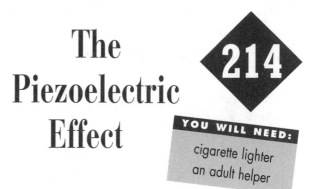

YOU WILL NEED:

cigarette lighter
an adult helper

A simple cigarette lighter can demonstrate the effect of pressure on quartz. Ask an adult to assist you.

What to do: Apply force with your thumb to the starter.

What happens: You get a spark.

Why: Inside the lighter is a wafer of quartz. When you apply pressure to it, you create electricity. In your watch, it is just the opposite. When electric current flows through, the wafer of quartz moves. Both of these changes in a crystalline substance like quartz—creating electricity from pressure and creating movement from electricity—demonstrate the piezoelectric effect. *Piezo* comes from a Greek word meaning to press or to squeeze.

Digital Clocks

At first quartz clocks had dials and hands, but these were often replaced by digital "readouts" of hours and minutes and sometimes even seconds. These numbers are formed by small luminous elements controlled by electrical signals.

There are different kinds of readouts. Some are LEDs (Light Emitting Diodes). When electric current runs through these electronic devices, it gives off a bright glow, either red, yellow, or green, depending on the material used. Readouts in small timepieces are generally LCD (Liquid Crystal Display). The creamy gray liquid crystals block the passage of light and thus turn black when current is applied. The result is a black digit on a gray background. Both result in squared-off digits formed from seven-section rectangles, parts of which light up and parts of which stay dark.

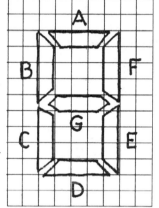

What to do: Copy the pattern above which is made up of seven straight lines forming a rectangle. Then blacken the sections of the form that make the number you want.

For instance, if you want to create a "6," blacken all the lines except F, the upper right one, and A, the top one. Then erase (or lighten) F and A. If you need to create a "5," blacken all the lines except F and C. For a "1," blacken only B and C and erase the others.

What happens: You can make all of the numbers by selecting which lines to highlight and which to eliminate. Digital clocks are coded to do this electrically.

Why: Perhaps you understand now why the shape of numbers and letters in digital readouts take some getting used to. They certainly don't resemble printed or cursive writing. The vibrations back and forth of the flake of quartz are counted by a binary logic gate, a kind of switch. Every time the count reaches the number of vibrations that a particular crystal makes in a second, the switch sends a pulse to the display unit and the watch records the passage of another second. Other switches on the same chip count 60 seconds and update the minute display; others count minutes to update the hour.

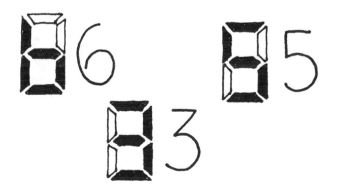

216 ◆ Glowing in the Dark

Early clocks and watches were made with chimes to give the time after dark. But during World War I, when a chiming watch might have given away the wearer's position to the enemy, watchmakers developed a watch that glowed in the dark. Hands and dials were painted with radium. When radium was found to be a hazardous substance, particularly to the workers who painted with it, less dangerous materials were used.

Available today are sports watches with phosphorescent hands that glow because the phosphorus coating converts the energy of sunlight into electronic vibrations and releases it in the form of light.

Also marketed are battery-operated watches with "Indiglo night lights." The watch face is coated with zinc sulfide diluted by a small amount of copper. When you press a button, electrical energy from the battery is converted by a microchip to a higher voltage, exciting electrons in the dial material than then provide a greenish light.

Timing the Past: The Radioactive Clock ◆ 217

Scientists tell time backward by using a radioactive clock that ticks away in ancient bones, in the wood of an ancient barge, and in every material that has lived in the past 50,000 years. This radioactive clock is a slowly disintegrating form of the carbon atom called carbon 14. Plants obtain carbon dioxide from the atmosphere and animals eat the plants. After the animals and plants die, radioactive decay begins. The rate of radioactive decay is measured in terms of half-life, the time required for half of an element to decay. A once-living organism loses half of its carbon 14 in about 5,000 years, half of what's left is lost in the next 5,000 years, and half of that in the third 5,000 years. Nothing detectable remains after about 50,000 years.

To determine the age of something that once lived—from cloth to seashells—scientists figure out its carbon-14 content and compare it with the content of a modern sample.

Radioactive atoms in earth, air, and water have also provided "clocks" by which the ages of rocks and fossils older than 50,000 years can be measured. Like that of carbon 14, the rate of radioactive decay is measured in terms of half-life. In one half-life, half of the original atoms decay; in a second half-life, half of that remains, and so on. Measurements of the decay of uranium, for example, give it a half-life of about 4.5 billion years.

Atomic Clocks

An atomic clock is based on the action of the electrons in an atom, which vibrates naturally and whose frequency is immune to the temperature and friction problems that plague mechanical clocks.

In 1967 the General Assembly on Weights and Measurements changed the definition of a second to the frequency with which the atom of the metal cesium vibrates back and forth—9,192,631,770 times a second. The more vibrations a timekeeper makes in one second, the more accurate it is. Atomic timetellers are accurate to one billionth of a second in 24 hours.

The first molecular clock, which used ammonia gas, was built in 1949 by H. Lyons at the United States National Bureau of Standards. In 1955 L. Essen and J.V.L. Parry built the first cesium atomic clock at the National Physical Laboratory in England.

You can see this latest method of keeping time at the laboratories of the National Bureau of Standards in Boulder, Colorado. It looks like no clock you have ever seen—more like a sewer pipe—a stainless steel pipe 20 feet (6m) long with a 16-inch diameter (40 cm), which is actually a cesium-beam tube. Cesium is a soft silvery metal that looks a little like mercury.

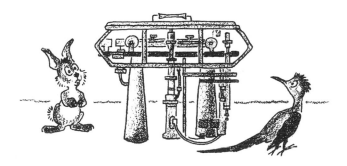

Time Machines— and More

A few scientists have been investigating claims that some people have actually gone back in time, that time can go backward. They are also looking into the possibility that some people see into the future. They debate whether dreams are sometimes a form of insight into what is going to happen, a form of "future time." Some philosophers through the years have suggested that time is a circle, doubling back on itself.

While it's easy to define the measuring of time, time itself is more difficult to describe. Some have questioned whether time exists at all. Everyone— from the physicist to the psychologist to the philosopher—has a different explanation. Einstein's theories—proved in laboratory atomic experiments—challenge some of our most basic beliefs about time. They indicate time slows down at speeds approaching the speed of light.

It takes light from the sun about 8 minutes and light from Pluto about 5 hours to reach Earth. But light from the nearest star—other than the sun—we now see twinkling in the sky actually has been traveling at the speed of light for more than four years. And some of the more distant stars' light has been traveling at that speed for more than 2 million years by the time astronomers see it on their telescopes.

With space exploration and the possibility of life on other planets, what more will the future teach us about the past—and the future?

Under Ground

When you walk through a park, over a hill, or down a dusty road, you probably don't give much thought about the ground under your feet. But the ground is an important part of nature. The soil we use to grow our plants and the rocks we use to build our homes and highways are valuable in many ways.

About Soil and Rocks

Soil is mostly made up of rock that has been broken up into very small pieces. This sand, created over many years (hundreds of thousands), is the result of weather, erosion, and freezing and thawing. The climate and the slope of the land (hillside or river valley) also affect how fast sandy soil forms in a particular area. Soil also contains air, water,

and decayed matter (known as humus). Basically, there are three types of soil: clay, sandy, and loam (a rich mixture of clay, sand, and humus that is good for growing plants).

There are also three different kinds of rocks. Igneous rock, such as granite, is formed from melted minerals, so it is often found near volcanoes. Sedimentary rock usually forms underwater, as a result of layers of material, called sediment, pressing down on other layers. Sandstone and limestone are examples of this type of rock. Metamorphic rock, such as marble, is formed by the great heat and pressure deep inside the Earth's surface.

The experiments here will help you learn about the soil and rock in your special part of the world.

Rock and Roll

YOU WILL NEED:

clean sand
white glue
small container
plastic spoon
oil or margarine
aluminum foil
coffee can (with lid)
water

The sand in soil is rock that has been broken up and worn down by a process called erosion. To demonstrate this, you need to make your own rocks (most outdoor rocks are much too hard).

What to do: Mix three large spoonfuls of sand together with three spoonfuls of white glue. Make small lumps of the mixture and place them on a lightly oiled piece of aluminum foil, so that they will not stick to it. Put the "rocks" in a dry, sunny location for two or three days, until hard. Then, put some of your "rocks" into the coffee can with some water. Hold the lid on securely and shake the can for four to five minutes. Remove the lid.

What happens: The rocks begin to wear down. Some rocks may be worn down into sand again.

Why: The water running over the rocks pushes them against each other, causing erosion that wears them down. In nature, this process takes many years, but the result is the same. Rocks are broken up, become smaller from rubbing against each other and, over time, wear down into sandy particles that may eventually become part of the soil near a river or stream.

It's a Dirty Job...

The surface of our Earth is made up of rocks, sand, humus, water, and air. All of these soil "ingredients" are necessary for plants and animals to survive. Let's find out how much air is in different soils.

What to do: Half-fill each jar with a soil sample from several places in your neighborhood. Then fill the jars with water, almost to the top.

What happens: Depending on the soil you are testing, you will see a few, some, or a lot of air bubbles rising to the top of the water in each jar. The number of bubbles tell how much air was trapped in the spaces between the soil particles.

Why: The more bubbles rising through the water, the more air was trapped which you can see escaping from the soil sample. Tightly packed soil has less space for air to be trapped than does soil that has a lot of humus or other organic matter in it to make "air pockets." Most plants tend to grow better in such aerated soil (soil with lots of air pockets) than densely packed soil (such as clay).

222 Soak It Up

Good soil, like that in a garden, always has some water in it. Here's how to find it.

What to do: Fill the can about half-full of garden soil. Tape a piece of black construction paper around the can, and place the glass or plastic plate over the top. Put the can in a sunny window or on a warm radiator for a couple of hours.

What happens: Water droplets begin to form on the underside of the lid. To prove that the water is from the soil, not the air, clean out and dry the can and repeat the experiment, but without putting in any soil. Compare the results.

Why: All soil contains some water. How much is held by the soil depends on what else is in the soil, the outside temperature, the weather at the time, and the climate in the area—wet or dry. Soil water is necessary for plant and animal growth, but most plants will need more water (from rain, rivers, or lakes) to keep growing.

223 Deeper and Deeper

Soil is made up of different layers. Here's how you can look for them.

What to do: Find a place where you can dig a hole (be sure to ask permission first). Try to dig about 2 feet (60 cm) or so straight down. Notice the colors of the soil layers along the sides of the hole as you dig. Measure the distance from the surface down to the different soil layers and write it down. Place a small sample of each layer's soil in a plastic bag.

At home, put some of each sample on clean white paper. Use a magnifying glass, or a microscope, to examine the samples.

What happens: Depending on where you live and dig, you may find one or more soil colors in layers as you dig down.

Why: The soil near the surface is usually a dark, rich color. This layer, called topsoil, is the thinnest and it usually contains a lot of organic matter (dead and decaying plants, insects, and animals which make up humus). Topsoil is best for growing plants and food crops. The next layer, known as subsoil, is often lighter in color and has a lot of sand and rocks in it. The last layer of soil is called the bedrock. If you dig down far enough to reach it, you will see it is the hardest layer to dig through. This is because there is no organic matter to soften it; bedrock is mostly made up of rocks, pebbles, and stones packed tightly together.

Note: Always remember to fill in any holes you make after you have finished obtaining soil samples

Nutrients Away

The food, or nutrients, in the soil can wash away when there is a lot of rain. Here's how it happens.

YOU WILL NEED:

¹/₂ cup of dry soil
blue powdered tempera paint (from hobby or art store)
measuring spoon
measuring cup
wide-mouthed jar
funnel
coffee filter
cups or containers
water

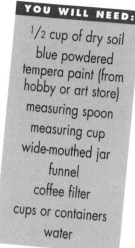

What to do: Add ¹/₂ teaspoon of the blue tempera paint to the ¹/₂ cup of soil and mix thoroughly. Set the funnel in the mouth of the jar and put a coffee filter in the funnel. Pour the soil mixture into the filter. Pour ¹/₂ cup of water into the funnel. Look at the color of the water running into the jar. Pour the water in the jar into a cup or container and put the funnel over the jar again; repeat this again with another ¹/₂ cup of water. Pour off the water, and repeat it another two or three times.

What happens: At first, the water that flows into the jar will be dark blue in color. Each time more water is poured over the same soil mixture, the color will get lighter. Eventually, the water will have no more blue in

it and run clean into the jar. How many half-cups of water did it take for that to happen?

Why: The blue tempera paint you added to the soil represents the nutrients that are naturally in the ground. These nutrients are necessary for plants to grow. However, when there is a lot of rain or water runoff, these nutrients are washed away, leaving a nutrient-poor soil.

Excessive rains and water runoff can remove from the soil the valuable food and minerals needed for plant growth. If you look at places in your area where a lot of soil has eroded away, you will see that there are very few plants growing there. Any plants still there are the kind that don't need much food to grow.

225

Making Bricks

You can make your own bricks using the same technique that the early pioneers did.

What to do: Put some ground clay (or your own "homemade" clay), straw, and enough water to make a doughy mixture in a bucket. Mix it together thoroughly. Place portions of the mixture into molds (frozen-vegetable packaging or small juice containers are good). Let them sit overnight in a warm place, then gently tear away the sides of the molds and let the bricks dry in the sun for several days. Use them to build something, like a little tower or house.

226

A Crystal Garden

Many of the rocks you find in the Earth's soil were formed by a process known as crystallization. This process goes on all the time and can easily be recreated in your own home. Here's how.

What to do: Wet a small piece of brick with water and place it in a small bowl. In a separate large container, mix together 1/2 cup of water, 1/2 cup of bluing, and 1/2 cup of ammonia (also from the grocery). Use a measuring cup to pour some of this mixture over the brick. Sprinkle the brick with salt and let it sit for 24 hours.

What happens: The next day you will see crystals forming on the surface of the brick.

What next: Add some more of the water + bluing + ammonia mixture to keep the blue crystals growing. Or, you can use drops of other food coloring and change some of the crystals from blue into a colorful display.

From Dust to Dust

When soil is blown from one place to another by the wind, it is known as wind erosion. This is a serious problem in many parts of the world. Is it happening where you live?

What to do: Stick some two-sided tape on one side of several different paddles. Stick the paddle handles into the ground in various places near your home. The paddles should face in different directions—North, South, East, and West (mark the direction on the paddles). At regular intervals, once or twice every week for example, look at the paddles and record the amount of dust, dirt, or soil sticking to the tape.

What happens: Depending on the amount of wind and the direction it blows where you live,

you will see that certain paddles collect more dust and dirt than other paddles do.

Why: More soil sticks on the paddles where wind erosion is taking place. If there are no barriers, such as trees, plants, and grass, to slow down or stop wind erosion, great quantities of soil can be swept into the air from one location and left somewhere else. One way to prevent wind erosion is to grow trees and plants to cut the wind and cover and protect the ground. This is why wind erosion is much less of a problem in dense forest than it is in the desert, which has sandstorms!

Erosion Explosion

Erosion can move large quantities of soil and seriously affect the lives of plants and people. Some examples of wind or water erosion are: a sandbar in a stream or off a beach, whirling dust devils, a muddy river after a storm, sand drifted against a fence or in a gully or canyon.

Some erosion quite common in and around the home is called wear. It's caused by friction rather

than wind or water. Here are some examples of wear erosion to look for:
1. Coins that are smooth from handling
2. Shoes with the heels worn down
3. An old car tire with no tread
4. A countertop with design or finish worn away

Can you list more evidence of erosion in and around your home?

229 Stem the Tide

Plants are important in many ways, but can they do anything to prevent or slow down soil erosion?

YOU WILL NEED:
2 cake pans
soil
grass seed
water
a pitcher
2 books

What to do: Fill two cake pans with soil. In one pan, plant some grass seed. Water the soil in both pans equally. Place the pan with the grass seed in a sunny location and water gently for several days. When the grass is about 3 inches (1 cm) high, place one end of each pan against a book or block of wood so that they lie at an angle. Fill the pitcher with water and pour it into the higher end of the first pan. Do the same thing with the pan that has grass growing in it.

What happens: In the pan without grass, the water flows freely across the surface. Some of the dirt is carried by the fast-running water toward the bottom of the pan. In the other pan, with the grass, less soil is washed away.

Why: The grass slows down the flow of the water over the surface and that stops much of the soil from being eroded away. You have looked at mountains or bare hillsides with very few plants and noticed that lots of soil has been washed away, except for rocks too big for the water to move. The use of plants helps keep soil in place and prevents erosion damage.

Did You Know? 230

· In the United States alone, more than seven billion tons of topsoil is eroded away into streams and rivers every year. Louisiana and Hawaii are the only states that continue to grow in physical size.
· About 75% of all the rocks on the Earth's surface are sedimentary rocks (rocks formed when small grains and particles of sediment are pressed together under tons of water for long periods of time).
· Each year, the world's deserts grow by as much as 16,000 square miles (41,600 sq km).

Water is one of the things we often take for granted. We turn on a faucet and water comes out. We turn the faucet off and the water stops. We usually don't think about what water is and just what it means to us, but we should. It is needed for our health, it is an important source of power for business and industry, and it is vital for maintaining life on Earth in all its forms.

One of the major concerns we have about water today is its purity (its cleanliness). Pollution of our water sources and resources is an increasing problem all over the world. We all need to work together to ensure that the water we want to use tomorrow is protected today.

The fun activities in this chapter will help you to learn more about water and its role in nature.

231 **Compact and Loose**

YOU WILL NEED:

measuring cup
potting soil
clean sandbox sand
3 same-size cans
(with ends removed)
cheesecloth
scissors
masking tape
water
3 clear jars
a helper, or a clock
with a second hand

Both water and soil are needed for plant growth. But water travels through soil at different rates, depending on how much, or the ratio of, organic matter there is to inorganic matter in the soil.

What to do: Cut three squares of cheesecloth. Shape a piece over one end of each can and tape the edges to the sides of the can. Cut out three more pieces of mesh and lay them over the tops of the glass jars. Turn the cans over, so the cheesecloth is on the bottom, and half-fill the first can with potting soil. Fill the second can halfway with sand. For the third can, combine potting soil and sand and half-fill the can with the mixture. Use your hand to pack down the soils in each can firmly, then place each can of soil on top of a cheesecloth-covered jar.

If you have a helper with you, add one-half cup of water to each can at the same time and see which one the water drips through first. If you are experimenting alone, pour the water into the cans one at a time, watch the jar and clock, and mark the time it takes for the water to leak through the soil packed into each jar.

What happens: The water you put in the can of sand runs through to the jar much more rapidly than the water in the sand and soil mixture. The water in the mixture leaks through at a faster rate than the water in the potting soil.

Why: Water flows through sand very quickly because this soil has lots of air space between the grains that lets the water pass through. Because the potting soil has organic material in it, this soil holds on to more of the water, stopping it from leaking through. This is one reason why gardeners and farmers add humus or other organic matter to the soil—to hold the water for their crops. The ability of a soil to allow water to pass through it is called permeability.

Well, Well, Well

YOU WILL NEED:
cardboard tube (toilet paper roll)
large (coffee) can
sand
aquarium or potting gravel
water

To get a drink of water, you probably just turn on a faucet. Many people, however, get their water from wells. How does this kind of system work? Let's build a small one and see.

What to do: Place the tube upright in the middle of the coffee can. Holding the tube, pour a layer of about 1½ inches (4 cm) of gravel on the bottom of the coffee can around the outside of the tube. Pour a second layer, this time of sand, on top of the gravel. Slowly pour some water onto the sand until the water reaches the top of the sand. Notice what happens inside the tube.

What happens: After a short time, water begins to rise inside the tube.

Why: When it rains, "groundwater" collects under the surface of the Earth. This collected water can be very shallow or deep depending on the rock formations and the kind of soil in a particular area. Some people think of this groundwater as a series of large underground lakes extending for miles and miles. Because there is a limit to the amount of water that can collect in an area, water pressure builds up in these "lakes." If a well has been dug nearby, the pressure forces water into it where it can be reached and used.

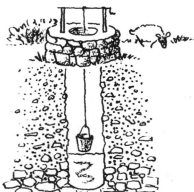

Often, when we think about water pollution, we think about rivers and streams. But we need to think about our oceans, too, because much of the food we eat, the weather that affects us, the air and even the moisture in it comes from our oceans. Unfortunately, even our largest oceans are becoming contaminated—oil spills pollute the sea, litter is thrown into the water, and garbage washes up on shores all over the world.

Even though we don't drink ocean water, it is still important to human life. If you have ever gone to a beach to swim or to walk along the shore, you may have seen some of the pollution that is destroying the world's oceans. Here are three things you can do to help:

1. If you go to a beach, take along a garbage bag to pack up your own litter or any you may find there. Put it in an available trash can or take it away with you when you leave.
2. Cut apart the plastic rings that come with six-packs of canned drinks. These often find their way into the oceans and can choke and kill sea birds and other marine life.
3. Ask your parents to buy soaps and detergents that are "biodegradable" and don't poison the ocean. Regular soaps contaminate the liquid waste, which is often pumped through sewers and into the oceans, and it kills large numbers of sea animals and plants. It is important to use biodegradable products even if you don't live anywhere near the ocean.

234 More Than You Know

YOU WILL NEED:
your eyes and your nose
clean container
a helper

If a stream runs near where you live, try this experiment to find out something about the water that flows there.

What to do: With your helper or friend, visit a nearby stream. Bend down and look closely at the water as it flows by. Sniff the air. Dip your container into the water and raise some to your nose. Smell it again.

What happens: Did you notice any of the following conditions?
• Some streams have a rotten-egg smell. Often, they are heavily polluted from a lot of sewage being dumped into the water source.
• If the stream has a shiny or multicolored film floating on it, that means that oil or gasoline is seeping into the water.
• If the color of the water is very green, there is probably a lot of algae in the water. Too much algae means there isn't enough oxygen in the water for fish and other plant life.
• Foam or suds floating on the water usually means that detergent or other soapy waste is leaking into the water from nearby factories or homes.
• Cloudy or muddy water usually means that the water contains large quantities of dirt, silt, or mud. Unfortunately, this means that the animals and plants that live in the stream aren't getting enough oxygen. It is possible that a lot of soil erosion is taking place somewhere upstream. Can you do something about it?
• Bright colors, such as red or orange, on the surface of the water is an indication that pollutants are being released into the stream by factories and industries.
• Clean, clear, or transparent water that has no smell to it is the best kind of water for aquatic plants and animals, and for us.

Why: For too long, people believed that it was OK to let streams and rivers carry away their pollutants and garbage. People put lots of things into their streams without thinking about the long-term effects. We now know that whatever we put into a stream will affect the plants, animals, and people who live downstream. Cleaning up our streams and making sure we don't put anything into a stream that does not occur naturally in that stream are important steps in maintaining these important, life-giving water resources.

235

YOU WILL NEED:

clean, plastic bottle
cooking oil
water
blue food coloring

Ocean Motion

Would you like to create an ocean that you can keep in your own home?

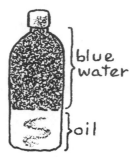

blue water

oil

What to do: Pour cooking oil into the bottle until it is one-third full. Fill the rest of the bottle to the brim with water and add a few drops of blue food coloring. Screw the cap on very tight and lay the bottle on its side. Now, tip the bottle back and forth.

What happens: The oily water in the bottle begins to roll back and forth, moving just like the waves in the ocean do. You have created a miniature ocean in a bottle.

Why: Waves are energy moving through water. The water of the wave itself doesn't move, it's the energy passing from one water molecule to another that forms the waves. Ocean waves are caused by the gravitational pull of the moon on the Earth's surface-water, the shape (geological formation) of the ocean floor, and the spinning of the Earth on its axis. You can create similar conditions artificially in a soda bottle and observe wave action that is very much like that which occurs throughout the oceans of the world.

236 You Crack Me Up!

Here's an experiment that demonstrates how large boulders are broken down into tiny pebbles—by water!

YOU WILL NEED:

pieces of sandstone (from hardware or building supply store)
sealable plastic bags
water

What to do: Soak pieces of sandstone in water overnight. The next day, place several pieces of the wet sandstone into sandwich bags and seal them tightly. Place the bags in the freezer overnight. Take them out and examine them the next day.

What happens: The sandstone cracks into smaller pieces.

Why: When water freezes, it expands. The sandstone absorbs some of the water, taking it up into the air spaces between the sand particles. When the stone was placed in the freezer, the water in it froze and expanded.

In nature, water seeps into the cracks of rocks, freezes in winter, and causes the rocks to break apart. After a while, the rocks are reduced to very small pebbles and eventually to sand.

237

Drip, Drip, Drip

With this experiment, you'll be able to remove salt from saltwater. Let's try it.

YOU WILL NEED:

water
table salt
measuring cup
measuring spoons
large bowl
small cup
plastic food wrap
small stone

What to do: In the large bowl, mix 3 teaspoons of salt into 2 cups of water until it is thoroughly dissolved. Use a spoon to carefully taste a small sample of the saltwater. Set the small cup in the middle of the bowl. Cover the bowl with plastic food wrap and place a small stone in the center of the wrap (directly over the cup) to weigh the plastic down.

Carefully, set the wrapped bowl, with stone in place, in the sun for several hours. Look at the wrap after a while and you will notice beads of water forming on the underside of the plastic food wrap and dripping into the small cup. Later on, remove the plastic wrap carefully and taste the water that has collected in the cup.

What happens: The saltwater inside the large bowl evaporates into the air inside the

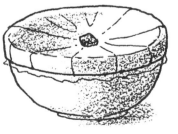

bowl. It then condenses as beads of water on the underside of the plastic wrap. With the plastic covering lower in the center, the beads of water roll down to the lowest point and drip into the small cup. The water in the cup is no longer salty!

Why: This experiment illustrates the natural process of solar distillation. Distillation involves changing a liquid into a gas (evaporation) by heating and then back into a liquid (condensation) by cooling the gas vapor. The sun's energy can evaporate water but not salt (salt molecules are heavier than water molecules), so the salt remains in the bowl. This entire process, often referred to as desalinization (removing salt) is used in many countries, such as those in the Middle East, to make fresh water from saltwater

Don't Rain on My Parade

YOU WILL NEED:

small (baby food) jars
pH paper and color chart (from aquarium or pet store)
rain and water samples (see below)
tweezers

Acid rain is a problem in many parts of the world, especially where there is a lot of industry. Here's how to find out if acid rain is a problem where you live.

What to do: Make sure each jar is thoroughly cleaned and dried. With an adult to help, collect several different samples of water (tap water, rainwater, well water, pool water, etc.). Collect each sample in a separate jar. Using the tweezers, dip a strip of pH paper into a sample of water and quickly compare the color that registers against the color chart. Do the same for each water sample and record the results. (You may want to collect some rainwater at the beginning of a storm and some at the end of the storm and compare the two different rainwater samples.)

What happens: You notice that the pH of the various water samples has different readings.

Why: pH indicates the amount of acid in substances. The pH scale goes from 0 to 14. Pure water, for example, has a pH value of 7 (it is neutral). Substances that have a pH value less than 7 are acids; substances that have a pH value more than 7 are bases. Acids and bases are common chemicals, many of which we have in our homes. Vinegar and lemon juice, for example, are acids; while baking soda is a base. The strength of an acid or base is determined by the pH scale (the lower the number the more acidic a substance is; the higher a number the more basic, or alkaline, it is).

Acid rain has a pH value of 5.6 or less. Rain that is considerably less than 5.6 will be more damaging to the environment than rain above 5.6 on the pH scale. Rain that falls at the beginning of a storm is usually more acidic than rain that falls at the end of a storm. Also, the rain that falls in the eastern United States is more acidic (because of the prevailing winds) than rain that falls in the western half of the country.

239

Acid Soil

There are many different types of soil. Certain plants (blueberries) like to grow in acid soils, and some plants (potatoes, peaches) prefer basic soils. You can test the pH (acidity or alkalinity) of soil with this experiment.

Collect several soil samples from various places in and around your community (about one cup of each will do). In clean jars, mix each soil sample with one cup of distilled water. (Distilled water, available in grocery stores, is neutral, having a pH of 7.) Shake each sample thoroughly. After a few minutes, dip a separate strip of pH test paper into each sample and quickly compare the strip to the colors on the pH chart. You should be able to see some difference in the pH of the soils even in your own neighborhood. Invite friends and relatives to give you soil samples from other places for testing, too.

240 Did You Know?

- It is estimated that about 14 billion pounds (6.3 billion kg) of trash and garbage are dumped into the oceans of the world every year.
- Americans alone consume about 450 billion gallons (1,710 billion liters) of water every day.
- Over 99% of all the fresh water on Earth is trapped in icebergs, icecaps, and glaciers.
- Mt. Waialeale in Hawaii averages 451 inches (1,146 cm) of rain per year, making it the wettest spot on Earth.
- There's about 9 million tons of gold dissolved in the oceans of the world.
- From the mouth of the Amazon River in Brazil pours one-fifth of all the moving fresh water on Earth.
- Canada contains one-third of all the fresh water on Earth.
- North America has more than 190,000 miles (304,000 km) of ocean coastline—more than any other continent.
- If all the world's ice melted, the sea level would rise 200 to 300 feet (600 to 900 m).
- Each year, about 2.3 trillion gallons (8.74 trillion
- liters) of liquid waste are discharged directly into United States coastal waters.
- It is estimated that acid rain costs American farmers about $4 billion a year.
- The smallest drip from a leaky faucet can waste more than 50 gallons (190 liters) of water a day.

PLENTY OF PLANTS

Plants are an important part of our environment. Without plants, animals and human beings could not survive. Plants provide us with food, oxygen, medicines, building materials, seasonings, candy, drinks, industrial products, dyes, manufactured goods, paper, and decorations.

About Plants

Plants are producers—the only living things able to make their own food. In order to grow, green plants use sunlight and store their energy in their leaves and stems. Sunlight enables plants to convert water—and also carbon dioxide, which all animals (including humans) give off as they breathe—into foods needed by the plants. This remarkable process is known as photosynthesis.

Plants are also responsible for producing oxygen—a gas necessary for animal survival. Plants add to the relative humidity of an area by releasing water vapor into the air. A plant's roots also help to reduce wind and water erosion by holding on to the soil. The fallen leaves of plants contribute to the quality of the soil, providing essential nutrients to other plants.

When the life cycle of plants is endangered by air pollution, when forests and plant life in certain areas are torn up or destroyed, or when poor farming methods are used, we are affected as well. Plants are a vital part of our daily lives and our survival

Hey, What's Inside?

Did you know that inside every seed is a very small plant waiting to grow? When the conditions are right, a new plant can begin life. What does it need?

YOU WILL NEED:

dried lima beans (from grocery store)
container of water
an adult helper with a dinner knife
magnifying glass

What to do: Soak several lima bean seeds in a container of water overnight. The next day, choose some of the seeds and place them on a countertop or some paper. Ask an adult to use a knife to pry along the edge of the seed's coat (the hard covering of the seed) and open it up for you. (Knives, especially sharp ones, are dangerous and must be handled carefully.) When the two halves of the seed have separated, use your magnifying glass lens to examine the embryo in the seed (it will look like a miniature plant). You may want to look inside other seeds for their embryos, too.

What happens: You will be able to see the three basic parts of a seed— the seed coat, the food storage area, and the embryo.

Why: Many plants, such as lima beans, reproduce sexually—that is, a sperm cell from a male plant and an egg cell from a female plant combine in the flower of a plant and a seed begins to form. Inside the seed is a miniature plant called an embryo.

There is also some food material in the seed so that a newly forming plant will have a ready food source as it begins its life. Covering the embryo and food source is a seed coat that serves as protection for the seed until the new plant is ready to start. Then, when the conditions are right (moisture and warmth), the seed germinates, or begins to grow. The embryo breaks out of the seed, like a chick out of an egg, and starts its life as a new plant.

Help Me Out

242

Do you know what seeds need to begin growing? Here's how you can find out.

What to do: Label each small bag with a number. Cut three paper towels in half. Moisten three of the towel pieces with water. As directed below, place the towels in the bottoms of the bags. Drop six radish seeds into each bag and then finish setting up each bag as follows:

Bag 1: moist paper towel (water), no light (put in a drawer or closet), room temperature

Bag 2: moist paper towel (water), light, room temperature

Bag 3: dry paper towel (no water), light, room temperature

Bag 4: no paper towel, water (seeds floating), light, room temperature

Bag 5: moist paper towel (water), no light, keep in refrigerator or freezer

Bag 6: moist paper towel (water), no light, room temperature, seeds covered by nail polish.

Record the date and time you began this activity and check each of the bags twice daily for any changes.

What happens: The seeds in Bag 1 and Bag 2 germinate (begin to grow). You may see some small difference in the seeds in Bag 4. The seeds in the other bags do not start growing. What is wrong?

Why: Seeds need favorable temperature, enough moisture, and oxygen to germinate. Light is not needed for germination (the seeds, after all, usually germinate underground), but light is necessary later for growth. The seeds in Bag 6 can't get any air or moisture through the nail polish, so they don't germinate.

Plant Requirements

Plants have certain needs for their growth and survival, just as we do.

Air: To live, plants take two gases from the air. They use carbon dioxide, a natural product of animal life, to make food by a process called photosynthesis, and oxygen as fuel for the energy that helps them breathe.

Water: To make their food, plants need water. Minerals in the water help plants to grow and replace damaged cells. Water is taken in through a plant's roots and is carried to the leaves.

Temperature: Each plant variety requires a specific temperature range. Over many years, plants have adapted and learned to thrive where other plants could not survive. For example, a cactus or a palm tree could not live at the North Pole, where the cold temperatures would be harmful.

Sunlight: Most plants, especially green leafy ones, need sunlight to grow. The light converts a plant's food into usable energy. But certain plants, such as mushrooms, don't like light and grow only in the dark.

Soil: Land plants need some type of soil in order to grow. It is usually a combination of organic material (decayed animal or vegetable matter known as humus) and sand or clay that also help hold the plant erect. Plants also get nutrients, or minerals, from the soil.

243 Swell Time

In order to begin the growing process, seeds need to take in water. Here's how they do it.

What to do: Fill each of the two bags with dry seeds (bean seeds work best). Finish filling one of the bags with as much water as it can hold, then seal both bags and place them outside or on a tray or in a container in a sunny location.

What happens: After several hours, the seeds in the bag with the water begin to swell up. Eventually, the expanding seeds pop the bag open and seeds spill out all over the place.

Why: To begin the growing process, or sprout, seeds need to take in water. Water is absorbed through the skin of the seed (seed coat), and the seeds begin to expand. Because the bag had been filled with the dry seeds and now all the seeds in the bag were absorbing water and expanding, there wasn't enough room in the bag. So, the expanding seeds forced the bag open and spilled out. In nature, seeds take in water and expand in the same way.

244 Top to Bottom

Plants need both roots and shoots in order to develop properly. To watch the growth of both plant parts at the same time, do this.

What to do: Trim the blotter to fit the glass or plastic sheets. Wet the blotter well and lay it on top of one. Arrange some seeds on the blotter, placing them at least 2 inches (5 cm) in from the edge. Put the other clear sheet on top. Tie the "seed sandwich" together securely with string and place it on edge in the pan. Support it upright, at an angle of about 45°, with one or more bricks. Put 1/2 inch (1 cm) or so of water into the pan. Add more when needed, to keep the blotter wet.

What happens: In a few days, the seeds will sprout, the shoots going up and the roots going down. Use a marker to make lines on the glass or a thin strip of masking tape to mark the daily or weekly growth of the seeds.

Why: The seeds sprout because you have provided them with water, light, and air. The roots always grow downwards and the actual plant upwards. Depending on the seeds used, you may see tiny leaves form. All seeds in nature demonstrate this same type of growth.

245 A Growing Enterprise

Some seeds are easy to grow, while others are more difficult. Fruit-bearing plants are very hard to grow from seed. That is why many fruit farmers use other ways to start growing new fruit trees, such as grafts (attaching a part of one plant to a part of another plant) or root stocks (sections of root) instead.

To try growing some fruit plants at home (keep in mind, however, that the success rate is very low), you need some seeds. The easiest way to get them is to buy a couple of your favorite fruits (not the seedless variety). Take the seeds from the fruit, wash the seeds in water (don't use soap), and let them dry well in a warm place.

Some fruits you can try growing from seeds: apple, pear, pumpkin, orange, grape, cherry, peach, banana, fig, apricot, plum, quince, nectarine, lemon, lime, tomato, melon, persimmon, grapefruit.

When you are ready to plant, get several small plastic cups and fill each one with some potting soil. Moisten the soil and plant four or five seeds from one of the fruits in each cup. Plant as many different varieties of fruit seeds as possible and note which ones were the easiest to grow and which ones were the most difficult.

After you have sprouted one or more fruits and then have reached a height of 5 or 6 inches (13–15 cm), you may want to transplant them outdoors.

Hawaiian Harvest 246

Almost everybody loves the taste of pineapple. Now you can grow this delicious fruit in your own home.

Buy a whole pineapple. Have an adult cut off the crown of the pineapple (top part, with the green leaves) leaving about 1 to 2 inches (3–5 cm) of the fruit attached. (Even with a sharp knife, cutting the pineapple may not be easy.) Let the crown dry for 36 hours, then put it in a large container of potting soil to root. Place the container in a warm location—about 72°F (2°C) is ideal. Keep the soil evenly moist (but not too wet).

Pineapple develops on the top of a long stem that may need to be supported by sticks or secured upright with string when the fruit grows large. If no fruit develops, put the whole plant (with its container) inside a large plastic bag. Place a rotting apple or lemon inside the bag, close it up, and leave it for several days (the ethylene gas produced by the rotting fruit will help stimulate fruiting).

Later, you may want to transplant the fruit to a larger container or, if you live where it is very warm, outside in loose, sandy soil.

247

YOU WILL NEED:
fresh stalk of celery
2 glasses of water
red food coloring
dinner knife

Green Highways

Plants must be able to carry water and nutrients to all their parts in order to grow, but can you prove that they actually do it? Sure, you can! Here's how.

What to do: Put the two glasses of water side by side. Place four drops of red food coloring into one of the glasses. Cut off the dried bottom end of the celery stalk and then cut the stalk up the middle from the bottom of the stalk to the leaves. Stand half of the celery stalk in the glass with clear water and the other in the glass with the red water. For the next several hours, go back every hour and check on your celery stalk experiment.

What happens: The celery in the glass of plain water shows no change, but telltale streaks of red move up the stalk of the celery standing in the colored water.

Why: All plants have special tubes in their stems that act something like drinking straws. These tubes move water, and the nutrients in it, from a plant's roots up into the leaves. Slight pressure differences in the long, tube sections actually "pull" the water up the stalk, using a process called osmosis. This allows the plant to get the water and food needed for it to grow and develop, By putting red food coloring into the water, you are able to track the water's path up the stalk, and prove your theory.

248

The Name Game

How would you like to spell your name with plants? Here's how.

Fill a large flat cake pan with soil. Smooth it over so that the soil is level and moisten it with water. Using a toothpick or the end of a knife, trace your name into the surface of the soil. Open a packet of radish seeds and carefully plant the seeds in the grooves you made for the letters of your name. Be sure to follow the directions for proper planting depth and distance between seeds given on the seed packet.) Cover the seeds with soil and place the pan in a sunny location and water occasionally. After a few days, the radishes will sprout into the shape of your name.

Later, you may want to write your name in plants again, using different varieties of seeds (grass seed and mung bean seeds work especially well).

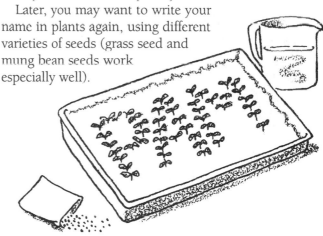

Water In, Water Out

YOU WILL NEED:

small potted plant
clear plastic bag
water
tape or string

Plants take in water in order to grow, but they also give off water.

What to do: Water the plant thoroughly. Place the plastic bag over the green, leafy part of the plant and close it up gently around the stem with tape or string. Place the plant in a sunny location for several hours.

What happens: Water droplets form on the inside of the bag.

Why: Plant leaves have tiny openings called stomata in them. In most plants, stomata are located on the underside of the leaves. During a plant's food-making process, air is taken in and released through these opening. Water, in the form of water vapor, is also released through the stomata into the atmosphere. You can see that water vapor, as it condenses and forms water droplets, on the inside of the plastic bag.

One of the reasons why a jungle is so humid is because of all the water vapor being released by the many trees and the vegetation in the area. The amount of water a plant loses varies with the weather conditions as well as the size and shape of its leaves.

Don't Crowd Me

YOU WILL NEED:

shoe box
potting soil
water
bean seeds

Do plants like togetherness, or wide-open spaces?

What to do: Fill the shoe box with potting soil. At one end of the box, plant six bean seeds very close together. At the other end of the box plant six more seeds, but space them about 1½ inches (4 cm) apart. Water the soil thoroughly, being careful not to wash it away from the seeds. Set the box aside and watch what happens to the seeds. Record the number of seeds that sprout, and continue to grow, at each end of the box.

What happens: The side with the seeds planted closer together has fewer sprouts, and they grow more slowly than the seeds planted farther apart at the other end.

Why: Plants need space in order to grow properly. When plants are crowded together, they have to compete for the limited resources available. As a result, the sprouts may not get all the soil nutrients, sunlight, and water they need to grow strong. To achieve full growth, there must be enough space left between plants. In nature, seeds are scattered over a large area, so that many are able to sprout and grow in an uncrowded environment. This is why gardeners and farmers are very careful not to plant their crops too close together.

Breathe Deeply

elodea plants (from aquarium or pet store)

aquarium or deep container

clear funnel

test tube

Do plants breathe? If so, how?

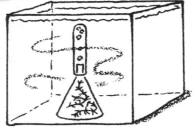

What to do: Fill the aquarium or container almost to the top with water. Place several elodea plants inside, close together in the middle, and cover them with the clear funnel (wide mouth, over the plants and narrow neck pointing upwards). Dip the test tube in the water, making sure that it fills with water.

Then, still underwater, turn the test tube over into the stem of the funnel, making sure no water escapes. Place the aquarium in a sunny location for a few days and watch what happens in the top of the test tube.

What happens: You will see oxygen building up in the top of the test tube (pushing out the water).

Why: The elodea plants (like other aquatic plants) produce oxygen. This oxygen is released into the water, where it becomes available to organisms that need it, such as fish. In this experiment, the oxygen collects in the top of the test tube, replacing the water.

252 Follow that Light

Do plants always grow toward the light? Here's a great experiment to prove that they do.

YOU WILL NEED:

2 shoe boxes
a healthy plant

What to do: Cut two corners of the cardboard from one of the shoe boxes. Tape the pieces inside the other shoe box as shown. Cut a hole in the top side. Place a healthy plant (a growing bean plant is fine) in the bottom and place the lid on the box. Put the closed shoe box in a sunny location. Every other day or so, remove the lid for a moment and quickly water the plant.

What happens: The plant grows toward the light source, even bending around the cardboard pieces to do it.

Why: All green plant life needs light in order to grow. Through a process known as phototropism, plants grow in whichever direction is toward the light. In your experiment, the plant grew toward the sunlight, even though the cardboard pieces were in the way. One of the reasons we turn our potted houseplants occasionally is so they will be able to get equal amounts of light on all sides and grow straight. If we did not, the plants would "lean" in the direction of the light.

Hanging On

YOU WILL NEED:
small potted plant with
a strong root system
2 large sponges
string

The previous experiment showed how plants always grow toward a light source. This experiment will now demonstrate how powerful that process is.

What to do: Carefully remove the plant from its pot (try to leave as much soil around the roots as possible). Wet the two sponges, wrap them around the root system, and tie them together with string. Turn the plant upside down (roots upwards) and hang it from the ceiling near a sunny window. Check the plant occasionally, and keep the sponges moistened.

What happens: After a few days, the stem and top of the plant will turn and begin to grow upwards toward the light.

Why: The leaves and stems of a plant will grow in the direction of a light source, following the process of phototropism, even if the plant is made to "stand on its head!" Also, a plant's roots will always grow downwards, trying to reach the necessary nutrients in the soil.

See Me Grow

YOU WILL NEED:
shoe box
sheet of clear acetate
or plastic
scissors
masking tape
variety of seeds
pebbles
potting soil
water

Have you ever wondered how plants grow under the ground? Here's a neat way to find out.

What to do: Cut a section from the side of a strong shoe box, leaving about a 1 inch (2.5 cm) border all around. Tape the acetate inside, tight against the opening. Punch some small holes in the bottom of the box. Put in a layer of pebbles and fill the box with potting soil. Plant several seeds in the soil, placing them up against the acetate so you can see them behind the sheet. Water the seeds, place the box outside or in a tray in the window. Watch the seeds for several days.

What happens: The seeds germinate and plants begin to grow. You can watch the growth of the plant upwards, and the roots reaching down underground as well.

Why: Plants need roots in order to take in water and other nutrients from the soil. They do this through tiny roots called root hairs. Roots generally grow in a downward direction to obtain the water and nutrients necessary for the plant's growth.

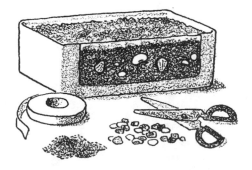

Flower Power

How can a little plant grow right up through a sidewalk? Let's see.

What to do: Put the potted plant on a sunny windowsill. Place the two boxes on either side of the pot (the boxes should be just a bit higher than the plant). Be careful not to shade the plant. Lay the clear acetate or plastic across the boxes. Make two identical "chains" of paper clips and lay them over the clear sheet so that the ends hang down the sides of the boxes. Arrange the chain ends evenly, and mark their positions on the sides of the boxes. Water and care for the plant as you would normally. Check the positions of the chains now and then.

What happens: As the plant grows, it pushes upwards against the clear sheet. The rate of growth is seen and measured by the markings made by the ends of the clip chains when they move up the sides of the boxes.

Why: Plants are incredibly strong. They are able to push up through the toughest soil as well as through rocks and cement to reach the light. This is why weeds can push up through the tiniest sidewalk cracks looking for sunlight—a necessary "ingredient" for their growth.

A Powerful Force

Plants often push their way up through even the tiniest crack in rocks or sidewalks, sometimes breaking up those hard objects. This is one way plants have of breaking apart large rocks into much smaller pebbles and stones.

You can see this for yourself. First, get some plaster of paris from a craft or hobby shop. Soak a few bean seeds in water overnight. The next day, plant two or three of them in a plastic cup filled with potting soil. Moisten the soil thoroughly.

Mix the plaster of paris according to the package directions, until it is like a thick milkshake. Pour a layer of the mixture, about ½ inch (0.5 cm) thick, on top of the soil in the cup. Put the cup in a sunny location and watch what happens (if you use a clear plastic cup and plant the seeds near the sides, you will be able to look through and watch the growth process). You will probably see the developing bean plants push up and through the plaster of paris—just like weeds are able to push up and through small cracks in a sidewalk.

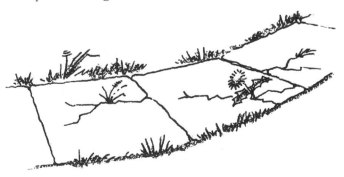

Hold That Mold

257

Would you believe that there are millions of plants growing right in your kitchen?

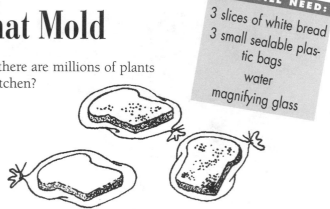

What to do: Take two slices of bread and wet them lightly (don't soak them). Carefully, rub one slice across a kitchen table or countertop (do it gently so you don't tear the bread). Place the slice of bread in a plastic bag and seal it. Then take the second moistened slice and gently rub it over the surface of the kitchen floor. Put it in a second bag and seal it. Now place the third (dry) slice of bread in the third bag and seal it. Place all three bags in a closet or other dark place for a couple of days.

What happens: You find mold growing on the surfaces of the two slices of bread that were moistened, rubbed over the kitchen surfaces, and placed in the bags. There may be some mold on the "dry" slice, too (some bakeries use preservatives to keep their breads fresh longer). Examine the moldy plants with the magnifying lens, or under a microscope. Try this experiment with other types of bread (wheat, rye) or rub slices over other surfaces (fence, wall, sidewalk, tree trunk).

Why: Molds and other microscopic plants are everywhere. In order to grow they need special conditions, such as moisture, warmth, and darkness instead of light.

258

My Bud-Bud-Buddy

Yeast is a plant used by cooks and bakers. The way it grows makes it a very special plant.

What to do: Put ½ cup of lukewarm water in each of the bags and add the contents of one yeast packet to each bag. Put the spoonful of sugar into the second bag. Close both bags, squeezing out as much air as possible before sealing them. Shake the bags well for a minute, then place them in a warm or sunny location.

What happens: The bag with just the water and yeast shows little change. But the bag with the water, yeast, and sugar has changed a lot. Bubbles have formed inside, and the bag is swelling up!

Why: Yeast is a plant that needs food in order to grow well. Sugar is a good food source for yeast. Yeast grows by producing one or more bumps, or buds, that break off and become new yeast plants. As it grows, the yeast also produces carbon-dioxide gas. Yeast is often added to bakery products, such as cake or bread, to make the dough rise. Without yeast, breads would be very flat.

All plants need food in order to grow. This is true for simple plants, such as yeast, and more complex plants, such as redwood trees; they all need nutrients. Without them, plants could not grow or survive.

Adopt a Tree

259

YOU WILL NEED:

string
measuring tape
plastic bags
drawing paper
pencil and crayons
your journal

Trees are some of the most beautiful plants in the world. Some are also so common that people don't even notice them. Here's an activity to help you learn more about one special tree.

What to do: Select a tree near where you live. If possible, locate a deciduous tree (one that sheds its leaves each year). The tree should be in a place that is easy to reach, because you will be visiting your tree for the next 12 months. To start, draw a picture of your tree (or photograph it) and write down in your journal any unusual markings, characteristics, or patterns you notice. Measure 3 feet (90 cm) up the tree trunk from the ground and tie a piece of string around the tree at that point. Measure the section of string to determine the circumference of the tree (how big around it is). Collect some of the tree's leaves and save them in small plastic bags. Place a piece of paper against the bark of the tree and rub a crayon over the paper until the pattern of the bark appears. What other kinds of learning activities can you do with your "adopted" tree?

What happens: Trees change during the year. They grow, shed their leaves, grow new leaves, serve as a home for all types of animal life, and contribute to the balance of nature in your local community.

Why: Since you will be focusing your attention on this one tree for a period of one year, you will undoubtedly notice many changes that you had never even seen or thought of before with other trees. Even one tree can have an influence on the environment in your small corner of the world.

260

Plants Breathe, Too

What do you think happens to plants if there are lots of pollutants in the air? Let's find out.

What to do: Place the plants on a windowsill so they will all get the same amount of sunlight. Label the plants "A," "B," and "C." Draw a picture of each plant and measure and record its height. Rub some petroleum jelly on the top side of all the leaves on plant A and under all the leaves on plant B. Leave plant C as it is. Water the plants every so often as you normally would. Every other day, record the height of each plant and draw pictures of any changes that have taken place.

What happens: Plant C shows the most growth. Plant A shows less growth. Plant B shows little growth and begins to die.

Why: Clean air is necessary for the chemical reaction called photosynthesis (when a plant produces its own food) to occur. The air enters the plant through the stomata on the underside of the leaves. When the air is polluted or when the leaves are covered by something (such as petroleum jelly) that acts as a pollutant, photosynthesis cannot take place and the plant dies.

261

Did You Know?

- The leaves of a Venus flytrap can close over an insect in less than half a second.
- The giant sequoia tree does not begin to flower until it is at least 175 to 200 years old.
- The roots of a redwood tree are capable of holding more than 130,000 gallons (494,000 liters) of water.
- There are more than 250,000 species of flowering plants in the world.
- Pacific giant kelp can grow more than 17 inches (43 cm) a day, and may reach lengths of up to 200 feet (9,000 cm).
- Bamboo may grow as much as 3 feet (90 cm) each day.
- An average apple tree will lose up to 20 quarts (19 liters) of water a day through its leaves.
- The plant life of the oceans makes up about 85% of all the greenery on the planet.
- Tree rings are a good record of earthquakes.
- In tropical rain forests, certain plants known as epiphytes grow on the highest branches of trees. They have no roots and get their water and nutrients directly from the humid air.
- A mature saguaro cactus may weigh up to 10 tons—and 80% of that weight is water.
- The largest seed in the world is the coconut.
- Lemons have more sugar in them than melons or peaches do.

262

I'm Impressed!

Preserve the flowers and leaves you collect by using a simple plant press. Get help to make this one.

HOT!

YOU WILL NEED:

an adult helper
use of hand or machine drill
2 sheets of plywood or fiberboard, 10 by 13 inches (25 by 33 cm)
standard size pieces of cardboard (cut from box)
white construction paper
4 bolts and 4 wingnuts

What to do: Ask an adult to drill holes (to fit your bolts) in each corner of the two sections of wood. The holes should be about 1 inch in from the top and side of each corner (drill the two boards together and the holes will be sure to match).

To use the press, put the connecting bolts through one board and lay it down so that the bolts stick upwards. Lay a piece of cardboard on top of this board. Next, place a sheet of paper on top of the cardboard, and whatever you want to press (a flower or leaves) on top of the paper. Put another sheet of paper on top of the specimen, and then other pieces of cardboard.

Repeat this process, making plant material "sandwiches," until you have a stack of several cardboard pieces. Put the second piece of plywood on top of the last cardboard piece on the stack, threading the bolts through the holes. Put a wing nut on each bolt and tighten them until you feel pressure. Then carefully tighten each bolt in turn as much as you can, putting even pressure on the stack.

The specimens will be pressed flat and will dry within a few weeks (check them occasionally if you wish). Later you may want to glue your pressed plants onto sheets of colorful construction paper and place them in paper frames from a hobby or arts and crafts store for display around your home.

What happens: The wooden press you made puts pressure on the plant specimens placed in it and keeps them flat. The pressure is gentle, but constant. Any "juices" squeezed from the plant material are absorbed by the white paper so that the plant dries out rapidly.

Why: People have been collecting and pressing plants, flowers, and leaves for many years. These pressings have been used in decorative displays and are a way of preserving some of nature's beauty long after a plant would normally die.

211

WONDERFUL WILDLIFE

Do you have a pet at home? Have you been to a zoo or an aquarium? Have you seen birds flying overhead, bees buzzing in the summertime, or snakes slithering through the grass? No doubt you have seen many kinds of animals wherever you live, for animals are a part of all our lives, and an important part of the world of nature, too.

About Wildlife—and You

Humans have always been fascinated by animals. We keep animals as pets and we observe animals in special places such as zoos and wildlife parks. But it is important to remember that animals are affected by the actions of humans. If we throw garbage into a stream, the fish and insects are affected; if we destroy nests and burrows during construction projects, those animals can no longer live there, and if we pollute the air, birds and, in fact, all breathing animals are affected. In other words, humans affect the survival of every living thing.

Learning about the animals in your area of the world will help you appreciate the rich variety of wildlife that surrounds you, and that look to you to help keep them safe.

263 ◆ Feathered Friends

Birds are important members of every environment and they are fun to watch. Here's how to attract more birds to your house.

What to do: Have an adult cut a panel from the side of the milk container, leaving a border around the opening. Tie the string tightly around the top, fill the container with some birdseed, and hang the new feeder in a nearby tree so you can see it from your window. Watch the birds that visit the feeder. What types of birds come to eat? How many, and at what time of day? Record your observations in the journal.

What happens: The feeder, if kept filled with food they like, attracts all kinds of birds. A book will help to identify the species, or types, of birds that live near you. You may learn to recognize certain individual birds that return often.

Why: Birds are affected by climate and by the availability of food. They adapt, or get used to, an environment and will stay as long as they have the food, water, and shelter they need in order to live and raise their young. Offering them clean water (bird bath), a bird house, and pieces of string and hair during nesting season are ways to encourage birds to stay nearby.

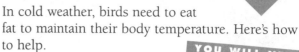

Well Fed ◆ 264

HOT!

In cold weather, birds need to eat fat to maintain their body temperature. Here's how to help.

What to do: Have an adult melt the fat or suet in a heavy pot. Then add birdseed (twice as much seed as fat) to the liquid fat and stir carefully. Let it cool and thicken overnight.

Carefully, using a hammer and nail, punch a small hole in the middle of the can bottom (an adult can help here, too) and the cardboard circle. Thread the string through the hole in the can and out the top. Pour the soft seed mixture into the can (if it is too liquid, you may have to seal the hole with clay or gum). When the fat has hardened, gently remove the can and push the string through the cardboard. Knot the string, then tie your seed feeder to a nearby tree, and watch the birds that visit it. (Experiment with other containers for different-shape feeders.)

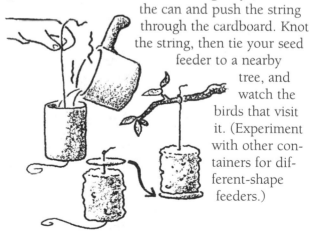

 Feed Me, I'm Yours!

With a little imagination, you can create bird feeders from almost anything in your home. Here are five ideas to get you started. Place them outside, and watch what happens. How many other bird feeders can you create?

1. Cut a half circle from the plastic lid of a coffee can. Nail or tape a small board to the side of the can and put some seed inside. Put the lid back on, so that it covers the bottom half, and lay the feeder outside.

2. Cut an orange in half. Scoop out the insides and make four small holes around the edge. Tie pieces of string to the holes around the orange half, fill it with seed, and hang it in a tree or bush.

3. Tie a string to a pinecone. Fill the crevices in the cone with peanut butter and roll the cone in some birdseed. Hang the cone from a tree branch.

4. Tie some unsalted peanuts onto various lengths of string. Hang these in a tree.

5. Tie a string to the stem of an apple. Roll the apple in some fat or bacon grease and then roll it in some birdseed. Hang it from a tree branch.

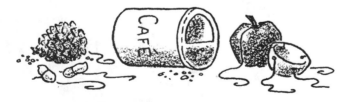

 Woodside Restaurant

Here's a great feeder for you to make for your feathered friends. Fill it with your own homemade nourishing treat or our super recipe for World's Greatest Birdfood (see page 215) and they will enjoy it all year long.

Find a 12- to 15-inch (30–40 cm) length of wood, about 2 inches (5 cm) square. Ask an adult to drill a number of holes in the wood with a 1 inch (2.5 cm) drill bit, staggering the holes down each side. The holes should be about ½ inch (2 cm) deep. Fasten an eye screw to one end of the stick and pass a long piece of strong string through it. Stuff the holes of the feeder with some sticky type of birdfood mixture, then hang the feeder in a nearby tree. Place it about 4 feet (125 cm), at least, off the ground so that the birds who come to eat will be safe from cats. Watch to see who comes to visit.

Remember to put fresh food in the holes every so often to keep your Woodside Restaurant open for business, and its feathered customers happy and coming back for more.

World's Greatest Birdfood

267

This nourishing recipe will keep birds coming back to your feeder all year—but especially in the winter.

What to do: With the help of an adult, cut the suet into small pieces and melt it slowly in a large frying pan. (Be very careful of spatters; hot fat can cause bad burns.) Let the melted fat cool until it becomes solid, then reheat it again and allow the liquid fat to cool off once more.

Thoroughly mix all of the other ingredients into the soft suet. Spoon the mixture into small plastic containers and put them in the refrigerator. When the mixture is firm, spoon some of it into the feeder holes of the Woodside Restaurant or some other bird feeder. Keep the remainder of the mixture refrigerated until needed.

Note: Because of the cost or availability, you may want to experiment with different quantities or ingredients—for example, mixing together just peanut butter and sunflower seeds during the summer months, and adding the suet (for the fat that birds need) only during the wintertime.

YOU WILL NEED:

suet, from butcher or supermarket (1 cup melted)

1 cup each, chunky peanut butter, chopped nuts, sunflower seeds, and cornmeal

1 tablespoon crushed eggshells

frying pan

an adult helper

use of the stove

Home Sweet Home

268

Some of the best "builders" in the animal kingdom are birds. Let's find out how they do it.

YOU WILL NEED:

binoculars

tweezers

magnifying glass

What to do: In late fall or early winter, take your binoculars outside to look for one or more empty bird nests. If, when you find one, it is high up, ask an adult to get it down for you. Be careful. Try to keep the nest as intact as possible and be sure that there are no eggs in the nest—that it is not still in use! At home, use tweezers to carefully separate the pieces making up the nest. Examine them closely with the magnifying glass. Make a list of what was used to build the nest.

What happens: You see the nests are constructed of many different types of materials, including twigs, grasses, straw, string, leaves, hair, feathers, etc. You will also notice that the sizes and shapes of nests vary depending on the species of bird that built it.

Why: Birds build their nests in different ways and use different materials. The construction of a nest depends largely on what material is available and how the eggs and young birds need to be protected while they are in the nest. As you continue to examine the nests of different species of birds you will notice many different variations in nest construction.

269

Look Ma, No Hands!

Can you imagine how difficult it is to build a nest from things like twigs, grass and feathers that you may find lying on the ground?

YOU WILL NEED:

twigs
dried grasses
yarn
scraps of paper

What to do: Take a walk around your neighborhood or park and locate several different bird's nests. Look carefully at how the nests are constructed (be careful not to disturb any occupants). Using the materials listed above (and any others you think might help you—but no glue!), try to build a bird's nest. Work with just your two hands and make a round nest that has room for two or three eggs.

What happens: You discover that nest building is not as easy as it may look. Hmmm, those birds must be smart!

Why: Birds are able to construct their nests with just their feet and beaks (no hands). And most birds seem to have learned the construction process by only seeing—and from sitting inside it—what their parents once built!

It's amazing to think that bird's nests are some of the most complicated homes in the animal kingdom—homes that are able to withstand bad weather and protect young birds as they grow and develop. So, the next time anyone calls you a "bird brain," be sure to thank them for the compliment.

270   Worm World

Would you be surprised to learn that earthworms are some of the most useful animals to human life? Be prepared to be surprised.

YOU WILL NEED:

large wide-mouthed (pickle) jar

tin can

gravel or small pebbles

soil

5 or 6 earthworms (from a garden, bait shop, pet store, or garden supply store) dark construction paper

What to do: Stand the tin can in the middle of the jar. Place a layer of gravel or small pebbles about ½ inch (1.2 cm) deep on the bottom of the jar, between the can and the jar sides. Fill the jar with garden soil up to the height of the tin can. Place the worms on top of the soil. Wrap the dark construction paper around the outside of the jar to keep out the light.

Note: Check the condition of the soil every so often and moisten it as needed.

What happens: The worms will begin burrowing into the soil. After several days, they will have dug a series of tunnels. You will be able to see these tunnels by carefully removing the construction paper from the sides of the jar. (Replace the con-struction paper after observing their work so the worms will continue to tunnel in the darkness.) You should be able to watch the worms' behavior, without harming them, for three or four weeks, but then you should put them back outside.

Why: Worms feed by taking soil through their bodies, creating tunnels as they go. These tunnels aerate the soil—providing plants with the oxygen they need to grow. If it weren't for earthworms, many varieties of plants would not be able to survive. Farmers consider earthworms some of the best "friends" they have.

live land snails
pieces of lettuce,
apple, celery,
or cereal
black construction
paper
large wide-mouthed
pickle jar
damp soil
magnifying glass
cheesecloth
string or rubber band

271 Creepy Crawlies

What do snails do? What do snails eat? How do snails travel? Here's how to discover the answers to those questions.

What to do: Find some land snails from around your home (look in the moist soil of gardens in the early morning hours). Put a 2-inch (5 cm) layer of damp soil in a large clear jar and place the snails in it. Place some cheesecloth over the jar opening and fasten it down securely with string or a rubber band to keep the occupants inside (snails can crawl up glass).

Sprinkle the soil every so often to keep it wet. Keep the jar in a cool shady place. Put in some pieces of lettuce every so often. You will be able to keep and observe the behavior of the snails for several days.

Move one or more of the snails to a sheet of black construction paper to see it better. Place a snail in the middle of the sheet and surround it with bits of

feed—a slice of apple, a lettuce leaf, a piece of celery, some cereal—and watch what happens.

What happens: The snails leave trails behind them on the paper as they slowly move toward the kind of food they prefer. Did you turn one over to see how it moves over the paper?

Why: As snails travel, using only one foot that pushes them along, they produce and leave a trail of mucus behind them. This mucus protects them from sharp rocks and other harmful objects they travel over in their environment. (A snail can even travel over a razor blade without hurting itself.) Most snails enjoy eating food that has a lot of moisture, such as fresh leaves and other vegetation. That is why they are considered a pest by home gardeners.

The Ants Go Marching...

You may not want to invite ants to your next picnic, but here's a way to invite them to your house for a short visit.

What to do: Look outside for a rotting piece of wood, which ants love, or an area with lots of ants. Scoop up into the glass jar some of the soil nearby, along with a healthy collection of ants. Put the lid on until you get the ants home. Then, cover the jar with black construction paper so that it is completely dark inside. Put some water in the cake pan, put the saucer upside down in the middle of it, and place the jar on the upturned saucer before removing the lid (the water prevents the ants from escaping from the jar). Sprinkle some sugar water over the soil and place two or three small bits of fruit inside.

What happens: The ants begin to dig tunnels in the soil. If it is dark enough, they dig their tunnels next to the sides of the glass. If you remove the black construction paper every week or so, you can see the progress they have made in their tunnel building.

Why: Many kinds of ants live in large colonies underground. Each of the ants has a job to do in order to keep the colony running smoothly. Many ants, known as "workers," are responsible for building the tunnels and the small caves that are home to the ant colony. It is in these tunnels that all the ants in a colony live, work, sleep, and eat.

Did you know that there are more than 12,000 different varieties of ants in the world?

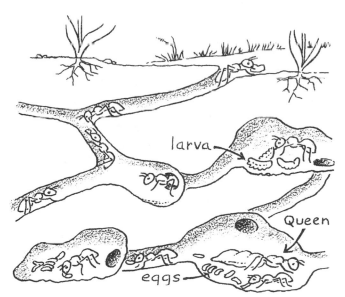

larva

Queen

eggs

273

Cricket Critters

You might never have thought of keeping crickets as house pets, but in some countries, such as Japan, they are valued members of the household.

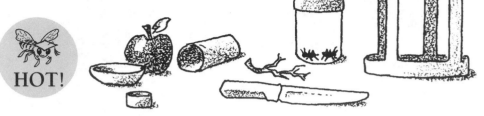

HOT!

What to do: Draw large "windows" on the sides of the empty round box. Leave frames around the windows as shown. Have an adult cut out the windows using a sharp knife (this can be very hard to do and you might get hurt, so don't do it yourself). Remove the remaining label from the box and decorate the outside with poster paint or markers.

Place the small bowl in the "cage." Fill the bottom of the box, and the bowl, with dry soil until you can just see the rim of the bowl. Push the bottle cap down on top of the soil. Carefully, pull a nylon stocking up over the box. Put shredded paper and a toilet paper roll or two in the cage. Water the soil in the bowl, and keep it moist. Fill the bottle cap with fresh water for drinking. Put in six or seven crickets and close up the top of the stocking to keep the critters in. The crickets can be easily cared for by feeding them some bran or oatmeal cereal, keeping the bottle cap filled with fresh water, and occasionally placing a slice of apple or potato in the cage.

What happens: The crickets thrive in this miniature environment. The females lay their eggs in the moist soil of the bowl (be sure the soil is always damp). If you're lucky you'll see the cricket eggs hatch into small crickets (called nymphs) and grow into adults in about eight weeks.

Why: Crickets enjoy simple surroundings. As long as they have a constant food supply and some moisture they will thrive in almost any environment.

Note: When you get your crickets from the pet store, be sure you have both males and females. Crickets look the same, except that females have a long slender rod, called an ovipositor, protruding from their back end. They use this ovipositor to lay their eggs.

274 ◆ Web Warriors

Spiderwebs come in all shapes and sizes. Here's how you can preserve a few.

YOU WILL NEED:

clear plastic adhesive sheeting from hardware or variety store

masking tape

black construction paper

hair spray

What to do: Taking hair spray, masking tape, and black construction paper, go outside and find a spiderweb nearby (make sure the spider isn't at home). Make five rings of masking tape, sticky side outward, around the fingers of one hand. (Now you can hold the construction paper flat and vertical, and it won't fall.) Carefully, place the hand with the construction paper just behind the spiderweb. With your other hand, gently hair-spray the web from the front, so that it pushes against the construction paper.

Slowly and gently (the web is fragile), move the web stuck on the construction paper away from where it is attached. When you get home, place some sticky clear plastic sheeting over the web and construction paper around the back. Collect several different kinds of spiderwebs this way and compare them.

Note: This takes practice, so don't get discouraged if everything doesn't work out quite right the first time around.

What happens: When you use the hair spray, the spiderweb is pushed against the construction paper and sticks to it. The sticky plastic sheeting seals the web against the paper. If the sheeting covers the back of the construction paper as well, the specimen is airtight, so it is preserved and doesn't get damaged.

Why: Spiderwebs are as varied as the number of spiders in the world. Spiders use their webs for homes and to help them collect the food they need to survive. When insects and other tiny animals become trapped in the threads of a spiderweb, they are food for the web's owner. Spiders also "wrap" trapped insects to eat later.

Did you know that a spiderweb, in the early morning with dew glistening on its threads, is considered one of the most beautiful sights in nature?

275 Net Gain

Here's a handy insect net to help you capture some of the bugs that fly or jump by.

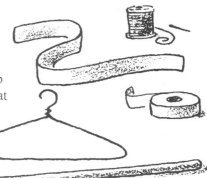

What to do: Shape the triangle part of the hanger into a circle, and straighten the hook. Tape the straightened hook to the end of the pole with the duct tape.

Using the measuring tape, measure the circumference (distance around) the wire circle. Cut the nylon netting into the shape shown here, making the straight edge the same length as the measurement around the wire loop. Sew the cotton strip to the straight edge of the net, and then sew the side seams. Attach the net to the hoop by folding the cotton strip over the wire frame and sewing it to itself.

Use your insect net to collect various types of bugs, but stay away from bees or wasps or you could be stung! When you catch something, twist the handle quickly to "close" the net and trap the insect inside. (You may have to practice with the net awhile to "close" it.)

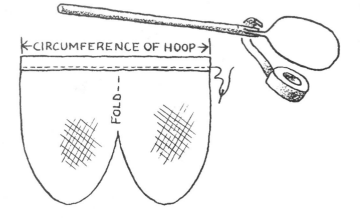

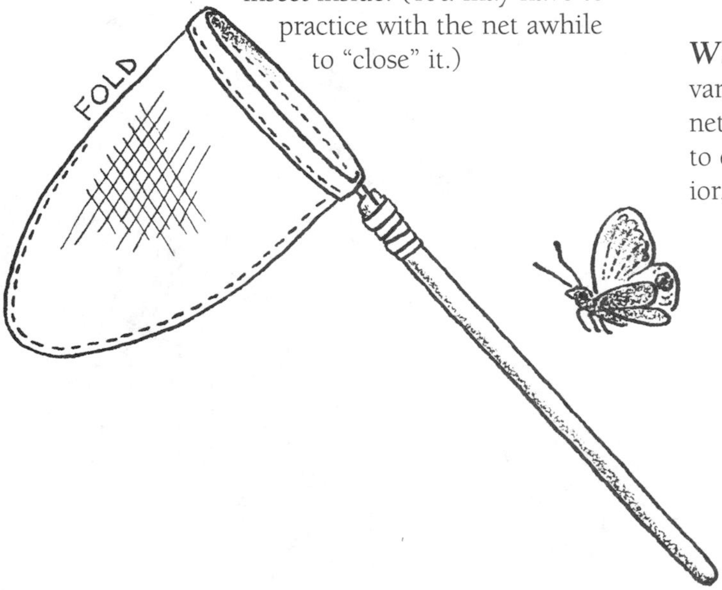

←CIRCUMFERENCE OF HOOP→

FOLD

What happens: You'll be able to capture a wide variety of flying insects with your nature collector's net. You may want to keep some insects a few days to examine them—noting their body shapes, behavior, and what they eat—before releasing them again.

FOLD

Mealworm Magic

Here's an animal you don't think about much, but you can keep in your home for a good while and maybe see some strange things.

What to do: Fill the plastic shoe box about two-thirds full with a mixture of bran, flour, and small pieces of bread. Place 20 to 25 mealworms in the box and put on the cover. Lift the cover every few days, or have an adult drill several small holes in the lid to let some air in. Keep the box in a warm location—between 75° and 80°F (24° and 26°C). Put in a slice of apple and replace it with a fresh piece every few days.

What happens: That depends on how long you keep and watch your mealworms and just how old they are.

Why: The mealworm is the larval stage (part of the life cycle) of the darkling beetle. The larvae, which are young mealworms, grow for about six months. They then turn into the pupae, a stage which lasts for about three weeks. Afterwards, the adult beetles emerge from the cocoon. The cycle is then repeated (male and female beetles mate, eggs are laid, the eggs hatch into mealworms, the mealworms turn into pupae, the pupae turn into adult beetles). You can watch each stage of insect growth (egg, larvae, pupae, adult) by looking through the sides of the plastic box or carefully sifting through the bran mixture with your fingers. The bran provides the nourishment these animals need, and the apple slices provide the necessary moisture.

Mealworms are raised primarily to serve as a food source for other animals (lizards and salamanders love them). They are a big part of many environments, living deep within the soil. By adding to the bran mixture and replacing dried-out apple slices, you can keep your "colony" of mealworms for some time. Later, you may want to release them to a new home, a warm and moist area near a rotting log, for example.

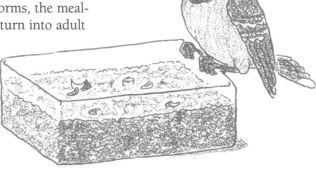

Bee Home, Be Careful

277

Bee stings can be dangerous, but bees are important to the environment. Here's how to help them survive.

YOU WILL NEED:

25 large drinking straws
masking tape
modeling clay
string
an adult helper (optional)

What to do: Gather about 25 drinking straws. Plug up one end of each straw with modeling clay. Mix up the straws so that some plugged ends face one way and some the other. Tape the bundle together tightly. With string or tape, fasten it sideways (horizontally) underneath a windowsill, rain gutter, or the roof overhang of your house (if high up, have an adult help you place the straw bundle). The bundle must be in a sunny location. You may want to place bundles in several places outdoors.

What happens: Bees may move into their new "home" and set up housekeeping. You'll see them coming and going.

   Note: Be careful not to interfere with them, or you might get stung.

Why: A bee's nest is full of small cells and tunnels. They use these to care for their young and to store the honey they make. Your "straw hive" offers the bees a place that is very similar to their regular hives. However, depending on where you live, the time of the year (early spring is best), and the type of bees that live in your area, you may or may not be able to attract bees to your nests. Several varieties of bees are very particular about where they live.

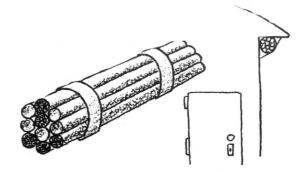

Sea Shrimp at the Seashore

Brine shrimp, though tiny, are some of the most amazing animals! Let's grow some.

What to do: Fill the pot with 2 quarts of water and allow it to sit for 3 days, stirring it occasionally. (Most city water has chlorine in it, which would kill the shrimp. By letting it "age" for a while, the chlorine gas can escape from the water.) Dissolve 5 teaspoons of non-iodized salt into the water. Add ½ teaspoon of brine shrimp eggs to the saltwater and place the pot in a warm spot. Use the medicine dropper to remove a few eggs from the water, and observe them with your magnifying glass or microscope. Examine a drop of water every day. You can draw a series of illustrations in your journal to record the growth of your brine shrimp.

What happens: The brine shrimp eggs begin to hatch in about two days. They will continue to grow in the water until they reach their adult stage. You can watch this growth process over a period of many days.

Why: The brine shrimp eggs purchased at a pet store are the fertilized eggs of very tiny animals known as brine shrimp. The eggs you buy are dried so that they can be stored for very long peri-ods of time (especially when kept in a dry place). When these eggs are placed in saltwater, however, they "wake up" and begin to grow. Although they are very small you can watch them grow for many days.

Note: Brine shrimp eggs are sold as food for aquarium fish.

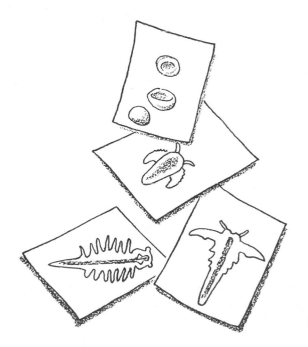

279 Can't See Me!

In order to survive, smaller animals sometimes need to hide from
larger ones. One way that certain animals avoid
being seen, and protect themselves from being
eaten, is to use a protective coloring as camouflage.
These animals match their body color to the colors
in their environment so that they "blend in" and
almost disappear.

What to do: Ask your helper or friend to mix up
all 200 toothpicks and to spread them out over a
certain area of grass (your front lawn or a section of
a park, for example). The area should be about 25
yards, or meters, square. As you pick up the toothpicks, have your partner time you for 1 minute, 2
minutes, and 3 minutes. Put the found toothpicks
aside in bunches each time.

What happens: After several
minutes, you probably notice
that you are finding and picking
up more red toothpicks than
green toothpicks. Later, you
can count the red and the
green toothpicks you found,
and record in your journal the
exact number of each color you found during each
time period.

Why: Because the green toothpicks were closer to
the color of the test environment (the green grass)
than the red ones, the green ones were harder to
see and find. Animals that are able to blend into
their environment have a better chance for survival
than those who have colors that make them easy to
see. The ability of animals to match the colors of
their surroundings, or use camouflage, helps them
to protect themselves. Green lizards are able to
hide better in an area with lots of green shrubs and
plants than would red or yellow lizards. Their
predators (animals that hunt and would eat them)
have a more difficult time locating them.

Find Me If You Can

Camouflage is the ability of an organism (plant or
animal) to blend with its surroundings. In doing so,
the organism is able to escape detection and "hide"
in certain parts of its environment.

The katydid, for example, is an insect that
looks like a leaf, making it hard to see in a plant
or tree. Because of their dull color, certain types
of caterpillars look like bird droppings when they
roll up, so they do it when danger is near and
avoid being eaten by birds and other enemies.
Some types of spiders have features that look like
the parts of a flower. By sitting on a flower, they
can avoid being a predator's next meal. Some
desert plants, called lithops, resemble small rocks
in shape and color and so avoid being chewed for
their moisture. It is only when water is easily

available that they bloom to spread their pollen.

Mimicry, the ability of one species to imitate the
coloring or behavior of another, is also a form of
protection. Some small animals or insects are
unpleasant or dangerous, so larger animals avoid
them. To survive, the other animals and insects
"copy" the colors and body movements of the
dangerous ones. By pretending to be what they're
not, these "copycats" are left alone and live longer
lives. One type of fly, for example, looks like a
dangerous and poisonous wasp; one very tasty
butterfly looks just like a bad-tasting moth; and
one caterpillar has body markings that make it
look like the eyes of a giant bird.

How many of nature's copycats can you name?

280 I'm All Yours!

"Adopt" an endangered animal. Write to:
The American Association of
Zoological Parks and Aquariums
4550 Montgomery Ave., Suite 940N
Bethesda, MD 20814
and ask about their animal adoption program. (Ask a parent first.) For a few dollars, you will be assigned an endangered animal and receive a photograph and a fact sheet about your "adoptee." The money you send will be used to feed and care for the animal.

Share this project with your teacher and classmates. By collecting money or contributing small amounts each, your entire class can adopt an endangered animal and learn about it.

281 Track Record

Animals leave tracks wherever they go. Here's how you can record those tracks.

YOU WILL NEED:
large-size milk carton, cut into 1- inch (2.5 cm) square strips (remove top and bottom)
old bowl or pot
plaster of paris (from craft or hobby stores)
water

What to do: Find an animal track or print in some soft dirt or mud (it can be a cat or dog track, or maybe a deer or some other wild animal in your area). Put a milk carton square around the track and push it partway down into the soil. (Be careful not to disturb the track.)

Mix the plaster of paris and water together in an old bowl or pot according to the directions on the package until it is like a thick milkshake). Pour it into the mold up to the top of the cardboard strip. Wait for about an hour until the plaster cast hardens. Remove the cast from the ground print and take off the cardboard strip.

What happens: You now have a model or cast of the animal's foot that made the print. (The cast is a raised model of the print.) You may want to make casts of several different animal tracks for display.

Why: When animals walk on damp ground, they leave impressions of their feet, or footprints, just as we do. By studying these tracks, we can tell a lot about the animal, and how and even why it was moving the way it was. If the track is very deep, the animal may have been very heavy. If the track is deeper at the front of the print than at the back, the animal was walking rapidly (or even running). If the depths of the four tracks (of a four-footed animal) are uneven, the animal may be limping from an old injury or may be hurt.

Sound Off

282

You may be surprised to discover the wide variety of animal sounds you can find in your neighborhood.

What to do: Tape the microphone handle to the end of the pole or broom (be sure not to put tape over the microphone itself). Go outside on a clear and calm day and place the microphone near one or more wildlife homes (a bird's nest, beehive or wasp's nest, for example). It helps if you know the animals are at home, but be careful.

You can either hold the microphone on the pole near the animal's home, or stick the pole into the ground. Take care doing this so that you do not disturb any birds or animals nearby. (It may be a good idea to have an adult along in case a "star" or friend nearby gets upset.) Turn on the microphone and record the sounds and noises the animals make.

Don't forget to take some "field notes" for your nature journal about the types or numbers of animals you see and have been able to "catch" on tape.

What happens: Your nature recordings will help you discover the many different sounds that the animals in your neighborhood make.

Note: It's important to make your recordings on non-windy days, since microphones often pick up wind sounds that "mask" the sounds animals may make.

Collect the neighborhood animal sounds and combine them with photographs, illustrations, and "field notes" on the behavior and habits of the animal. This data can be collected into an attractive notebook or display box for sharing with friends and family.

Why: Animals such as birds and insects make all different kinds of sounds as they go about their daily chores. Some of the sounds they make are used to "talk" to others of their species, some are for protection, some to help locate mates, and some sounds they make can call others to a food source or tell them where food nearby can be found.

Did You Know?

283

The roundworm lives for only twelve days; the lake sturgeon (a fish) can live more than 150 years.

- Crickets have hearing organs in their knees.
- An ant can lift 50 times its own weight—with its mouth.
- The common snail has close to 10,000 teeth—all on its tongue.
- A frog must close its eyes in order to swallow.
- Texas horned toads can squirt blood from the corners of their eyes.
- The tumbler pigeon can do backward somer saults while flying.

- The praying mantis is the only insect that can turn its head without moving any part of its body.
- If it were possible to weigh all of the land animals on the surface of the Earth, ants would be 10 to 15% of the total weight.
- Scientists have determined that the common housefly hums in the musical key of F.
- To make one pound (2.2 kg) of honey, bees must collect nectar from approximately 2 million flowers.
- Most mammals live for about 1_ billion heartbeats.
- A mosquito has 47 teeth.

Ecosystems Near and Far

An ecological system, ecosystem for short, is made up of organisms that live together. These ecosystems include plants, animals, and a combination.

About Ecosystems

All living things that come together in one place make up a community. Plant or animal, community members depend on one another for survival. Some animals eat plants, some plants live off other plants, and some animals eat other animals. All living things are part of one or more food chains—energy and materials are passed down the line from one living thing to another in the form of food.

While living things depend on one another, human life needs a variety of plants and animals in order to survive. Understanding how all living things rely on each other is an important part of nature study. The experiments in this chapter will allow you to journey into the ecosystems that exist where you are.

284 ▸ Life in a Square

You may be surprised to discover a wide variety of life—right in your own backyard!

What to do: Go into your yard or a nearby park. Push the pencils into the soil in a 1-foot (30 cm) square pattern. Tie string around them, making a miniature "boxing ring" on the ground. Get down and look closely inside the square. Make a note of all the different types of plants you see there, as well as the varieties of animal life and their behavior as they travel (jump, crawl, slither) through it. Go back regularly over several weeks to observe and record what you see.

What happens: You have a long list of natural life that lives in or has passed through your marked-off square. In fact, you are probably amazed at the many different forms of life that you found in just that very small space!

Why: Life is everywhere! Take the time to stop, see what is going on around you, and wonder at all the life forms that share the environment you call home. You may discover animals and plants, living in your own backyard, that you never knew existed!

285

Houses and Homes

Where do animals live? What kind of dwelling places or "houses" do they call home? Let's take a look around.

What to do: With an older friend or adult, take a walking "field trip" around your town or neighborhood. Look for places where animals live. These may be nests, burrows, tree trunks, ant hills, under rocks, in and near logs, holes in the ground, even cracks in the sidewalk. If you have a camera, take a photograph of each habitat, or place where an animal lives, or draw a picture of it. Later, name the animals and match their pictures with the pictures of their "houses." An older brother or sister, parent, or high school student might enjoy helping you learn the scientific names of the animals to add to your journal or field trip report.

What happens: You will be amazed to discover the wide variety of animals living in homes in and near your own house. You will probably discover that you've found many more than you thought you would.

Why: Animals are everywhere: from high in a tree to far under the ground. The homes that animals live in are designed to protect their young, shelter the animals from the weather, help them defend against their enemies, and are located where they can find the food they need. In fact, aren't those the same reasons why humans live where they do?

286

Happy Habitat

How would you like to be the creator of your own miniature ecosystem?

What to do: Have an adult cut off the top of the plastic soda bottle. Cover the bottom of the bottle with a layer of small pebbles mixed with bits of aquarium charcoal. Put in a layer of soil about twice as deep as the first layer. Sprinkle the soil with just enough water to keep it moist (you may have to add water occasionally.

Place several plants, such as mosses, ferns, lichens, or liverworts (available from garden or aquarium shops), into the soil. You could sprinkle a few grass seeds on the soil, too. Place several rocks or pieces of wood into the bottom of the bottle.

Some small land animals (such as snails, earthworms, a tiny turtle or frog) can also be added. Cover the top (to allow the humidity to build up), then open and ventilate (allowing some fresh air in) by placing some lightweight cloth over the top and holding it on with a rubber band or tying it there with a string. Keep the bottle out of direct sunlight and be sure to feed the occupants of your habitat regularly.

What happens: Your miniature ecosystem will grow and flourish as long as you add some moisture occasionally. If you put animals in the bottle, check with your local pet store for an appropriate food supply.

Why: This ecosystem is similar to a wetlands or woodlands ecosystem in nature. Plants and animals are able to survive because they are dependent on each other and because all of their "needs" (air, water, food) are provided in their immediate environment.

A Simple Community

Here's how you can construct a simple and inexpensive aquarium in your own home.

YOU WILL NEED:

large (commercial-size) mayonnaise jar (from your school cafeteria or a local restaurant)

gravel

washed sand (from an aquarium store)

aquatic plants (see below)

guppies or goldfish

water snails

wire screen

What to do: Wash and rinse out the large jar thoroughly. Wash and rinse the gravel and sand, too. Washed (clean) sand can be obtained at an aquarium store. Place a ½ inch (1 cm) layer of gravel and a 1 inch (3 cm) layer of sand on the bottom of the jar. Fill the jar almost to the top with tap water and allow the jar to sit undisturbed for three to four days so that the chlorine that is in the water can evaporate.

Get two or three aquatic plants (such as elodea) from an aquarium store and place them in the bottom of the jar (make sure they are firmly rooted in the sand). Place a few, two or three, goldfish and also snails in the jar. Place a piece of wire screening over the top of the jar—to keep in the snails!

What happens: This miniature environment will be able to sustain itself for some time (so long as you put in some fish food occasionally). The plants and animals will thrive for a good while, but you may need to obtain an inexpensive air pump later to keep your aquarium going.

Why: Plants and animals need each other in order to survive. In an aquatic environment, such as your aquarium, the plants provide necessary oxygen for the fish and snails. The fish provide nourishment (with their wastes) for the plants (and the eventual growth of small plants such as algae). The algae serve as a food source for the snails.

When properly maintained, this miniature ecosystem will be "in balance."

My Own Backyard

Did you know that your backyard can qualify as a nature preserve—a place where plants and animals are protected?

The National Wildlife Federation has what is known as a Wildlife Habitat Program. If you ask, they will provide you with information and details about establishing your backyard as a wildlife preserve. Then, for a small fee, you can send them a plan of action and they will certify your backyard as an official Backyard Wildlife Habitat.

For more information write:
National Wildlife Federation
Backyard Wildlife Habitat Program
1412 16th Street, NW
Washington, DC 20036

Bags of Bananas

289

Decomposition, the natural decay of dead organisms, is a continuing process in nature. You can learn about it by doing this experiment in your own home.

YOU WILL NEED:

4 sealable plastic sandwich bags
1 banana
knife
2 packets of yeast
water

What to do: Label each one of the four bags: "A," "B," "C," and "D." In Bag "A" put several slices of banana; in Bag "B" put several slices of banana and a packet of yeast; in Bag "C" put several slices of banana and some water; and in Bag "D" put several slices of banana, some water, and a packet of yeast. Seal all the bags and place them on a sunny windowsill for a few days.

What happens: The banana slices in bag "A" darken slightly. The yeast in bag "B" grows very slowly, but there is some change in the banana slices. The slices in bag "C" show some decay and some mold. The banana slices in bad "D" show the most decay. In that bag, the banana is breaking down. The liquid is bubbling, and carbon-dioxide gas is forming and

expanding the bag. The bag may pop open and release a powerful odor into the room.

Why: When plant and animal life die, they serve as a valuable food source for micro-organisms. These micro-organisms feed on the dead materials and break them down. Yeast is made up of millions of such micro-organisms that grow under the right conditions: when moisture, food, and warmth are present. As they grow, the micro-organisms in bag "D" break down the banana slices.

The same process takes place in nature. As a result, micro-organisms can reduce large animals and plants into valuable nutrients for the soil. In other words, when an organism dies it provides what other organisms need in order to live.

It's Absolutely Degrading!

290

YOU WILL NEED:

slice of fruit (apple, orange, peach)

slice of bread

piece of lettuce

plastic or foam cup

piece of aluminum foil

shovel

water

ice cream sticks

pencil or felt-tip marker

Do you know what the word "biodegradable" means? Here's how you can find out about this continuing process and how it works.

What to do: Find a place in your or a friend's yard where you can dig some small holes for this experiment. Dig five holes, each about 8 to 12 inches (20-30 cm) deep. Place the fruit slice in one hole, the bread in another hole, the lettuce in another, the cup in the fourth hole, and the foil in the last hole. Cover each hole with soil and water each one thoroughly. Place a marker stick labeled with the words "slice," "bread," "lettuce," "cup," or "foil" (or anything else you are testing for biodegradability) at the location of each hole. After 4 to 5 weeks, return to the filled holes and dig up what you buried.

What happens: The fruit, bread and lettuce have probably "broken down" or disintegrated (in fact, you may find it difficult to even locate these

items). The rate at which these items have biodegraded depends on the amount of moisture in the soil and the soil's temperature. The cup and the piece of foil, however, will be whole and easy to locate.

Why: When organic matter (fruit, bread lettuce, even dead plants and animals) is left on or in the soil, it starts to "break down." This natural (and constant) biodegrading process caused by micro-organisms releases nutrients into the soil so that other organisms can grow. The cup and the foil are not biodegradable, the micro-organisms can't affect them, so they will never decompose. Landfills are filled with lots of non-biodegradable materials that take up valuable space without returning anything to the environment.

Did You Know?

291

- Americans consume about 55 million tons of food from the oceans each year, and dump 90% of their garbage into landfills.
- Homeowners in the United States use ten times more toxic chemicals per acre (on their gardens and lawns) than do farmers.
- Each year, more than 27 million acres (10.8 million hectares) of tropical rain forest are destroyed—an area about the size of the state of Ohio, or of Iceland.
- Although rain forests cover only about 6% of the Earth's surface, they contain more than half of all the plant and animal species.
- The rain forests of the Amazon region produce about 40% of the world's oxygen.

NATURE PROBLEMS TO SOLVE

How we care for the Earth and its inhabitants today will have a big impact on the world we live in twenty or fifty years from now. It will determine the kinds of food, recreation, and quality of life available to us in the years to come. Becoming a conservator (a caretaker) of the Earth is important for every man, woman, and child.

About Nature's Problems
We are faced today with many problems that affect the way we live and the ways in which our plants and our animal friends live, too. Air and water pollution, toxins and trash, and the destruction of the ozone layer (which filters out the harmful rays of the sun) may someday threaten all our lives.

These problems are not simple ones, and they require more than simple solutions. But if we care about our environment, and understand how we and the animals and plants must all exist side by side in order to survive, then we need to start now to work together to preserve nature.

Preserving nature won't be easy. It will take lots of planning and people working together to ensure a natural and healthy life for ourselves and for our biological neighbors. The experiments in this chapter will alert you to some of the problems we face, and suggest what you and your friends can do to help preserve our fragile environment.

A Plethora of Pollution

292

Pollution can take many forms. Some of it can be seen, but many types that we don't see are just as dangerous

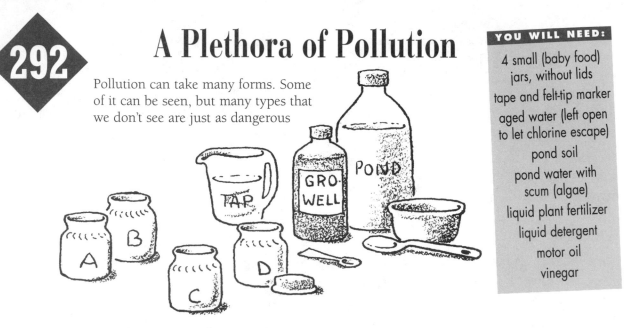

YOU WILL NEED:

4 small (baby food) jars, without lids

tape and felt-tip marker

aged water (left open to let chlorine escape)

pond soil

pond water with scum (algae)

liquid plant fertilizer

liquid detergent

motor oil

vinegar

What to do: Label the four jars "A," "B," "C," or "D." Prepare each jar as follows: fill the jar halfway with aged tap water (see page 00), put in a ½ inch (1 cm) layer of pond soil, add 1 teaspoon of plant fertilizer, then fill the jar the rest of the way with pond water and algae. Allow the jars to sit in a sunny location or windowsill for 2 weeks.

Next, treat each separate jar as follows: in jar "A" add 2 tablespoons of detergent; in jar "B" add enough motor oil to cover the surface; in jar "C" add ½ cup of vinegar; and leave jar "D" just as it is. Allow the jars to sit for 4 weeks more.

What happens: With the addition of the detergent, motor oil, and vinegar to the first three jars, the healthy growth that took place in the jars during the first two weeks of the experi-

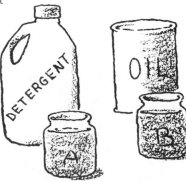

ment has severely changed. In fact, those jars now probably show little or no growth taking place, while the organisms in jar "D" continue to grow.

Why: Detergent, motor oil, and vinegar are pollutants that prevent organisms from obtaining the nutrients and oxygen they need to continue growing. The detergent shows what happens when large qualities of soap are released into an area's water; the motor oil shows what happens to organisms after an oil spill; and the vinegar shows what can happen when high levels of acids are added to an ecosystem such as a pond or stream. When industry, factories, homeowners, and other consumers put these and other kinds of pollutants into streams, rivers, and other sources or water, it can seriously affect and even destroy the plants and animals that live there.

293 Eggs Over Easy

Pollution is a problem all over the world. Let's take a look at one specific pollution problem: oil

What to do: Label the four bags "A," "B," "C," or "D." Fill each bag with ½ cup of water and ½ cup of motor oil. Place a hard-boiled egg in each bag. Remove the egg from bag "A" after 15 minutes; remove the egg from bag "B" after 30 minutes; remove the egg from bag "C" after 60 minutes; and remove the egg from bag "D" after 120 minutes. Each time you remove an egg from a bag, carefully open and peel off the egg shell.

What happens: The eggs in the oil-polluted water the longest showed the most pollution. The egg in bag "D," for example, had more oil inside its shell than the bag "A" egg.

Why: When an oil tanker accident spills oil into the water, the oil slick that forms affects all manner of living things. The oil sticks to the bodies and surfaces of birds, plants, fish , and other aquatic creatures and prevents them from doing what they do naturally. (Birds cannot use their wings or fly, fish cannot breathe, and plants cannot carry out the process of photosynthesis.) The longer the oil remains on the organism, the more damaging it is. Many living things die as a result of oil spills.

294 Oil Change

Repeat the "Eggs Over Easy" experiment opposite, but this time also put ½ cup of liquid detergent into each bag. Shake each bag gently and allow it to stand for the designated time. Notice what effect the liquid soap has on the pollution of each hard-boiled egg.

For another variation, put the ½ cup of detergent into each bag just before you remove the eggs. While the soap might remove some of the oil pollution from the outside of the eggs, does it have any effect on the eggs themselves?

295

Not in My Air!

YOU WILL NEED:

petroleum jelly
3 index cards
masking tape

Do you know if there is air pollution in your area, and how much? Here's a way to find out

What to do: Smear a thin layer of petroleum jelly on one surface of each of the three index cards. Tape two of the cards in different locations outside. For example, one card can be taped to the side of your house and the other hung from the tree branch in your backyard. Or, one card can be taped to a mailbox and the other to a garage door. The third card should be taped someplace inside your home. Check the cards every week or so to see how much particulate matter (dust, odd bits and pieces of material, pollen, and other small particles that float in the air) have collected on them.

What happens: After some time (depending on where you live) you will find that the two cards placed outside have collected a good amount of particulate matter (the one placed inside the house may have considerably fewer particles on it). The amount of matter collected on the two outside cards indicates the amount of pollution that is in

your air, and that you are probably taking into your lungs as well. (Do this air test several times throughout the seasons, to see if pollution is better, or worse, at some times than at other times.)

Why: Air pollution is a serious concern in many industrial areas. Factories, trucks and cars, and incinerators are just a few of the causes of air pollution. The polluting particles, often very small, can affect the environment nearby and far away (blown great distances by the wind). The pollutants settle on the ground and on buildings, and sometimes we inhale them into our lungs. Your cards will show you how serious the air pollution is where you live.

A Band of Bands

Here's another experiment to demonstrate how much air pollution is in your area.

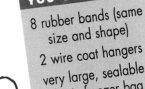
What to do: Bend each coat hanger into a rectangular shape. (Some hangers are harder to shape than others; you may need help with this.) Slide two rubber bands onto one end of a coat hanger and two over the other end. The rubber bands should be fairly tight to be sure to stay on. Do this for both hangers. Hang one of the coat hangers outside (in a tree, for example), making sure it is out of the sun. Place the second hanger in a plastic bag and seal it. Keep it in your room.

What happens: Depending on the amount of air pollution in your local area, the rubber bands on the hanger hung outside start to deteriorate. They begin to decompose, split, or break apart.

Why: Pollution in the air can affect all kinds of things, even those made of rubber, so the condition of the rubber bands on the hanger placed outside is a good indication of the severity of this problem in your area. If the rubber bands break down in only a few weeks, then it probably means that there is a great deal of air pollution in your area. If, however, the rubber bands take longer to break down, there may not be as much pollution. You'll also notice that the rubber bands on the coat hanger that you kept inside the plastic bag showed no breakdown at all. This shows what can happen when air pollution is reduced or eliminated.

297 Acid from the Skies

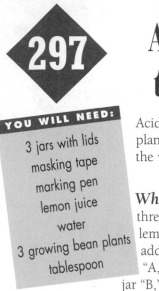

Acid rain is a danger to plant life in many parts of the world. Here's why.

What to do: Label the three jars and put ½ cup of lemon juice in each, then add water as follows: jar "A," add ½ cup of water; jar "B," add ½ cup of water; jar "C," add ½ cup of water. Label the three bean plants A, B and C, and place them on a sunny windowsill. Every day, water each plant with four tablespoons of the lemon juice solution assigned to it (plant "A" gets solution "A").

What happens: Plant "A" shows the effects of the "acid rain" first. The leaves start to curl and shrivel. Its growth slows down or stops, and it starts looking sickly. The other two bean plants eventually show these problems, too.

Why: Acid rain is caused by air pollutants pumped into the atmosphere through the smokestacks of factories and industry. The pollutants gather in dense clouds and fall back to earth when it rains. The pollutants, which are acidic like the lemon juice, build up in the soil and affect the growth of plant life (like the lemon juice solutions did to your plants). The more acidic the rain (like solution "A"), the sooner the plant is affected. Over time, the plants will die; and new plants won't be able to grow because of the highly

298 That Cookie Is "Mine"

When resources such as coal are taken from the ground, does it affect the local environment?

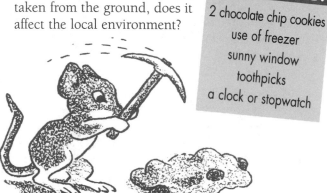

What to do: Put one cookie in the freezer for an hour, and the other in a sunny window. Then, pretending you are a coal miner, take a toothpick and "mine" as much hard "coal" (chocolate chips) from the cold cookie as you can for four minutes. Then stop, and try for four minutes more to dig the soft chips out of the cookie left in the window. How many chips can you remove from each in four minutes?

What happens: You find it hard to "mine" the chips and, in both cases, probably had to destroy or alter the "landscape" of the cookie in order to get chips out. You also notice that it is easier to "mine" hard chips than to remove soft ones.

Why: The hard and soft chips in the cookies represent two basic types of coal: anthracite (hard) coal and bituminous (soft) coal. When coal is mined, it can damage the surrounding area. Over several years, a good deal of harm can be done to the environment. It is often difficult or impossible to reverse the damage done by mining, just as it would be difficult to repair your cookies after removing the chocolate chips.

Gumming Up the Works

YOU WILL NEED:

chunk-style bubble gum
pie plate or shallow pan
water
household machine oil
toothpick
hand-held grater
an adult helper
paper

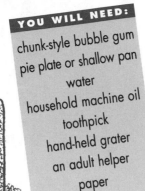

Oil spills are dangerous to the environment, so we are always looking for ways to prevent them, and to contain them when they do happen. How? Try using bubble gum to contain your own home-grown oil spill!

What to do: Put a piece of chunk-style bubble gum in the freezer and leave it overnight. Fill the pie plate halfway with water. Carefully release about 10 drops of oil into the middle of the water (use a toothpick to pull the oil-spill drops together). Take the bubble gum from the freezer and ask an adult to grate it into small strips onto a sheet of paper. Carefully, lift the sheet and sprinkle the grated gum onto the oil spill. Let a little of it fall into the water as well. Wait for about thirty minutes.

What happens: The gum begins to absorb the oil in the water. Depending on the amount of gum you sprinkled into the oil, all or most of the spill will be absorbed. The gum strips that fell on the water don't absorb anything.

Why: Gum consists of a type of particle known as a non-polar molecule. A non-polar molecule will absorb another type of non-polar molecule. Water, however, is made of polar molecules. Thus, the gum (which is non-polar) will not absorb the water (which is polar), but will absorb the oil (which is also non-polar). So, in order to contain or absorb oil spills in the ocean, it is necessary to put a non-polar absorbing material on the spill. In this way the oil is absorbed by the material, but the sea water is not. The material and the oil spill can then be skimmed or pumped from the surface of the water.

Did You Know?

- The average American family produces about 100 pounds (45 kg) of trash and garbage every week.
- According to some scientists, more than 99% of all the plant and animal species that have ever lived are now extinct.
- In California alone, more than 200 million tons of pesticides are used every year.
- In the Imperial Valley in California, there is a power plant that burns about 900 tons of cow manure daily.
- Every year, landfills in the United States are crammed with 24 million tons of leaves and grass clippings that could have been composted and recycled for use in gardens.
- By recycling a ton of paper, we can save close to 10 cubic feet (.28 cubic m) of landfill space—and 17 trees!
- Every year, humans add six billion tons of carbon dioxide to the atmosphere. Most of this comes from burning fossil fuels, such as coal and oil.

Making a Difference

Kids can and do make a difference! When you and your friends, classmates, or other neighborhood kids take an interest in preserving nature, we can all work together to care for the plants, animals, and environments that are part of our world. Sometimes it may mean putting up a bird feeder in your backyard, picking up litter along the side of a road, or writing to groups and organizations for information and brochures on what you can do to help. All our efforts are important, because if we don't take care of nature, who will?

A group called Renew America collects stories about people and groups who are working to preserve the environment. You may be interested in learning about some of the nature activities that kids all across the country are participating in—true stories about kids who are making a difference. If so, write to them and ask for information:
Renew America
Suite 710
1400 16th St., NW
Washington, DC 20036

You're on the Air

Yes! You're definitely on the air in this chapter. You'll learn about the principles of flight, or Bernoulli's Law. Once you understand this, you'll know what keeps aircraft in the air.

About Air and Air Travel

Besides constructing many types of airfoils, or models of an airplane wing, you'll learn about air currents and how they circulate around and act on a plane's surface. This circulation of air, both fast and slow, lifts the airplane up into the upper atmosphere.

In addition, you'll construct toy helicopters, rotary motors, flying propellers and real cardboard plane models that fly.

The simple everyday materials needed are explained clearly, but if you have any trouble measuring and cutting out parts, get help.

With a few simple materials, and a little effort, you'll be on the air in no time.

302 Ruler's Uprising

This is one ruler that will be uplifted, even do a back flip! And it's all due to Bernoulli's Principle.

What to do: Place the cardboard strip on the ruler so that it is touching one end and extends toward the middle. Push the strip upward a bit to form a slight arch, or curve, about an inch (1.5 cm) in height. Tape both ends of the strip to the ruler.

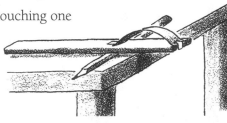

Place the ruler on a table and balance it on the pencil. The ruler should extend about 3 inches (8 cm) off the edge of the table.

Now, blow a steady stream of air over the top of the cardboard strip and down the length of the ruler. If nothing happens, or if the ruler just moves down the table on the pencil, adjust the balance point of the ruler on the pencil and try again.

What happens: The ruler rises, springs up and does a back flip.

Why: Bernoulli's Principle is used when a plane lifts into the air. The same principle applies to our cardboard wing, or airfoil, taped to the ruler.

The air traveling over an airplane or cardboard wing has to travel farther and faster, so the pressure over the wing is less. Because the flow of air is slower on the wing's flat underside, it produces greater pressure and forces, or pushes, the aircraft upward.

303 Blowhard

Blow hard and recreate Bernoulli's Principle of Liquid Pressure. Simulate, or copy, an airplane's wing in this simple but uplifting experiment.

What to do: Place one end of the paper just below your lower lip and blow hard over the top of it.

What happens: The paper rises and flaps in the air.

Why: Again, a fast-moving flow of air passes over the top of the paper, producing lower pressure, while the slower air flow beneath the paper causes greater pressure. The difference causes lift and pushes the strip of paper upward.

Let's Wing It!

Do you love experiments? This one's a breeze!
Design an airplane wing, or airfoil, and see how it reacts
to a rapid air stream.

What to do: Prepare two pieces of notebook paper, about 4 by 5 inches (11 by 14 cm). (You can also cut a sheet of typing paper into quarters, use two now, and keep the other two quarters for the next experiment.) Keep one piece of paper flat and form a slight arch, loop, or hill on top with the other, as shown.

Tape the curved piece of paper to the outer edges of the flat piece, and you have made a copy of an airplane wing, or airfoil.

Now, carefully straighten a large paper clip (adult help may be needed) and poke it through the middle of both pieces of paper. Bend the clip slightly underneath, if needed, to hold the paper.

Gently but rapidly, blow some air over the short, front side of the airfoil, followed by blowing again just underneath it. Be careful to blow only for short periods, and to rest in between blowing. (Your body needs air, too!)

What happens: When you blew a short burst of air over the curved side of the airfoil, it lifted; while no movement was noticed when blowing a stream of air under the wing.

Why: Again, Bernoulli's Principle, or Rule, explains it. The lower air pressure on the top of the wing and the greater pressure on the bottom caused lift. (See "Ruler's Uprising.")

Foiled Again!

This time you're going to start rolling, and then square off, and find out what happens.

YOU WILL NEED:

notebook paper
straightened paper clip from "Let's Wing It"
tape

What to do: From a notebook, take a small sheet of paper and roll it into a cylinder or tube, and tape it. Take another piece of paper, fold it in half, then open and fold each end to the center crease. Shape the creased sheet to form a box. Tape that, too.

Again, have someone poke the straightened paper clip into the middle of each shape and test each separately. Make certain the hole is large enough so the airfoil slides up and down the paper clip.

As you did in "Let's Wing It," blow over the top of each shape and then under it. Again, remember to rest between blowing. Did you notice any difference in the movements between the airplane foil, the cylinder or the box? Do you think how an airplane wing is designed is important?

What happens: The cylinder airfoil rises very little, while the box wing does not move at all.

Why: The push of air against a wing of a plane is called drag. Instead of helping the plane move smoothly through the air, it breaks up or blocks the airflow, so holds the plane back.

This is why the design of an airplane wing is so very important. Out first airfoil created a smooth flow of air around the wing, while the curves and angles of the cylinder and box caused much drag, or breaking up and blockage of air.

BLOW

BLOW

306 Oddballs

YOU WILL NEED:
2 balloons
a yard/meter length
of string

Air affects aircraft in many ways, both lifting and pushing. See how two balloons react to each other in this oddball experiment.

What to do: Blow each balloon up to large-orange size and knot them closed. Tie a balloon to each end of the string. Hold the string up in front of your face, or arrange the string over a high fixture or lamp, so that the two balloons hang evenly, next to each other, about 2 inches (5 cm) apart.

Now, blow a rapid stream of air between the two balloons and try to separate them more. Be sure to rest, stop blowing, a few minutes between tries. You do want to do your best…and not run out of breath!

What happens: The fast-moving air stream does not separate the balloons, as you might think, but instead brings the balloons closer together.

Why: When you blew between the balloons, the fast moving air between them caused a reduction in air pressure there, and the greater pressure on the outside of each balloon pushed them together.

Try "High Rollers" and other Bernoulli experiments for more air pressure information.

High Rollers: A Big Wind! 307

Sound like a Las Vegas game? No, you won't have to gamble on this simple and successful experiment. It's just Bernoulli's Principle of Air Pressure again, demonstrating lift.

YOU WILL NEED:
2 cardboard toilet
paper rolls
drinking straw
a flat, steady table

What to do: Place the two cardboard tubes about an inch (2.5 cm) away from one another. With the straw, blow a steady stream of air between them. (Place the tubes on a thick, heavy book to raise the experiment higher off the table, and easier to do.)

What happens: The stream of air blown through the straw causes the two cardboard rolls to come together. (Now you know why this experiment is called "High Rollers.")

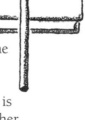

Why: As the fast-moving air from the straw passes between the two tubes, the air pressure there is less than on the outer sides of the tubes. The difference in air pressure is enough to bring the two tubes together.

Whirlybird

YOU WILL NEED:

scissors
strip of light cardboard, about 1½ by 16 inches (3 by 40 cm)
pencil with an eraser
thumbtack

In the next two experiments, you'll become an expert on helicopter flight. With a simple pencil and piece of light cardboard, you'll duplicate the effect of the spinning blades, or rotor, of a helicopter.

What to do: Place the middle of the cardboard strip on the top of the pencil eraser and press the tack through the strip to attach it. Make certain the tack is in tightly, as you bend the two ends of the strip upward from the middle. Your rotor blade, or cardboard strip, should have a slight V-shape at the eraser.

You are now ready to launch your model. This experiment can be done indoors or out. For best results, it can be launched from a height, such as a deck or staircase. Because high places can be dangerous, ask an adult to help you—you'll want someone to witness your launch anyway!

To launch properly, rapidly roll the pencil between your hands and release it. Be certain you roll and drop it the same way each time you conduct the experiment. (It should spin and turn as it drops downward.)

Do this many times, conducting many trials, before you decide how your model helicopter performs or flies.

What happens: With practice, your model helicopter with the cardboard-strip rotor should turn and spin and whirl through the air as it gently floats downward.

Why: Like an airplane, the rotors, or wings, of a helicopter are an airfoil and are designed to catch the slower-moving air under them rather than the fast-moving air over them.

These crowded or dense air molecules cause the rotors and craft to be pushed upward. The small side rotor on the tail end of the helicopter stops what is known as torque, balancing it and keeping the whole craft from turning, while the main rotor helps the craft to lift and turn, according to its position.

Although, our cardboard/pencil model with its rapid hand-spin thrust does not lift the model very much, it still reduces the fall rate as it descends.

Twirly-Whirlies

YOU WILL NEED:

3 pencils
light cardboard
scissors
thumbtacks

Twirly-what? Whirlies! In "Whirlybird," you made a simple pencil-and-paper helicopter-like toy. Now, let's replace that straight and simple blade with a circular pinwheel-and-cross rotor. Will the design of the different rotors make your model stay up in the air longer? Turn and fly better?

Do longer or wider rotors make a difference? Let's try different shapes, sizes, and widths of rotors to find out what works best.

What to do: Cut a circle between 4_ and 8 inches (11 to 20 cm) in diameter from the light cardboard. Cut four slits opposite each other in toward the center, but leave the center uncut. Fold one side of each slit to form a pinwheel.

Next, cut a strip 2 by 8 inches (5 by 20 cm) long and fold the strip in the center to form a V. Lastly, cut a 6-inch (15 cm) square of cardboard and cut out 2-inch (5 cm) squares from each corner to form a cross. Turn the cross ends up.

Now, tack the middle of each cardboard rotor to the top of a pencil eraser. Make certain the thumbtack is securely in place on all three models.

To launch, rapidly roll a pencil between your hands and release it. Again, see "Whirlybirds" for help and hints!

What happens: With our test models, the 2-by-8-inch (5 by 20 cm) strip worked fairly well but was somewhat clumsy. The pinwheel airfoil was very clumsy, did not turn or rotate, and fell to the ground without catching the air currents. However, the 6-inch (15 cm) cross rotor flew very well, with smooth and gentle spinning or rotation as it softly fell to the ground.

Why: The cross rotor was probably more like a real helicopter's airfoil than the other models. The wide blades with the four upturned ends, when rotated by hand, caught the denser, closer air underneath it and reduced the rate of drag from air holding it back as it fell to the ground. See "Whirlybird."

What now: Do this same experiment but see if you can make a perfect airfoil, or helicopter rotor, by adjusting the variables, other things that can affect spinning and flight.

For example, will longer or wider rotors make a difference? Or heavier or lighter paper or cardboard? Will making a drive shaft or spinning launcher help? In the next experiment, you'll find out!

310 ◆ Rotor Motor

You can make a jet-propelled, helicopter-like rotor, or blade, whirl, using nothing but 100% balloon power.

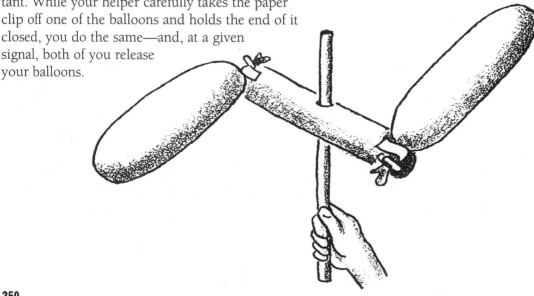

What to do: Ask an adult to help by using a sharp scissors tip to punch two holes completely through the cardboard tube, through both sides, at a point midway along its length. The holes need to be exactly opposite each other so an inserted dowel will fit right across. Place the dowel through the holes in the tube and turn, or rotate, the tube on the dowel many times until it spins freely.

Next, blow up one of the oblong balloons, twist and clip it, and carefully tape it to one end of the tube. (Be sure to fasten it well.)

Blow up the second balloon, twist and clip it, and fasten it to the other end of the tube, making certain the balloon opening is facing opposite the first balloon.

Now, get ready for the action! To do two things at once, you'll need the help of your assistant. While your helper carefully takes the paper clip off one of the balloons and holds the end of it closed, you do the same—and, at a given signal, both of you release your balloons.

YOU WILL NEED:

cardboard paper towel roll

scissors

2 large oblong balloons

paper clip

wooden dowel, 1/2-inch by 18 inches (45 cm)

tape

a helper

What happens: As soon as you release the balloons, the tube whirls and spins.

Why: The rush of air from the balloons mounted on opposite ends of the tube pushes them forward, turning the tube around the dowel. The air being expelled by the balloons causes this push. Sir Isaac Newton's Third Law of Motion explains it best: for every action there is an equal and opposite reaction. The reaction of the balloons is to move forward. What would happen if the two balloons were placed on the dowel with their neck openings in the same direction?

An American Yank

If you are careful to follow these clear and simple directions, this spinning airfoil won't let you down. It's time to pull some strings, give your helicopter a good old American yank, and watch it take off. You'll be flying high in no time!

What to do: Wrap the cardboard rectangle around the pencil to form a cylinder and tape it. Make certain the tube is loose enough for the pencil to turn inside it (drive shaft).

Next, cut 2-inch (5 cm) squares from each corner of the construction paper, forming a cross (see "Twirly Whirlies"). Place this cross-shaped rotor on top of the pencil eraser and fasten it with the tack. Make certain the tack is in tight enough so the rotor won't fall off. Bend the blades upward for better flight.

Lastly, place just the pencil point, or about an inch (2.5 cm) of pencil, into the drive-shaft cylinder. Wrap the thread around the pencil above it, as you would wind kite string around a stick—keeping it smooth, straight and tight.

Although it is not necessary, it's best to test-fly this experimental craft from a higher point to a lower area to observe the results. Ask for help if needed.

Pull the thread rapidly but smoothly and watch your helicopter turn with a whir and lift into the air.

If your helicopter doesn't work as it should, look for these variables, or other things that could be affecting its upward flight:

1. Is the thread wound too high on the pencil?
2. Is the pencil too deep in the drive shaft?
3. Is the tack holding the rotor loose or crooked, or still tight and in place?
4. Is the drive shaft too tight around the pencil?
5. Did you use string instead of thread? (String fibers are rough and cause drag by catching on the drive shaft and pencil.)

What happens: As you pull the thread away from around the pencil, the pencil is made to rotate, or turn, making a gradual but noticeable whirring sound and the craft lifts into the air.

Why: The rapid action of the rotating, or spinning, pencil causes the moving rotor blades to lift up in reaction to the air being forced or pushed down.

I'm Banking On You!

Would you like to make the kind of instrument that helps pilots determine an airplane's position in flight? The artificial horizon will tell you whether you are flying level, or banking, or tilting, right or left. You're bound to crash in on the fun.

What to do: Flatten and cut the ends off the shoe box lid and cut the flat, rectangular piece of cardboard in half. Cut one of the halves an inch (2.5 cm) shorter.

Cut a 3-inch (8 cm) square from the plastic bag. With one of the marker pens, draw a straight line across the center of the piece.

Now, cut a 2½-inch (7 cm) circle from the center of the longer piece of cardboard and tape the clear plastic piece with the line on it to one side. Again, make certain the line is centered in the middle.

On the second, shorter piece of cardboard, draw a different colored line. It should be in the center, so as to divide it. Now draw a 90° straight line vertically or straight up from the center of the other line. You should have what looks like an upside down T.

Lastly, place the two cardboard pieces together—the window-lined piece on top of the inside shorter T-piece. Make certain both lines are matched up with each other.

Have someone punch a hole in the top center pieces of the cardboard, as you would a hanger on a picture, and position the bolt and nut, or fastener, in it.

The back, shorter, piece should move freely back and forth, much like a pendulum on a clock. Your flight instrument is now ready to be tested.

The line you drew on the plastic window represents the wing, while the cardboard with lines attached to the window shows the horizon, the line between the earth and sky.

Hold the attached longer piece level with the floor and slowly but gradually tip the instrument to the right and then to the left.

What happens: When tilting, if the horizon line is below the wing, the airplane is headed upward. If the line is above the wing line, the plane is angled downwards.

Why: A real artificial horizon helps a pilot navigate accurately even if he or she cannot see ahead. It tells the pilot whether the plane is going up, down or flying level.

The instrument shows two lines, one of which represents the horizon, the other, the wing. The horizon line is balanced by a gyroscope or a spinning wheel that keeps the horizon line level with the real horizon. This instrument is so accurate, that it keeps the two horizon lines steady, even if the airplane is not.

Note: Your artificial horizon must be matched up, line for line, carefully in order to register correctly, to give you an accurate reading.

◆ 313 ◆ Meter-Made

Make an aneroid barometer, which is similar to an airplane's altimeter (altitude meter). Although your liquidless barometer won't measure altitude above sea level, it will teach you the highs and lows of air-pressure changes.

YOU WILL NEED:

16-ounce wide-mouth jar

scissors

straw

ruler

tape

clay

large balloon

What to do: Cut the neck off the balloon and make a 1-inch (3 cm) cut on its side. Open it up and stretch it over the mouth of the jar, as you would spread skin over a drum. It should be put on tight, but not too tight. Done correctly, it will not slip off the mouth of the jar but will form an airtight seal.

Next, place the straw in the middle of the balloon skin and carefully and gently tape it.

Lastly, form a ball with the clay and stick the end of the ruler with the lower numbers into it. The clay will form a stand for your ruler-scale. Place the ruler close to the straw and record any numbered up and down movements.

What happens: The straw will move up or down to record any air pressure changes in the jar.

Why: When the straw moves up the numbered ruler, the pressure is higher; when it falls, the pressure is lower.

The aneroid barometer you made is similar to an airplane's altimeter, but it has no liquid in it. Too, unlike the airplane's device, it only shows altitude changes above sea level.

As a plane ascends, or climbs, the air pressure becomes less and is recorded as a drop on the altimeter. Air pressure at sea level exerts a greater force and affects all things on Earth.

Note: In order to show accurate barometric pressure changes, keep your barometer safe and undisturbed in a sheltered area for an extended, or long, period of time.

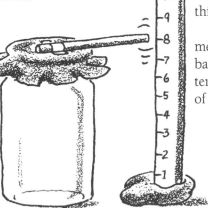

314

HOT!

Tailspin

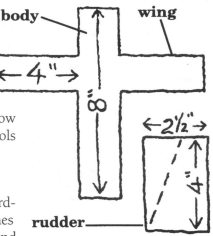

body — wing

← 4" →

∞

← 2½" →

4"

rudder —

You'll get into a real tailspin when you learn how the rudder, or tail section, of an airplane controls its left and right turns.

What to do: In the middle of the piece of cardboard, draw a line with the ruler, about 8 inches (20 cm) long. Place the ruler next to the line and draw the remaining lines around it to form the outline of the ruler. You should have drawn a long rectangle.

When done, you want an airplane pattern, with a wingspan, on each side, that measures 2 by 4 inches (5 by 10 cm). So, about 2 inches (5 cm) down from the top of the rectangle, draw a line, from one side 4 inches (10 cm) across. Do the other side the same way as to form a cross. This is the wing. Since it is wider than the body of the plane, draw a line opposite each end of each 4 inch (10 cm) line that measures 2 inches (5 cm). Fill in the remaining opposite 10-cm lines on each side to form the complete wing section.

With the remaining cardboard, cut out a rectangle, that measures 2½ by 4 (6 by 10 cm). This piece will represent the rudder.

Now, cut out both plane and rudder patterns. Cut out a slanted piece on one side of the rudder.

Align the plane pattern and attach it with thumbtacks to the narrow side of the toothpaste carton.

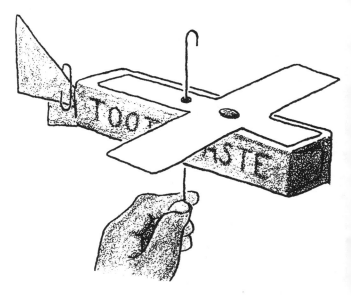

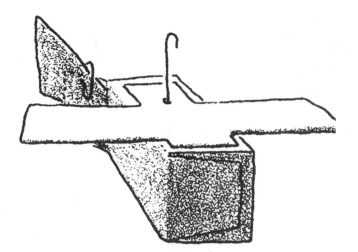

Pull out the main end flap of the toothpaste carton (near the tail-end of the airplane pattern) and attach the rudder to the flap with a paper clip (with the straight side of rudder facing away from the airplane pattern).

Puncture wounds can be dangerous, so get an adult to open and carefully straighten part of a paper clip. The straight end of the paper clip needs to be pushed through the middle underside of the box (underneath your attached plane pattern and behind the wing) and up through the top side. For safety, and to keep the plane on the clip, the straight, exposed part of the paper clip should be bent downward. (A small nail may be helpful in starting the holes.)

Your model plane is finished and is now ready to be tested.

To do this, look behind the model and push the rudder toward the right wing. Now position the plane, the front toward you, while carefully holding the underside paper clip, and gently blow a stream of air toward the rudder.

Now, repeat this action while reversing the rudder as far as it will go to the left. (Since the rudder is attached to the right side of the flap, it will be necessary for you to push and press it to the left as much and as hard as you can.)

What happens: Blowing on the rudder at different angles will move the model plane right to left.

Why: When you blew a stream of air against the rudder, while it was turned to the right, the air hit its right side, turning the plane's nose to the right. When you blew a stream of air against the rudder, while it was moved to the left, the air force again pressed against it, this time moving the plane's nose to the left.

What next: Keep your model airplane for more flight experiments (see "Flap-Happy").

315 Flap-Happy

YOU WILL NEED:

toothpaste-carton airplane from "Tailspin"

pencil

scissors

ruler

In "Tailspin," you made a model airplane with a rudder that controlled left and right turns, called "banking." Here, you'll go one step further, and cut flaps in the wings of your model airplane. These flaps will further control turns. In addition, you'll learn a lot about giving right-left directions—right? No, left!

What to do: Using your "Tailspin" model, mark off a 2-inch (4 cm) space on each side of the wings, making certain the marked space is in the same area on both wings.

Now, draw vertical or straight lines about an inch long (2 cm) from the end marks of each two-inch area on each wing. These will represent the wing flaps, or ailerons. Now make a cut on each vertical line—you should make two cuts on one wing; two cuts on the other. By folding, you will now have movable flaps on each side of the wings.

Look in the back of your model's wings to determine right wing, left wing. Turn the right aileron up and the left aileron down and the rudder to the right. Now blow a steady stream of air against the upturned flap. Which way does the airplane turn? Remember, to consider right-wing/left-wing, consider the turn from the back side of your model and not the front, and also remember to line up the model with your right and left hand.

Now, turn the flaps in the opposite direction, with the left aileron up and the right aileron down and the rudder pushed to the left. Again, blow a stream of air toward the front of the model. Which way does the airplane turn?

What happens: When you turned the right aileron up and the left aileron down and the rudder to the right, the model turned to the right. The plane turned to the left when the left aileron was up and the right aileron was down and the rudder was pushed to the left.

Why: Again, as in "Tailspin," the model turned to the right when the right aileron was up and the rudder was pushed to the right. The plane turned to the left when the left aileron was up and the rudder was pushed to the left.

Again, in both cases, the air stream hit the flat surfaces that were turned toward it and moved the model accordingly.

316 ◆ Flight Pattern

When you take your plane outside and throw it, you must remember that this is a scientific experiment. Like all scientific experiments, launching your model plane must be conducted scientifically. If your plane does not fly well or does not fly at all, there's probably a scientific explanation.

Again, go back to "What's All the Flap About?" Did you correctly trim and adjust the weights on your plane? Did you streamline the wings, body (fuselage), rudder and stabilizer by cutting rounder corners? If not, your plane may be too clumsy and awkward to fly.

Adjust paper clips on the nose of your plane and do not be afraid to add more, take away some, reposition clips, or add larger and heavier clips.

Remember, this is an experiment and you want to know which features will make your model fly best. Be adventurous and don't be afraid to try different things to make your plane fly longer, higher and straighter.

Also, you might want to try making different sized models with different designs by slightly changing the directions in "What's All the Flap About?" Larger planes usually glide longer distances and turn less. The possibilities for having your plane do what you want it to do are endless.

To make the best throws, find the center of gravity of your plane. If it has clips on its nose, place a finger and your thumb under the wing. When your model does not fall off your fingers and is perfectly balanced, you'll have found the center of gravity. This is where you should hold your plane; for ours, it was just behind the wing.

When you hold your plane at its balancing point, you'll get straighter, smoother and longer flights every time.

So have fun! Your plane experiments will never be boring but will leave you flying high with excitement.

What's All the Flap About?

You know something about aileron and rudder flaps; testing a practically stationary or non-movable model. Now, you'll go further. You'll throw and fly a real model with movable flaps. You'll even add a stabilizer, the horizontal, flat piece of the tail, to your experimental aircraft. Both will make your model even more interesting.

WING

STABILIZER

What to do: Draw the parts of your model plane. First, draw a 10-inch (25 cm) long rectangular box (ruler width) across the middle of the cardboard. When folded as shown, this will form the fuselage, or the body of the plane, with slits for the wing and stabilizer pieces.

Add a tailpiece to the fuselage, by drawing a 3-inch (8 cm) line up from the top left end of the rectangle; and then a 2-inch (5 cm) line across to the right, toward the front of your model. Finally, draw a line diagonally downward, to meet the top of the rectangle. This up-and-down part of the tailpiece, attached to the fuselage, is the rudder of your plane.

For the wing, draw another ruler-width 10-inch (25 cm) rectangular box.

Next, draw another, shorter rectangle. Make it about 2 by 5 inches (5 by 12.5 cm). This will represent the plane's elevator, or stabilizer; the flat and even part of your model's tailpiece.

To assemble your model plane, cut out the fuselage (body) with its attached rudder, the wing, and the stabilizer (flat part of tail assembly).

Make a crease, or fold, down the center of the fuselage. Fasten it with a paper clip. The clip can be removed later, as the plane is further assembled.

Now, 2 inches (4 cm) from the front of the plane, in the middle of the folded-over fuselage, draw a 2-inch (4 cm) line. Here, have an adult cut through the doubled-over fuselage to form a slit. This is where the wing will go. Make a similar line and slit toward the back of the plane, at the base of the rudder. Insert the stabilizer and the wing into their slits and adjust them. Reinforce the positions of your stabilizer and wing by taping them to the fuselage.

If your model's parts are large and it flies awkwardly, streamline it. Cut the areas at the ends of the wings, rudder and stabilizer to round them off. Cut the nose at an angle, trimming it, and place 4 or 5 paper clips on the nose assembly to balance and weight the model while removing any unnecessary clips on the fuselage.

Last-minute trimming and the adjusting of weights is necessary to make your model stable, steady, and most important, able to fly well.

Before cutting flaps in your plane's wing, rudder and stabilizer, take it outside and test it for flight. How you launch, or throw, your plane and the scientific methods you use are important variables. See "Flight Pattern" for help.

Once your plane flies well, cut flaps an equal distance apart on the wings, stabilizer and rudder. Adjust flaps up on the stabilizer to make your plane climb, or down to make it dip. Adjust ailerons (wing flaps) and rudder (flap at back) to the left or right to make turns. Let it fly!

What happens: Your model plane flies differently depending on how the flaps are positioned.

Why: When you turned the left wing's aileron up and rudder flap to the left, the air stream pushed toward the flaps and turned the model in that direction. The opposite applies when the right aileron and rudder is in the opposite direction.

Also, the movable flap in the stabilizer, the flat tailpiece, moves the plane according to how the air stream is hitting it. When lowered, the plane dives, when raised, it ascends, or climbs.

318

Forward, March!

In the last experiment, you learned about Newton's Law of Motion. Simply put, it states that for every action there must be an equal and opposite reaction.

YOU WILL NEED:
balloons
standard sheet of paper
masking tape
scissors

When rushing fueled-air in a jet plane's engine is activated or ignited, the heated air that is released from the rear of the plane, pushes the plane forward. This is a perfect example of thrust. You can further see this law in rockets and planes by doing a few important but simple experiments:

What to do: First, blow up a few balloons and release them. When you blow the balloons up and let them go, the air comes out of the neck and propels them forward. A similar reaction occurs in planes and rockets.

You can make a simple rocket (you'll construct and develop more interesting rockets later on) by rolling a piece of paper into a cylinder and taping it.

Next, cut a piece of masking tape about 6 inches (15 cm) long and stick it on the neck of the balloon. Forming a bridge with the balloon and tape, stick the sides of the tape to the cylinder. You should be able to put your finger in the space between the tape and the cylinder. Also, the neck of the balloon should be facing the inside of the cylinder but with the opening out far enough to allow you to blow into it.

Now, blow a stream of air into the balloon and hold the end until it is ready to be released. If the tape starts to loosen or the balloon is stuck hard to the tape, readjust the tape or the balloon or start over. When ready, release the balloon and watch what happens.

The simple cylinder rocket is propelled forward as the air released from the neck of the balloon rushes through it.

319 ◆ A "Prop-er" Engine: A Wheel Deal!

Modern jet planes use a mixture of fueled, hot, compressed rushing air to turn a series of wheeled fans on rods, or axles, called turbines.

This compressed, or flattened and pressed, air is then forced out of the plane's tail and pushes, or thrusts, the craft forward. Early turboprop planes used propellers and turbines to do the same job, but not as well as modern jet crafts. Find out how early jet-prop planes worked in this simple, easy, and fun experiment—it's a "wheel" deal!

What to do: Cut a rectangular section in the middle side of the cup that extends half way down its sides. Poke a hole in the middle of the bottom of the cup and cut the flap off the straw hole in the plastic lid.

Draw two circles 3 inches (8 cm) in diameter on the cardboard and divide each into eight parts, like circles used for teaching fractions.

Next, make _-inch cuts on the lines in the circles and bend the sections back and forth to represent the blades of a fan. Use tape to reinforce cuts and repair any tears.

Poke holes in the middle of the circular fans and push the straw through them. Each fan should be in the middle of the straw and about 2 inches (5 cm) from the other.

Fit the fan-and-straw assembly through the bottom hole of the cup while securing the plastic lid and straw into the top. Test the assembly to see if it turns easily. If not, cut larger holes to accommodate the straw, so that it will turn freely.

To make the propeller, cut a 1- by 5-inch (2.5 by 13 cm) propeller-shaped piece out of the cardboard.

Cut small slits into the center of each side and gently bend each part in opposite directions. This will give the propeller its third-dimensional shape.

Assemble the propeller by wrapping the rubber band around the straw securely where it pokes up through the lid. This will act as a buffer between the propeller and the lid, so that the propeller will stay forward and turn more freely. Next, place the propeller on the end of the straw (it will be necessary to poke a hole in the middle of the propeller), in front of the wrapped rubber band.

Finally, secure the propeller in place by shaping a nose for your plane out of clay and pushing it into place on the straw in front of the propeller.

Now you are ready to test your model jet prop. Blow a steady stream of air to the sides of the propeller and watch what happens.

What happens: By blowing a stream of air to the sides of the propeller, the compressor-turbine fanned parts are turned around.

Why: Although our experimental turboprop model is fun to make and test, it does not necessarily show how a real turboprop works. This model essentially was made to show how the movement of turbine parts is needed in the jet propulsion process. In a real turboprop engine, the turbines turn the propellers; while in our model, it is the propeller that turns the turbine parts.

Again, in a modern jet engine, incoming air at the front of the plane is compressed or squeezed together by engine parts. The jet's fuel is ignited or burned in a chamber and the hot gases are blown out of the rear of the plane. The thrust, or the forward push of the plane, is explained by one of Newton's three laws of motion, put forth in the year 1687, that every action has an equal and opposite reaction.

Traveling Bags: They're High and Mighty

Mankind could never keep eyes, and feet, on the ground. Watching birds soaring high, people dreamed of joining them—they never stopped trying.

About Hot Air Balloons

As early as the 1600s, long before the invention of the airplane, people talked of attaching baskets to flying spheres or balls. For years, they experimented with such balloons and large bags filled with lighter-than-air gases. Finally, in 1783, a French papermaker, Etienne Montgolfier, was credited with the first successful man-balloon launch—using hot air.

Air expands when heated, becoming lighter than the air surrounding it. One problem with early hot-air balloons was that the air inside would cool off. Then came the propane burner, which could be made to hang beneath a balloon, and the problem was solved.

Today, hot-air ballooning enthusiasts still enjoy just floating quietly on air currents. But balloons have been used to explore the atmosphere, gather data and weather information, even communicate. So, get ready for some "air-raising" experiences with air pressure and heated and expanded air, and learn about communication using helium balloons.

Airbag Balancing Act

You'll have lots of fun learning how hot air behaves in this enjoyable, magical experiment. It's easy to put together and involves everyday materials you'll find around the house. However, you will need an assistant and a steady hand.

HOT!

Note: An adult assistant is recommended. This experiment involves work with a lighted lamp bulb. Also, keep your materials for next experiment.

What to do: Open fully the two lunch bags. Place a paper clip on each flat, closed end of the bags.

Cut the string in half and tie each piece securely to each paper clip on each bag. Finally tie each stringed paper bag to each end of the ruler. You have now made a simple balance.

Ask your adult helper to remove the shade from a table lamp. The lamp should be low enough so you or your assistant can hold one

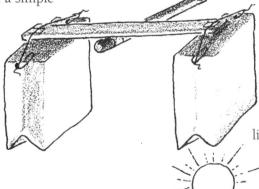

end of the bag-balance over it.

Now, you or your assistant should balance the ruler on the end of the pencil. When equally balanced, notice how both sides are the same.

For a few minutes, hold one of the bags slightly over the heated bulb. Again, you'll need a steady hand, and you and your partner will need to watch what happens. Can you or your helper tilt one end of the balance, with the heated bulb, so that it will fall?

What happens: After a few minutes, one end of your bag-balance should slightly tip or lean to one side and finally fall.

Why: The molecules of warmed air rising from the light bulb are moving very fast and are expanded or farther apart. It is this warmer, expanded air that is responsible for pushing against the bag and slightly lifting it.

Toy Balloons and Old Bags: Still Rising to the Occasion

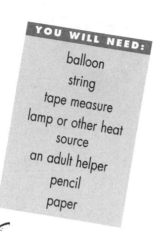

YOU WILL NEED:

balloon
string
tape measure
lamp or other heat source
an adult helper
pencil
paper

You can simply and easily prove that air expands when heated—very hot news for toy balloons and old bags (hot-air balloon bags, that is). So go ahead and blow up a few balloons and measure some hot air. You're sure to be bursting with excitement! It's definitely nothing to take lightly!

What to do: Blow up a balloon and tie it off with a string. Measure the circumference of the balloon, distance around the widest part. Write down the measurement. Now, with the help of a parent or adult friend, dangle the balloon above a lit lamp bulb. (It's not necessary to remove the shade.)

To thoroughly warm the balloon, you'll need to rotate, or turn, the balloon above the bulb for two to three minutes. Then, without removing the balloon from the heat source (you really need an extra hand here), measure the balloon's circumference, widest part, again. Record your information.

What happens: The balloon measurement is bigger than before!

Why: When the balloon was heated, the air inside became warmer, causing the air molecules to move faster, bump into each other and spread out. This action, in turn, increased the size of the balloon.

322 Spinning Wheel: It's Wheel Science At Work!

Because air molecules expand when heated, the hot air in a hot-air balloon is much lighter than the surrounding air. It's this difference that causes a hot-air balloon to lift off from the ground.

Now you can discover how another gas rises to the occasion to turn a toy's head (a pinwheel, that is).

HOT!

What to do: Cut six 1-inch (2.5 cm), equally-spaced slits around the aluminum disk or circle. Fold the shiny side down and bend the cut sides downward and back to form vanes or flaps. You should have something that looks like an upside-down pinwheel. Poke a very tiny hole directly in the center of the disk.

Cut a 1-inch (2.5 cm) piece from the bendable straw to use as the balancing piece. Have an adult poke the needle or pin through the center of the straw to form a T. The eye or pin head should be sticking out above the crossed section.

Now, shiny side down, place the upside-down pinwheel over the eye of the needle. Also, adjust the flaps or vanes of the circle so that they lay smoothly, with a slightly downward bend.

Bend the flexible straw to form a pipe and place the pointed end of the needle into the bent end of the straw.

The next step must be done carefully and with help. Have an adult put about a cup of water on the stove to boil. When the water begins to simmer and steam, have them hold the straw and extend the pinwheel over the hot water. Watch carefully.

What happens: The aluminum pinwheel disc gradually and slowly begins to turn.

Why: Although hot air and steam are not quite the same, they are both gases. Both can "lift" and do work, such as steam engines, hot-air balloons.

The steam here is hot water vapor, a gas. Like hot air, the molecules move faster and take up more space. In turn, they have much energy to move or push an object. Here, the foil pinwheel is turned by the loose, escaping, uprising heated gas molecules.

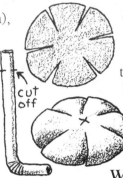

piece of straw

needle

A MATTER OF GRAVITY

Astronomers, mathematicians, and scientists once believed the planets followed circular paths or orbits around the sun; holding constant speeds as they orbited. Actually, the planets move around the sun in an ellipse, or oval, and according to their distance, or nearness to it and its gravitational pull, they speed up or slow down just enough to keep from being pulled in!

But getting down to Earth! As a resident, your body is being pulled down toward the center of the planet. Your weight on its surface reflects this pull.

About Gravity

In other words, your weight is the result of the pull of Earth's gravity on your body On Mars, your weight would be one-third of your Earth weight, because Mars is smaller. On the moon, with only one-sixth of Earth's gravity, you would weigh even a smaller fraction of your weight on Earth.

Another way of looking at it: the bigger the planet or moon, the more mass and gravity it possesses. So, on larger planets you would weigh more; and on smaller planets you would weigh less.

In this chapter, you'll not only do experiments about the speeds, orbits, and gravity of other planets, but learn how this important force affects our world as well. We know you'll find this chapter very attractive; we're pulling for you!

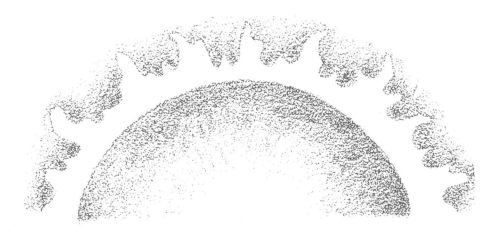

323

Curve-Ball Trajectory

YOU WILL NEED:

soft, light ball
(for safety)

a helper (optional), to
throw and return ball

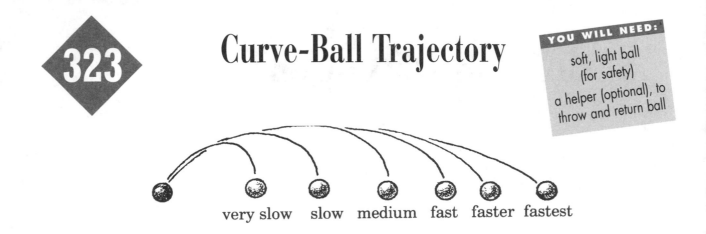

very slow   slow   medium   fast   faster   fastest

Throw a slow or fast ball and watch what kind of curved path, or trajectory, it takes.

What to do: Throw a ball upward into the air and follow the path, or trajectory, it takes each time you throw it. Repeat the throws, varying or changing the speed of your throw each time; for example, from slow, to slower, to even slower.

Then, throw some fast balls and notice if the speed has anything to do with changing the curved path or trajectory the ball takes.

What happens: All the thrown balls take a curved path once they are released, some following a steeper curve than others.

Why: The balls you threw into the air curved and were pulled back to Earth by its gravitational, or pulling, force. This curved path, called the trajectory, in all cases imitates the curvature of the Earth.

When you threw the ball slowly, you could see the curve it took more easily than when the ball was thrown fast. A slower throw, then, will definitely take a steeper, more noticeable path.

Spooling Around

YOU WILL NEED:
rubber eraser
paper clip
string, 20 inches
(50 cm) long
empty thread spool

Make a simple twirler, an eraser suspended from a string through a spool, and learn about centripetal force—while spooling around!

What to do: Tie the string tightly around the eraser and then thread it through the spool. Wrap the other end of the string around the paper clip and tie it securely. The clip will act as the anchor, to stop the string and eraser from flying off.

Now you're ready for a test. Hold the twirler straight out, away from your body and above your head. Make sure no one is nearby or in your path.

Gently but rapidly rotate, or spin, the spool, and then allow it to slow down and then to stop.

Continue to repeat this action and carefully watch what happens. Please note! It's not necessary to do this with any great force or movement.

What happens: As you rapidly spin the spool, the eraser will spin away from the spool and will rise upwards. When you slow or stop the spinning, the eraser will be pulled downwards and eventually stop.

Why: The eraser on the string is like gravity on the Earth. The string (gravity) pulls the eraser toward it (the spool). What actually is happening is called centripetal force. This is the force that directs movement to the center of the object. When you spun the spool, string and eraser around you, you pulled the eraser toward you and the force caused the string and eraser to move up and away from its center.

325

Weight Lifter: Stringing You Along!

YOU WILL NEED:

5 similar rubber erasers

paper and pencil

scissors

a helper

string, about 40 inches (100 cm)

watch or clock, with second hand

spool

In these whirling experiments you'll use several eraser weights, and learn what this tells you about the planets, their gravitational pull, and how they revolve around, or circle, the sun. So, enjoy twirling and whirling away with no strings attached—well, maybe one!

What to do: As in "Spooling Around," tie one end of the string around an eraser and thread the string through the spool. Tie an eraser to the opposite end of the string. For each trial, you will add one eraser to the bottom of the string. Your assistant's job will be to use the watch or clock to time each 15-second trial and then to record the number of weights and the results.

When you're ready to start each trial, have your helper stand at a distance, ready to start timing. First, get your twirler spinning well, before the official start time. Be sure to pull, hold, and keep the bottom-weighted string in the same position for every experiment.

At your start signal, have your helper silently count off 15 seconds as you quietly count the number of turns the eraser makes around the spool before your assistant calls "Time." Call out the number of turns to record, then add another eraser—to two, three, then four—and repeat the trial. After each trial, your helper writes down the number of weights used and the revolutions, or number of turns.

What happens: The more weights or erasers you add to the bottom of your twirler, the more revolutions, or turns, the top one will make in the 15-second allotted time.

Why: The planets, like Mercury and Venus, that are closest to the sun have to travel faster than those that are at a distance. If these planets did not orbit fast enough, they would be pulled into the sun by its powerful gravitational force.

The twirler with many weights represents the greater gravitational force of the sun on its nearby planets (such as Mercury) and therefore such bodies need to make more revolutions. However, the sun's gravitational pull on the more distant planets—Uranus, Neptune and Pluto—is much less than on the planets closer to it—Mercury and Venus.

The twirler with one weight (again, the weight represents the gravitational pull of the sun) is like Pluto, with fewer revolutions, or turns, around the sun and, therefore, a smaller number of spins around the spool.

326

The Big Three:
Mercury, Jupiter, Neptune

What to do: Cut three circles from the cardboard, one 10 inches (25.5 cm) across, the other 12 inches (30.5 cm), the third 14 inches (35.5 cm). Next, cut a slit from the outside edge of the circles to the center or middle. Form the circles into cones and tape the outside slits together. Make certain you shape each cone so the angle or height of the walls are the same. (The trick to doing this accurately and easily is placing the second and third cones inside the first!) When finished, get ready for the fun!

Orbiter I: Operation Mercury

Take the first 10-inch, orbiter cone and drop the marble into its center. The center will represent the sun; the marble, Mercury; and the cone, Mercury's orbital path around the sun.

While holding the cone in the palm of your hand, gently rotate or whirl it, keeping the marble orbiting as close to the center as possible without it actually dropping into the center.

Once the marble starts moving in a continuous orbit, with smooth, even rotations or circles, use the watch with the second hand, to time its orbits.

To do this, time and record, the number of times the marble makes one full revolution or circle in 15 seconds.

Since Mercury is closest to the sun, our hypothesis, or guess, will state that it will have to move faster around the sun in order to avoid being pulled into it. After you complete the other two experiments, you can chart and compare your results.

327

Orbiter II: Operation Jupiter

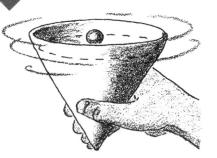

Next, place the marble (Jupiter) into the center hole (the sun) of the 12-inch orbital cone.

Again, repeat the steps as in "Orbiter I," but this time, whirl or rotate the marble so it makes a wider path or orbit, almost touching the cone's edge. The wider cone represents Jupiter's wider orbit or path around the sun.

The Big Three: Countdown!

328

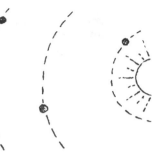

Using what you already know about the orbits of these three planets, write down or chart your experimental orbital speeds and compare them with our real planetary average estimated speeds.

Mercury speeds around the sun at 108,000 mph. It takes Mercury only 88 Earth days to revolve around the sun.

Jupiter has an average speed around the sun of 29,400 mph. It takes Jupiter practically 12 Earth years to move around the sun.

Neptune's average orbital speed around the sun is 12,200 mph. It takes Neptune over 160 Earth years to travel around the sun.

Is there a connection between your experimental orbital speeds, the distances of orbits from the sun, and the actual estimated speeds of the planets?

To be certain there are no other variables, or things that can change the results, make certain the cones are all evenly smooth circles, and securely taped. For best test results, do at least three or four such trials and compare them to the actual estimates.

Orbiter III: Operation Neptune

329

Now that you've done the first two experiments, try the third. Yes, you've guessed it! Neptune has a much wider orbit around the sun than the other planets. Use the larger, wider, 14-inch cone for this one. Repeat the steps, but now whirling the marble in a much wider orbit.

I Get Around

A marble's in a bottle The bottle is turned upside down. The marble stays inside! How? A full-of-surprises trick that will have your friends standing on their heads.

What to do: Drop the marble in the bottle and ask your friends if they can turn the bottle upside down without having the marble drop out. And no, they can't simply hold the marble inside!

Impossible, they say. Now it's your turn. Holding the bottle upright, with your hand underneath, move the bottle to start the marble whirling in a circular orbit within it. While continuing to swirl the bottle and the marble within, gradually move the bottle to a horizontal and then to an upside-down position.

What happens: The revolving whirling marble doesn't fall out of the bottle, even when the bottle is turned upside down.

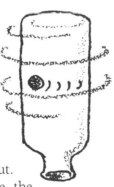

Why: When your friends simply turned the bottle, not whirling it, the Earth's gravity pulled the marble down and out. However, by whirling the bottle, the marble was pulled up away from the neck to the side of the bottle by centrifugal force.

Slam Dunk

Gravity is a lot like a slam dunk, pushing a basketball forcefully down through a hoop. But gravity's force pushes everything down. In order to fly, an airplane's lift, must be greater than the downward pull of gravity. This experiment shows that gravity is a persistent force; the results are the same, even if you try to change them.

What to do: Place the book on the table so one end hangs off the end. Place a ruler about an inch (2 cm) away from the book, with an end hanging over it. Place one coin on the end of the extended part of the ruler; the other at the top of the end of the book in the space next to the ruler. Now, use the other ruler to forcefully strike the end of the extended, overhanging ruler so that both coins are pushed to the ground.

Will forcefully pushing the ruler to the side to hit one of the coins greatly affect its fall? Which coin will hit the floor first?

What happens: Both coins hit the floor at the same time.

Why: The force of gravity is always the same. In our experiment, a forceful side hit to the coin by the ruler was greater than the force that caused the coin to drop off its extended end. However, even this effect was not enough to alter or change the rate of fall.

Gumdrop

Will a large eraser hit the floor before a small paper clip? What about a flat sheet of paper or aluminum foil? Does size, shape, and weight affect the rate of fall, or how fast an object falls to Earth? Try these experiments and erase all doubt!

What to do: With an aluminum foil sheet laying on one hand, and a paper sheet on the other, extend your arms. Drop both sheets at the same time and observe what happens.

Now repeat the experiment, but replace one sheet with an eraser. Follow this by dropping the paper clip and a sheet. Lastly, drop the eraser and paper clip at the same time.

What happens: The paper and the foil, in general, float down to the floor at the same rate, while the eraser and the paper clip hit the floor before either the foil or the paper sheet. Finally, both the eraser and paper clip hit the floor at the same time.

Why: The size and the weight of the clip and eraser do not affect the rate of fall. This is because most of their mass is inside. The amount of metal and eraser forming their surface areas are small, so drag from air resistance is reduced. Gravity pulls on both objects with the same equal force, ounce for ounce.

However, the flat sheets of paper and foil, with their masses spread out over a wider surface area, met much more air resistance. It was this greater drag that affected their rate of fall.

Balance Beam & Airheads

Here you'll stretch one experiment into two. First you'll find the center of gravity in "Balance Beam" and then the "Airheads" will show you their stuff.

Balance Beam

What to do: Loosely tie one end of a long piece of string to something high up and let the string hang down. Tie the dowel to the other end of it.

Yes! That's right! All you have to do for this experiment is simply adjust the dowel on the string so it is perfectly balanced. In other words, find the dowel's center of gravity, the point on the dowel where its weight, or mass, is centered. At this point, the dowel will be balanced on the string, and hang there horizontally. You'll find the dowel's center of gravity somewhere in the middle of it.

Airheads

What to do: Cut four more 15-inch (40 cm) strings. Tie and space two on one side of the dowel, and two on the other.

Inflate the four balloons equally. Knot the necks or tie the openings tightly with string, then tie each balloon onto one of the four separate strings on the dowel. The balloons should be equally spaced and the dowel's center of gravity balanced.

With the safety pin, pop one of the balloons. Adjust the dowel's center of gravity. Pop a second balloon. Now, with only two balloons remaining, readjust the balance and pop one of the last remaining balloons.

What happened: When you popped one of the two remaining balloons, the dowel, and the one remaining balloon, dropped and fell to one side.

This proves you should never take air lightly. It has weight and it is heavy—it's definitely a weighty subject!

Flypaper

A long time ago, someone took a sheet of paper, folded it, aimed it, and threw it. It became the first flying paper, or glider.

Here's your chance to build an assortment of gliders and, in the interest of science, your teacher or parents can't really complain. You'll find out which materials are best to use, what designs fly best and which attachments or parts make a difference to flight.

Now, get ready to build gliders with different designs, parts, and with ailerons or flaps—and prepare to soar.

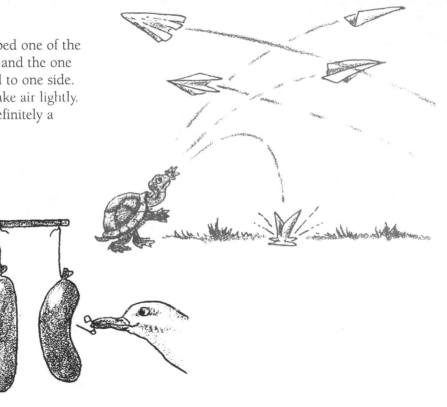

334 Flight: Up in the Air?

YOU WILL NEED:
sheet of paper
measuring tape or stick

Still confused about the ups and downs of flight? No problem. You'll start out working with a basic glider and add or take away "extras," the variables, that make your plane fly great, good, well. Well, maybe not so well!—but you'll be air-minded in no time.

What to do: Fold the paper in half lengthwise and crease. Open the fold, and fold the two corners at one end in toward the center line. Crease at the fold.

Now, bring each of the two folded edges of the triangle to the center line. Align the folds against the center line, and crease the new folds.

Finally, turning the glider, align one fold against the center line and crease. Then do the same on the opposite side. Hold the glider up and position the wings outward. If done correctly, the nose tip of the glider should point slightly downward.

You're now ready to test your craft. It should be thrown each time by the same person and in the same way. After each throw, the distance traveled should be carefully measured and noted.

What happens: With each throw, your glider should soar, circle, swoop or descend swiftly, traveling a good distance.

Why: Your glider is an excellent example of an airfoil. If you examine the wings, you'll notice they curve slightly on the top and are flat on the bottom. The air passing over the top of the wing is forced to travel faster, due to the raised shape, and the faster air becomes thinner than the air passing under the wing.

Because the air underneath is denser, or thicker, because it is traveling more slowly, the denser air pushes the plane upward, into the thinner air. It is this process, or law of nature on air movement, that keeps your glider soaring aloft, or in flight.

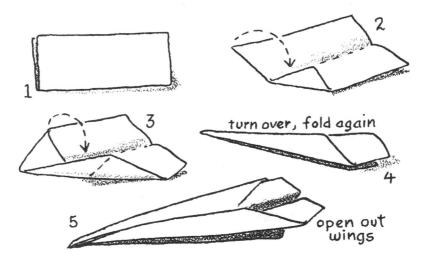

turn over, fold again

open out wings

335 Clipped Wings

Flaps or clips, which do you prefer? Maybe both? Try flight experiments with paper clips placed in different places on the planes to stabilize them, make them fly steadier and straighter.

Fly each separate design against your basic, no-frills model. In each case, test distance traveled and smoothness of flight. For example, test the basic plane against one that has a clip on the end of each wing, then test another design, and so on. This example of experimentation, comparing a basic model against one that has been altered or changed in one way, is called controlled.

You can also try taping the wings of one model together, cutting adjustable flaps in each wing-ending of another, or attaching a rudder or tail to a third.

There are countless combinations or possibilities—try them all or just a few. After you have thoroughly experimented with your altered or changed models and compared them with the basic glider, form a hypothesis, or guess, on why some models fly better than others.   Can you now test out your hypothesis? With each test, keep accurate and careful records: distances traveled, smoothness of flight, less than successful landings. Remember, you can learn more from mistakes and failures than from smooth sailing. Every obstacle provides an opportunity to learn. By making and flying gliders, you can learn a lot about flight.

Kite Tales

A legend tells that once upon a time in the land of Woo, a Chinese province, a man named Sun-Wing was very lonely. Waion, the god of the wind, was very lonely too.

To please Waion, Sun-Wing tied and placed two thin birch sticks across very thin paper and attached it to cord. Sun-Wing let Waion catch his paper windbird and lift it on high. Suddenly, both Sun Wing and Waion realized they were no longer lonely. On Waion's command, the paper wind bird danced, glided, swooped and dived.

You, too, can make your own paper windbird and, under Waion's command, maybe it, too, will dance, glide, swoop and dive.

336 Our Fantastic Mini-Box Kite

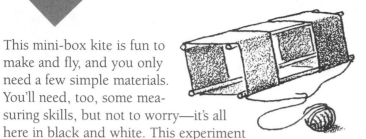

HOT!

YOU WILL NEED:
sheet of paper
scissors
hole punch or nail
ruler
tape
string

This mini-box kite is fun to make and fly, and you only need a few simple materials. You'll need, too, some measuring skills, but not to worry—it's all here in black and white. This experiment won't leave you up in the air—but the kite will.

What to do: On the paper, measure and draw a 6½-by-8-inch (17-by-20 cm) rectangle. Cut the rectangle out, then fold it in half, and crease. Next, open it and fold in each end of the sheet to the center line and crease again. Open and you have the makings of an open-ended box shape with sides measuring 2 inches (5 cm).

Now, you need to make four fairly equal rectangular "windows" in each of the four box sides. To do this, flatten the sheet, lay a ruler against the inner side of each crease and draw lines across, to help guide you. Now, ³⁄₈ inch (1 cm) in from each guide line and ½ inch (2 cm) in from each edge of the paper, draw the 1½-by-5 inch (3-by-13 cm) windows in each side. Lay the ruler across the windows to check that they align and are centered, then cut them out.

A real, old-time box kite looks more like the one shown in the illustration. Using straws and long strips of light paper, why not try making a small model and see if it flies. Then, you can try toothpicks and smaller strips of tissue paper for an even smaller version! Where will it all end?

Build a Simple Kite!
It's a Breeze!

HOT!

YOU WILL NEED:

dowel or stick, ¹/₂ inch (0.5 cm) by 30 inches (75 cm)

dowel or stick, ¹/₂ inch (0.5 cm) by 28 inches (70 cm)

tool for cutting and notching dowels

a large work area

newspapers

tissue paper

scissors

string

tape

glue

pencil

tape measure

an adult helper

Get the family together for some high-flying fun! Kitemaking is an "exact" science and an art involving designing work, stringing, framing, and bridle, so it's nice to have adult help.

You can learn a lot about the principles of aerodynamics when you build and fly one of the earliest and oldest flying toys and machines, the ever-fantastic kite!

What to do: Ask an adult to cut small grooves or notches on the ends of each wooden dowel or stick. String will be run through these slits to make the frame, so the notches need to be deep enough to hold it.

Find the middle of your 28-inch (70 cm) cross stick—14 inches (35 cm) in from the ends. Mark it.

Next, mark a place on the upright main, or mast, stick, 8 inches (20 cm) from one end. Placed toward the top, this is the point where the two sticks will meet to form a cross. Using a figure-8 wrap, tie the two sticks together carefully with string until they are fastened.

Work a long piece of string into the end notches of each dowel as you form the frame of the kite. Pull the string slightly to tighten it around the frame, then tie it off.

You will probably need two sheets of tissue paper to form the skin, or sail, of the kite. If so, lay one tissue paper sheet over the other, leaving a 1-inch (2.5 cm) margin overlap. Carefully tape the sheets along the seam, both front and back.

Lay the kite frame on the tissue paper. Leave an edging of at least 2 inches (5 cm) of paper to fold and glue down. Cut around the frame as shown.

When finished, glue the overlap or end flaps (a glue stick works well) down over the string frame. Keep your scissors handy. It's important to trim away extra paper so that the end sticks are free and clear. Also, pull the tissue slightly so that it is taut on the frame, but be careful not to rip the paper.

What happens: If all the variables are right (kite construction, bridle, tail, wind direction and speed), your kite should be lifted up high into the air and stay there, dancing against the sky.

Why: The action of air lifting a kite is similar that on an airfoil or an airplane wing. The air flowing over it has a longer way to go and has less force than the air against its near surface. As a result, the air pressure exerts a greater force on the front of the kite than on its back and the kite is pulled up, up, and away!

The string you pull toward you, on the other hand, holds and steadies the kite, balancing it in the air

338 Hightail It to the Bridle Party

Let this be a family project—a bridle party and a kite launching. Your tail and bridle, the string harness attached to the main or flying string on your kite, needs to be made and attached carefully—and with your aerodynamic mind, you should be highly successful.

To make a bridle, or kite harness, attach a long string to the ends of the upright stick. The string should be slack, or loose, enough so it pulls out.

Next, attach a shorter string to the ends of the dowel that make up the cross stick and make them meet a little below it. Adjust the bridle

strings so they are equal and tight, and tie the flying string to where the bridle strings meet.

At this point, it's important to test your kite to see if it "catches the wind" properly—if not, it will not fly at all or will fly incorrectly. With the bridle and flying string attached, stand in the wind and pull the kite toward you. If the top of the kite pulls upwards and the kite tilts and seems to be gathering in the wind, your bridle is correctly attached. If this is not the case, adjust the cross string to a higher or lower position and try again.

To add a tail (to help balance the kite), cut rectangular pieces of colored tissue (multi-colored or a variety of colored pieces show up best). Space and tie them, using smaller pieces of string, every 7 to 8 inches (18–20 cm) along a 6 to 8 foot (2–3 m) tail string.

Tie the tail to the bottom end of the upright stick and get ready to soar—and have a high-falutin,' high-flyin' time!

EXPLORATION IN OUTER SPACE?
OUT OF THIS WORLD!

From Skylab, the American space station put into orbit in 1973, to the space shuttle *Endeavor* launched in 1993, to recent cooperative efforts in the long-lasting Russian *Mir,* and Pathfinder's invasion of Mars, space exploration has never been more exciting.

In this chapter, you'll do experiments that teach you about the conditions in outer space, watch the reentry of a space capsule, make your own space food, and even design a space station and man it.

And, you'll create conditions and craters on the moon and design logo space patches for imaginative and creative fun. So, get ready to blast-off for an out-of-this-world adventure!

Signs from Space: An Emblematic Concern

Astronauts often wear specially designed emblems, known as patches, on their clothing to indicate their unit and tell, in pictures and words, something about the unit's mission in space. The Gemini and Apollo crew members wore such patches on their sleeves, and future astronauts will certainly wear their own similar emblems proudly.

You can design your own emblem, or badge, simply and easily. First, pick up some heavy posterboard—sold at stationary and variety stores, art supply or drugstores. Use your imagination and brightly colored markers, crayons, or pencils, creative lettering and a variety of space scenes to turn out exciting, creative crew badges.

Create a space scene, circling suns or draw some alien terrain, or ground surface. Will your badge-emblem show a planet with several moons, or a landscape with huge craters, deep surface cracks, or volcanoes? Will you have a rocket on your badge or a futuristic space shuttle or space station? The possibilities are endless and with ideas all around you, you'll have no problem getting started.

Give your pretend outer-space mission a name—remember the Discovery and Columbia missions?—and include your mission name on your badge. Use imaginative lettering for an extra-special effect. Select an interesting shape—square, triangle, circle, oval, or maybe a shield—for each badge. When you finish your emblem, cut out the shape and attach a small safety pin to the backside of each badge, using small precut strips of masking tape. Now, your crew is ready to explore flight and space and to let their imaginations soar.

Reentry Splashdown

YOU WILL NEED:

disposable cup from a fast-food restaurant

eraser

paper towel sheet

tape

string, about 80 inches (200 cm)

hole punch

4 lengths of string, 12 inches (30 cm) each

scissors

Ever wonder how early astronauts used to get back to Earth, before shuttles, after rocketing into space? This simple experiment will show you, with a few simple, easy-to-find materials, how it was done.

What to do: Cut away the top of a disposable cup, leaving only a 2-inch deep bottom portion. With the hole punch, make a hole about _ inch (1 cm) from the top of the cup and tie the long string to the cup.

Next, assemble the parachute and space capsule portion of the experiment. To do this, tape the four 12-inch (30 cm) strings to each corner of the paper towel. Gather the other ends of the strings together and tie them around the eraser. Test your parachute-capsule. Try balling it up in your hand and tossing it into the air a few times. The parachute should open easily and be balanced to float the eraser to the ground.

Now, to demonstrate how an orbiting space-capsule re-enters Earth's atmosphere, take all your experimental props (chute-capsule and beverage cup) outside. You'll need room to whirl your space capsule over your head without worrying about it hitting things or someone nearby.

Place the eraser in the bottom of the cup. Gently pack the paper chute on top of the eraser. Don't stuff it all the way down into the cup. It is easier to do the forced re-entry simulation if it is loosely packed.

Find a clear spot outside and begin whirling your space capsule overhead. Start slowly, and gradually increase the speed. The parachute will stay in place in the cup as long as you continue to whirl it smoothly. Now, slow the whirling motion and purposely jerk the string sharply. You may have to do this several times and in different ways before you get the hang of ejecting the parachute-capsule.

Always remember that scientists often try many different ways of doing something before they find not only an acceptable way, but the best way. If, after several tries, your capsule does not eject or the parachute does not open properly, check the weight of your eraser, how it fits the cup—maybe too tightly?—and readjust and repack the parachute.

What happens: After you slow the whirling motion and jerk on the string, the parachute and capsule eject, or pop out of the cup. The chute opens and floats the capsule easily and gently to the ground.

Why: You have demonstrated how space capsules used to be recovered or brought back from Earth's orbit and make a soft landing. The slowing of the whirling motion and the jerking of the string represented the firing of retrorockets that slowed the capsule's forward motion so that gravity would pull it toward Earth.

The string represents the balance of gravity and centrifugal force that kept space capsules in orbit so they would not fly out into space. The space capsule's orbit was similar to your turning and whirling the string-cup parachute.

To prepare for and deploy your parachute capsule for re-entry, you slowed the whirling motion and jerked the string. This was like firing retrorockets and, once a space capsule reached Earth's atmosphere, the parachute automatically opened to float the capsule to Earth.

The real space capsule landings were made at sea—called "splashdowns!" Today, astronauts travel into space in modern spacecrafts, called shuttles. They are pushed into orbit by orbiter and booster rockets that return to Earth, are recovered and reused. Astronauts now fly their shuttlecraft back to Earth like planes, to be used again and again, unlike space capsules. Some early capsules that were saved and studied after splashdown are on display in space museums.

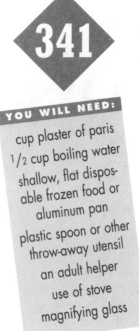

341 Moonscape I: Mark-It Research

YOU WILL NEED:

cup plaster of paris
1/2 cup boiling water
shallow, flat disposable frozen food or aluminum pan
plastic spoon or other throw-away utensil
an adult helper
use of stove
magnifying glass

HOT!

To really see close up, and even touch the moon, make your very own model moonscape. It's easy and you'll find out how some lunar features or surface marks were formed. As a bonus, you can name the craters, mountains, and seas on your moonscape after anyone you want!

What to do: While a parent or adult brings the half-cup of water to a rolling boil on the stove, pour the half cup of plaster of paris over the bottom of the shallow, flat pan.

Then, again with help, pour about half of the hot, boiling water carefully into the pan and stir it briefly to moisten all the plaster. If needed, add more water to dry sections. Don't worry about a few lumps. They're meant for great things!

When the mixture cools slightly, and is partially solid, pour off any excess water. Place the pan where it can be left undisturbed for about an hour to dry.

After the plaster mix has completely dried, take your model moonscape and observe its features, the surface areas, with a magnifying glass. Map out and pencil in names and areas on your model; name the seas, or maria; the rougher, patchy areas; the mountains; lumpy areas; and the craters, those different-sized holes you find. Look at the moonscape in the early morning or late afternoon sunshine, or use a flashlight to see how the different features cast shadows on the moonscape.

What happens: As the plaster of paris hardens, the lumpier areas grow in size to form mountains, holes of various sizes appear in the surface to form craters; and rough, flat surfaces become the seas or plains.

Why: Billions of impact holes or craters cover all of the moon's surface, the mountainous areas as well as the flat sea, or plains, areas known as maria. These "seas" (not bodies of water at all but wide areas of volcanic rock) were formed billions of years ago as the flowing hot lunar surface cooled.

Evidence from the Apollo explorations and moon landings have proven that many lunar features or surface marks were caused by underground forces, as the moon's molten, or hot liquid, center cooled deep beneath the hardened crust.

When our hot plaster mixture cools, like the surface of the moon did long ago, it also forms craters, rough areas, and large lumpy, mountainous, areas. These features are due, again, to the heating and cooling of the surface, the contraction or shortening and the expansion or lengthening of its crust.

342 Moonscape II: A Heavy Hitter!

Go one step further and find out how the size of asteroids and meteorites, speed and distance affect the size and distance of moon craters. Careful, this is messy! Do it outside, wear old clothes, and put newspapers under your experiment pan to make it easy to clean up your mess when you're done.

What to do: Pour the cup of flour, baking soda or sand into the container. Mound it first into a hill in one corner of the tray then level it down, smoothing it off with your hand from that corner to the others. This will represent the surface of the moon.

Next, take the "meteor" and drop it from a height of 4 to 5 inches (10-13 cm) above the filled tray surface. Measure the hole or crater it made in the powdery surface, across from one rim, or outer circle, of the impact, or hit, to the other. Record the distance of the "meteor" fall to the surface in the tray and the diameter of the crater the drop made. If it helps, draw a picture and put in both measurements as labels.

Level or smooth off the surface powder and try again. Double the distance of your last drop. Again, use the yardstick to measure the height of the drop and the ruler to find the diameter of the crater made by the impact. Repeat several times, and gradually increase the height of your drops, smoothing the surface powder before each. Keep good records and illustrations.

According to your notes and measurements, what did you observe between greater-distance drops and closer-distance ones?

Moonscape III: Making a Good Impression

Simulate or copy the conditions on the moon and Earth and then compare each. Unlike the Earth, the moon has little or no erosion or surface breakdown. A crater, footprint or any other impression or mark on the surface could last for millions of years!

What to do: Fill each container with _ cup of soil and 1 cup of sand. Mix each well with a trowel or spoon. Press the imprinting object firmly into each surface. If the print does not come out well, smooth over the surface and try again.

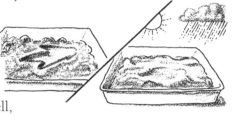

Place one of the trays in an undisturbed location and label it "Earthscape". Also write day one and date. For clearest test results, place the exposed "Earth" sample in an unprotected, open area where wind, rain and other elements can do their work.

Place the other dish labeled "Moonscape" in an additional undisturbed location. Also, place the box lid over the dish and weight it with a heavy object. Better yet, if an outdoor cabinet or shed is available, use it to enclose your "moon sample," with or without the lid.

Again, label the experiment as you did in the "Earthscape" sample. Observe each sample over a 7-to-14-day period and write down what you see.

Why: Since the moon has no atmosphere, there is no wind, water, rain and snow or other atmospheric elements that would cause surface break-down or erosion. This, too, is somewhat like our protected experiment.

When comets, asteroids and meteors hit the lunar surface, there is no weathering force to affect the impact or craters they form.

The Earth's atmospheric conditions, however, produce wind, water, rain and snow. These same conditions, similar to our exposed experiment, cause weathering and erosion or a natural wearing away of rocks and soil.

What happens: The Earthscape experiment tray that was left outside unprotected, soon is broken down, wears away until little or any of the original print or impression is left.

The Moonscape experiment dish covered with the box lid and/or in the closet remains as it was originally. There is little erosion and the impression or print remains clear.

Moving Picture

344

Since the moon revolves or moves around the Earth, how does a space craft going to the moon hit its moving target? Find a couple of friends and try this fun demonstration. It definitely will move you to think.

What to do: Mark off a large circular running area or arrange to use a school track.

Have someone time how long it takes a runner to go around the large outside track once at a constant rate of speed. Record the time. Have a second runner run a smaller circular track within the larger track. Again have someone time this runner and record the results.

Now, start both runners running their tracks at their same rates of speed. When ready, or at your signal, the runner moving on the inner track should gradually and steadily increase the diameter of the running circle in order to join up with the runner on the outer track.

Again, the person with the stop watch should record the time it takes for the inner runner to join the outside runner.

What happens: The inside runner has a hard time trying to join up with the runner on the outer track, and likely has to speed up or slow down to do it.

Why: In order for a spacecraft to intersect the moon, timing is very important. Calculations are made before launch so that fuel is not wasted in slowing down, speeding up, or changing course in flight. The speeds of both the craft and the moon have to be taken into account, and also the speed necessary for the craft to overcome the force of Earth's gravity. Actually, to "catch" the moon, the spacecraft must be directed ahead of it, where the moon will be. Now have your runners try joining up again and see if they can better their time.

Plan-It Plus

345

Now that you've mastered the compass and distances of inner planets and sizes, why not do a large diagram of all the planets. You'll need a large white poster board and some information on the outer planets.

With the information provided below, you can mathematically calculate or figure out the scaled distances of orbits and the sizes of the outer planets.

Jupiter	over 483 million	about 90,000
Saturn	over 886 million	about 71,000
Uranus	1.783 billion	30,000
Neptune	2.790 billion	over 27,000
Pluto	3.670 billion	over 3,000

346 Plan-It!

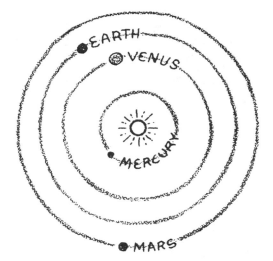

Plan a diagram or chart of the inner planets, showing their orbits and sizes. It's simple and easy and these instructions show you how.

Find a cleared desk or table for a workspace. First, you'll need an inexpensive pencil compass for making circles. For additional accuracy, an inexpensive circle stencil or template, showing the diameter of circles, can be bought at the same store. However, if you insist on drawing freehand, that's okay too!

Finally, you'll need a standard sheet of paper. For a bonus effect, you can use colored markers, pencils, crayons or colored construction paper.

Our sun is about 865 million miles in diameter (almost 1.4 million km across). One hundred Earths could fit inside the sun.

Draw a circle in the middle of your paper about the size of a quarter. If using a stencil, a 5/16-inch circle will do. If you wish, you can decorate your sun with flame-like spokes to represent the sun's outer area or corona.

Next, set your compass to the 1/2 inch (2 cm) mark and place its point in the middle of the sun. Carefully move the paper or the pencil around so the compass pencil-point marks the paper.

Helpful hint: Holding the center pointer down as you move the pencil around will help prevent skipping or moving. This circle represents Mercury's orbit around the sun.

Place a small pea-size circle on this path or 3/16 inch on the stencil to represent Mercury. Actually, next to our sun, Mercury is merely a grain of sand. Mercury is only about 3,030 miles wide and is 36 million miles or (58 million km) away from the sun.

Position your compass on 1_ inch (4 cm) for Venus's orbit and follow the same marking procedure as you did with Mercury's orbit. Venus's path around the sun is over 67 million miles (about 108 million km) from the sun. Nearly Earth size, it is about 7,500 miles across (about 12,000 km). Draw a circle on the orbit about the size of a large pea or 1/2 inch (0.8 cm) circle on the stencil.

Our planet Earth comes next. Set your compass to the 2-inch (5 cm) mark and follow the marking procedure for the other orbits. Since Venus and Earth are close to the same size, use the same circle for Earth as you did for Venus. Our Earth is just under 8,000 miles in diameter (7,927 actually, or about 12,757 km). It is about 93 million miles from the sun, or about 150 million km.

The last inner planet is Mars. According to its orbits, it's at least 50 million miles away from Earth; 142 million miles away from the sun and over 4,000 miles wide (over 6,700 km). Use a 6.5 cm setting on your compass for an orbit and a slightly smaller size than Earth or Venus for diameter or width of this planet. For continuation with the outer planets, see "Plan-It Plus."

347 Shuttle Wrap-Up: A Closed Case!

How do space shuttles withstand the extreme cold and heat of outer space? Do this heated experiment and find out. It's cool!

What to do: Layer the three types of paper, with the foil in the middle, the paper bag on the inside and the paper toweling on the outside.

Fill both cans with hot tap water. With your' assistant's help, form two clay balls (about the size of a quarter) and press one against the hole in each can. The clay ball should be pressed against the hole and not into it.

Work quickly as you wrap the paper layers around one of the cans and secure it with rubber bands. The other can should remain as it is, without a wrapper

Four hands are faster than two and this experiment must be done quickly before water cools and thermometer temperatures change.

Patiently wait 30 to 40 minutes for the water to cool. Record the time. Again, you must work quickly to get accurate results. First, make certain both thermometers register the same temperature. If not, run them under warm or cool water to get similar readings.

While leaving the wrapper on the can, quickly pour its contents, the water, into one of the jars. Do the same with the other can into the other jar. Place the cans behind each jar so as not to confuse the sample test waters. Place a thermometer in each jar and let it stand for 2 to 3 minutes. Do not remove the thermometers from the jars when recording temperatures. Rather, press each to the side of the clear surface as you write down each number.

What happens: The can with the wrapper showed a 3 to 5° recorded temperature difference. In other words, the water in the wrapped can was 3 to 5° warmer than the can that was unwrapped.

Why: There are extreme areas of heat and cold in outer space, so space craft must be protected by wrapped blankets of insulating materials. These materials can be used to prevent or stop the loss of heat or even to cool.

Scientifically speaking, molecules vibrate more quickly in warm parts of a material and transfer heat energy to their slower moving cousins in colder parts. This process is called conduction. Knowing about this process, space scientists use materials to absorb heat or to reflect it. In general, metals conduct or carry heat best, while wood, paper, plastic, water and air are poor conductors.

348 Thermal Underwear: A Heated Problem

In places where it's very cold, people often wear thermal underwear. These long coveralls, worn under regular clothes, are designed with air pockets to keep body heat in.

In "Shuttle Wrap-Up: A Closed Case!" we put a type of thermal wrap on a can, best described as thermal outer wear. Try doing the same experiment, but substitute different layers of wrapping and rearrange them in different ways. Does what is inside or outside the other layer make much difference in final results or do the results remain the same?

Also, create some new experiments with thermal outer wear. Try using different containers with different coverings and thicknesses to scientifically "wrap-up" your final results.

349 Travel Agent

How well does heat travel through metal, plastic or wood? The right answer, important to space exploration, will keep you out of hot water.

What to do: Heat water on a stove or microwave a cup of water on high for one minute. (Get adult help, as very hot water can cause a bad burn.) Put all three objects in the cup with ends separated and upright, like wheel spokes.

After five minutes, touch the middle of each object, where they meet the lip of the cup. Also, remove each object and feel the ends that were covered with the hot water. Of the three, which feels the warmer?

HOT!

What happens:
Parts of the metal object feel warmer than that of the wooden or plastic object.

YOU WILL NEED:
fork, nail or metal object
cup of very hot water
pencil, stick or wooden object
plastic spoon, drinking straw
an adult helper

Why: Metals are better conductors of heat than plastic or wood. Electrons are looser in metals and can carry heat better. This explains why the metal object in our experiment felt warmer than the plastic or wood.

Now, you can see how this information would be helpful and very important to space scientists for insulating or protecting spacecraft and astronauts for the extreme temperatures of outer space.

350 Space Food: Can't Keep It Down!

Want to pretend you're an astronaut, and eat space-style? Enjoy this easy and fun experiment.

What to do: Pour the drink mix into the freezer bag. Fill it one-third full with milk. Seal the bag securely and shake thoroughly. Open one small corner of the bag and insert the straw. Sip your astromeal!

What happens: The food-in-a-bag demonstrates how food is eaten in space—sucked through a straw.

Why: Astronauts need to keep their foods contained in outer space. Without closed pouches, liquids and other loose foods would simply separate, and float away—all around the cabin! Messy, huh?

Space foods are dehydrated (dried), like our powdered breakfast drink, and rehydrated (water added) in outer space.

What next: Look for other dried foods found here on Earth and rehydrate them by adding water or milk. Also, experiment with ice cream, and other juices and foods that you can serve and eat spacestyle using plastic bag containers. It's a neat and fun way to eat—without all the mess.

351 Man Your Station

Make a simple space station and then man it, or place a crew member or members on its deck, whirl it, and learn what centrifugal force can really do.

What to do: Cut a rectangular opening in the narrow side of the box, leaving an inch of cardboard at either end. Have someone poke a hole on each side of the box, thread the string through both ends, and tie each side off. You now should have a string handle and a rectangular opening in the box.

With tape, attach a pair of cardboard rolls to each side. You should have what looks like an opened box with a pair of doubled-tube wings.

Lastly, place one object, followed by two to four, inside the box, or module, of your space station. While holding the string, rock the model slowly, then make several full circle swings. Start the string whirling slowly, gradually increase the speed, and then, very slowly, come to a stop.

What happens: With a slow, rocking swing, the objects move and rattle around in the box. With a faster, full, over-the-head whirl, the objects stay in place and do not move, while a slower, coming-to-a-stop type swing starts the objects moving and eventually they fly from the box.

Why: The overall force that kept the objects in your make-believe space station module from flying out, was called 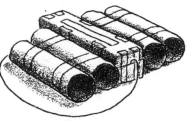 centrifugal force. When you rapidly whirled the station above your head, you pulled the objects inside the box toward you (centripetal force, see "Spooling Around") and the objects, in turn, pulled outward or away from you.

352 ◆ So You want to be an Astronaut

The future is waiting for you. If your goal is to be a part of it, out there, now is a good time to start thinking of how to turn your dream of going into space into reality. Here, from the agencies involved in space work and exploration, is information on how you can take your place as an astronaut.

353 ◆ Designer Craft

To design a more authentic, realistic space station, bring out marker pens, scissors, cardboard, toilet paper and towel rolls, tape, string and lots of imagination. The illustration on this page will help you.

For starters, use a paper towel roll for the different parts, or modules, of your craft. Since the roll is similar to the cylinder shape of a real station, this will add realism.

Also, cut out two or three rectangular pieces from the ends or middle of the tube. You might need an adult to help with this task. This will make the modules look authentic, or real. You may wish it to hold objects and put it into orbit as you did in "Man Your Station."

Draw circular and side lines to show the different modular parts. Add rectangular cardboard pieces to your model to show the many solar panels that are attached to such crafts.

Lastly, if you wish, attach string and astronauts, and put your craft into orbit as you did in "Man Your Station." Have fun!

Astronaut Selection and Training

In the future, the United States, with its international partners Japan, Canada, and the European Space Agency, will operate a manned Space Station. From that orbiting depot, explorers will continue on their journeys to the moon and Mars. As these plans come closer to reality, the need for qualified space-flight professionals will increase.

To fill the upcoming need, NASA accepts applications for the Astronaut Candidate Program on a continuous basis. Candidates are selected as needed, normally every two years, for pilot and mission-specialist categories. Both civilian and military personnel are considered for the program. Civilians may apply at any time. Military personnel must apply through their parent service and be nominated by their branch of service to transfer to NASA.

The astronaut candidate selection process was developed to select highly qualified individuals for human space programs. For mission specialists and pilot-astronaut candidates, there are several education and experience requirements: at least a bachelor's degree from an accredited institution in engineering, biological science, physical science, or mathematics. Three years of related, progressively responsible professional experience must follow the degree. An advanced degree is desirable and may be substituted for all or part of the experience requirement (i.e., master's degree = 1 year of work experience, doctoral degree = three years of experience)....

Applicants who meet the basic qualifications are evaluated by discipline panels during a week-long process of personal interviews, thorough medical evaluations, and orientation.

Selected applicants are designated astronaut candidates and are assigned to the astronaut office at Johnson Space Center for a one-year training-and-evaluation period. During this time, candidates take part in the astronaut training program designed to develop the knowledge and skills required for formal mission training upon selection for a flight and are assigned technical or scientific responsibilities. However, selection as a candidate does not ensure selection as an astronaut.

Final selection is based on satisfactory completion of the one-year program. Civilian candidates who successfully complete the training and evaluation and are selected as astronauts are expected to remain with NASA for at least five years.

Portions reprinted courtesy of the National Aeronautics and Space Administration and the Lyndon B. Johnson Space Center, Houston, Texas

Rocketry: The Three R's (Ready! Reaction! Replay!)

The many mini-experiments in this chapter are based on a balloon-straw-string rocket. You may have seen balloon-string rockets in experiment books before, but not the way they're presented here. This experiment absolutely shot the works, with balloons, weights, balances, and counterbalances to explain the concepts or ideas of thrust, acceleration, deceleration, and booster and retro rockets.

You'll be doing experiments with rockets, space shuttles, and retrorockets in mind. This even adds a jet-propelled toy car for fast thinkers, and you won't need expensive or dangerous propellants or fuels—it's all 100% balloon power.

So, power up! You'll need lots of balloons, both large round and oblong ones, and perhaps a helper, but you'll soon be bursting with fun and ideas. And all the experiments are fuel-proof!

354 Rocket Scientists Don't Fuel Around

YOU WILL NEED:
aluminum foil (enough to make a tightly packed 5-inch rocket)
coffee filter
3 teaspoons baking soda
3 rubber bands
1-pint (500 ml) plastic beverage bottle filled with vinegar (5% or more acidity)
a helper

Space scientists are very serious when it comes to getting a spacecraft off the ground. Fuel is a very important part of any space launch and this fuel-proof experiment will have you sputtering, hissing and roaring with excitement. An assistant is recommended

What to do: Place 3 teaspoons of baking soda on the coffee filter and spread out evenly into a long column. Fold over evenly to form a long tube package and secure with rubber bands. This will represent your fuel package. Pack the aluminum foil into a 5-inch (13 cm) rocket, making certain the bottom end fits snugly but not too tightly into the bottle. It should be still loose enough to move up and down. Take your bottle of vinegar, fuel package and rocket outside to a location that can be easily washed down.

The next steps must be done carefully and quickly. Make certain the long fuel tube is not broken or leaking and can be easily inserted into the bottle.

Next, drop the fuel package into the bottle, quickly followed by the rocket. When the chemical reaction occurs, poke the rocket down into the bottle and watch what happens.

Continue to poke the rocket down into the bottle until the reaction stops.

What happens: The vinegar and baking soda chemically combine to produce CO_2 gas. The gas in turn, overflows from the bottle, hisses, steams and slightly moves the rocket.

Why: Your model rocket on its launch pad (bottle) simulates or copies a real rocket or spacecraft launched into outer space. In a real craft, two liquid fuels are combined and explode, causing pressure and giving the craft its lift or thrust. The chemical reaction, hissing, steam and overflow and slight lift when the model rocket is pushed back into the bottle copies the built-up pressure, exhaust and lift of the real thing.

Designing a Rocket

How about being creative and designing special features on your 5-inch (13 cm) aluminum rocket? And, since the rocket is waterproof, you can use it over and over. Better yet, why not try modeling extra rockets of different designs and sizes for future launches?

With a little imagination, waterproof permanent markers, extra aluminum foil, straws and other waterproof household materials, you can do much to change the design and shape of your rockets.

Try forming strips of foil in separate bands around the width of your missile to show the different parts or stages of the rocket. Also, reshape the nose of your model or construct tail fins. You might even add booster or end rockets (straws work best) to make your craft look more realistic.

Lastly, use permanent markers to draw U.S.A. or other logos or signs on your project. Have fun!

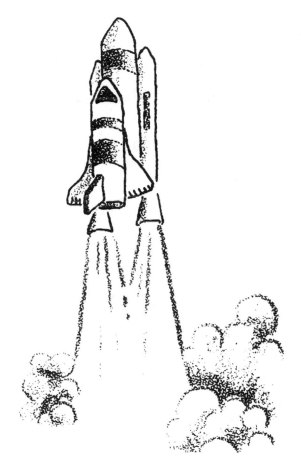

Shuttled About

YOU WILL NEED:

outdoor location

thread

a helper

tape

drinking straw

paper clip

large, long balloon

scissors

large foam cup

stopwatch or watch
with second hand

paper

pencil

clip, clothespin, or
pushpin

Watch the space capsule fall off your model rocket as it reaches its target. Although modern spacecraft use a space shuttle system with a plane-like orbiter, your simple rocket will demonstrate how one part of a spacecraft can be launched into outer space with the help of another.

What to do: Tie 4 to 5 yards (or meters) of thread lengthwise from one chair or object to another as a free, or removable, line. On the end of the free or removable line, thread the straw (see "Line Item"). An assistant is recommended for the following steps:

Blow up the balloon, twist the end and clip it. With a very long piece of tape, fasten the balloon to the underside of the straw, making certain the hole faces the chair. Next, loosely fit the cup over the nose or the front of the balloon. This will represent earlier space capsules which were fitted onto the end of rockets.

You now are ready to launch your rocket. Remove the paper clip from the balloon while holding the end of it closed. When ready, release the balloon and time how long it takes your rocket to leave its launch pad and reach its target.

What happens: When released, the balloon races along the string and reaches its target while the cup or capsule falls off.

Why: Your balloon rocket demonstrates the law of Sir Isaac Newton: for every action there is an equal and opposite reaction. Your rocket shows how the principles of jet propulsion work. The backward push of the air escaping from the balloon, propels or pushes the balloon forward.

357 Line Item

The clip, clothespin, or push-pin is used to attach or pin one end of the rocket-balloon thread line from one object to another, such as a chair. One end of the line can be permanently tied to an object but the other should be free. This is done so balloon rockets (slipped on a thread line through a straw attached to a balloon) can be changed or altered when needed. Since there are many mini-experiments with these balloon rockets, this free line should be helpful.

To easily get the thread through the straw, tie one end of it around the head of a straight pin and drop it through the straw. Leave the pin on the thread to act as a plumb or weighted line. The pin can be draped over a push pin or attached by a clip to another object.

358 Booster Shot

Now that you've got the bang of it, why not try a booster shot! You'll keep the same set-up and do the same experiment as in "Shuttled About," but now you'll add an extra balloon or booster rocket. Will it make any difference in the rate of speed and time your rocket reaches its target? Be a big shot and find out!

What to do: As you did in "Shuttled About," again blow up the original balloon taped to the underside of the straw. (If the balloon is now too stretched out or doesn't work well, replace it with a new one.) Twist the end and clip it.

Now add a new long balloon to the side of the original balloon. Again, tape, twist and clip the end of the balloon.

With your assistant's help, and the clock ready, unclip and release both balloons at the same time. Time how long it takes for your booster rocket to reach its target. Is there a big difference between the booster's time and the one in "Shuttled About?"

YOU WILL NEED:

outdoor location
thread
a helper
tape
drinking straw
paper clip
2 large, long balloons
scissors
large foam cup
stopwatch or watch with second hand
paper
pencil
clip, clothespin, or pushpin

What happens: Your balloon rocket with its booster rocket, races along the string with more force than your original rocket.

Why: With two rockets, the jet propulsion rate is doubled and thus the rate of travel is faster.

Completely Exhausted

You'll love this effect for your balloon rocket. It simulates, or copies, the real thrust and propulsion of the jet rocket engine. It also gives you an idea how the stages of a rocket work. Now as a surprise bonus, there's a bit of fake smoke for realism! The materials are easy to find and it's absolutely guaranteed not to leave you exhausted.

What to do: Do this experiment as you did the others. However, before you blow up the balloon and attach it to the straw, place the funnel inside the opening of the uninflated balloon and fill it with about 1 teaspoon of flour. Use the spoon to

stir the flour around in the funnel and into the balloon. Inflate the balloon, shake it so the flour reaches the opening, attach it to the straw, tie it off with the clip and get ready to shoot the works.

What happens: If done correctly, the balloon rocket races along the string, leaving a trail of smoke behind it.

Four Going Retro

Now, using the same thread line and materials used in "Shuttled About," try doing these next four mini-experiments on retrorockets, those small secondary or additional rockets that produce a thrust opposite to that of the main rocket. Retrorockets are often used to slow down a spacecraft's reentry or to "soft land." You can also try

extending your thread line, buy larger balloons, or increase the number of balloons for added thrust.

Get your whole family, or at least a friend, involved in these experiments. You'll need the help of an assistant anyway! Now get moving and have a blast!

361 Retrorocket I: Watch the Tube!

With cardboard tubes, this rocket looks and acts like a real one, with retrorockets.

What to do: With tape, attach the two cardboard tubes from the top sides of an inflated balloon and attach it to the straw.

Hint: It's easier to tape from the inside of the tube out. Release the balloon from one end of the line and observe what happens.

What happens: The balloon pushes or shoots down the line, but with less force, and does not reach the end of it.

Why: The rolls, like retrorockets, act as a counter-force, a force or action acting against the main thrust of the rocket balloon. This, in turn, slows down the main thrust of the rocket balloon and makes it unable to reach its target.

Retrorocket II: A Perfect Roll Model 362

Now try the same experiment, but with a difference!

What to do: Inflate the balloon and, with tape, securely fasten the cardboard tube to the bottom of it and then to the straw.

Next, roll and tape the newspapers into a tight cylinder and place them into the attached balloon roll. Release the balloon from one end of the line and observe what happens.

What happens: The rocket moves only to the middle of the thread line, and then stops.

Why: The retrorocket-like tube-cylinder, due to its weight, acted as a greater counter or opposite force, and it slowed down more than its tubed cousin.

Retrorocket III: Bully for You!

YOU WILL NEED:

line hook-up with
2 straws

scissors

3 oblong balloons

tape

3 paper clips

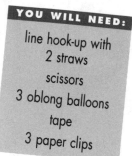

The balloon rocket in this experiment is a regular bully, but it shows you, forcefully, the opposite thrust of a retrorocket.

What to do: Thread two straws at the beginning of the removable end of the free thread line.

Next, inflate three oblong balloons; two fully inflated, the other, half inflated. With tape, attach the two fully inflated balloons together on one of the straws—twist and clip the end of each balloon. Do the same with the half inflated balloon on the other straw.

Important: The balloons should be facing each other, with back openings facing the ends of each line.

Hold your balloons about a quarter of the distance away from the end line while your assistant does the same with the half inflated balloon.

At an announced signal, release the balloons and watch the action carefully.

What happens: The two-balloon rocket pushes the half-inflated balloon to the other side of the line.

Why: The two-balloon rocket represents a forceful retrorocket, slowing and forcefully pushing the small rocket (representing the main rocket) back to its end line.

Retrorocket IV: You're Canceled!

YOU WILL NEED:
line hookup with
2 straws
2 oblong balloons
2 paper clips
tape

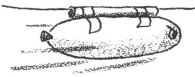

What will happen if two fully inflated balloons, moving in the same direction, meet?

What to do: Repeat the steps in "Retrorocket III: Bully for You" but replace these balloons with two fully inflated balloons facing each other with openings behind and facing the end lines.

What happens: The two balloons shoot to the middle of the line and stop.

Why: The thrust or push from each balloon was the same and, when they met, pushed against each other, stopping or canceling one another out.

Forgoing Retro

A toy car moving in one direction can be redirected into an opposite direction. How? Not rocketry, but a reverse trick using counter forces.

What to do: Fold the strip of cardboard in thirds lengthwise to make a walled track. Push it up against a wall. Then blow up the balloon and knot or twist it closed. Clip or tape the balloon to the lower wall and floor, or to the track so it becomes a barrier at the end of the it.

Hold the long tube at a downward angle, adjusting it as needed at the track opening opposite the balloon, and drop the car into it.

YOU WILL NEED:
toy minicar
long cardboard tube
strip of cardboard, 6-inches (15-cm) wide
paper clip
round balloon
the floor near a wall
tape

What happens: The car slides down the tube and onto the track. When it hits the balloon, the car is pushed backwards on the track. It's not a retrorocket, but another way a forward-moving object can be sent in another or opposite direction.

GLOSSARY

The following terms appear in the section containing experiments with food:

acids—a large class of compounds that are capable of neutralizing alkalis and which range from benign sour-tasting citric acids, like lemons, limes and oranges, to hazardous, poisonous sulfuric and hydrochloric acid.

alkalis—also known as bases—any of numerous bitter-tasting, soapy-feeling substances that dissolve in water and neutralize acids to form salts. These include carbonates, like sodium bicarbonate (baking soda) and sodium carbonate (washing soda), and caustic hydroxides like lye, limewater and ammonia, useful commercially and in the home.

amino acids—the building blocks of proteins. The body manufactures all but nine amino acids. These must be obtained from the food we eat. Meat, fish, poultry, dairy products and eggs contain all nine essential amino acids.

baking—dry heat method of cooking, especially in an oven.

boiling point—point at which a liquid turns into a gas.

broiling—cooking by direct exposure to high heat, over a grill or under an electric element.

calorie—a measure of energy. A calorie is a quantity of food capable of producing the heat and energy needed to raise the temperature of one kilogram of water one degree centigrade. An ounce of carbohydrates or protein is equal to 115 calories; an ounce of fat is equal to 255 calories. A person's daily calorie need depends on age, weight, and level of activity.

carbohydrates—the sugars and starches that supply energy help the body use fat efficiently, or provide fiber. They are compounds made of carbon, hydrogen and oxygen, most of which are formed by green plants. Simple carbohydrates are honey, sugar and fruits. Complex carbohydrates are grains and cereals, dried beans, root vegetables and potatoes.

enzyme—protein molecules that break down or build up materials inside the body but are not changed themselves (catalysts). Human digestive enzymes break up proteins into individual amino acids and starch into individual glucose units.

digestion—the changing of food to a form the body can use.

fiber—the parts of cereal grains, fruits and vegetables, seeds, legumes and nuts that cannot be digested. Fiber aids digestion and elimination by carrying waste products with it as it leaves the digestive tract and by absorbing fluids that make wastes soft enough for easy passage.

fungus—a plant like mushrooms or yeast that cannot manufacture its own food but lives off decaying organisms around it. This kind of plant is called saprophytic.

minerals—small amounts of minerals such as magnesium, phosphorus, flourine, potassium, chlorine, copper, iron, iodine, sulfur, and zinc are needed for teeth, bones and health. Larger amounts of calcium and sodium are needed.

molecule—one or more atoms that are the smallest particle of an element of compound that retains the properties of the substance.

organic compound—a group of compounds containing the carbon necessary for life.
proteins—a group of organic compounds containing nitrogen, which our body needs to build and repair tissue, red blood cells and enzymes.

osmosis—the flow of a liquid through a thin membrane from an area of greater concentration to an area of lesser concentration of water.

vitamins—special nutrients needed in small quantities but essential to life. A, D, E and K dissolve in fat and can be stored for a long time in the body. Eight B vitamins and vitamin C dissolve in water. Because they are not stored in the body very long, foods providing them must be eaten daily—whole grains, meat or beans for the B's, citrus fruits, melons, berries or leafy green vegetables for the C.

yeast—a group of about 160 species of single-celled microscopic fungi, some of which spoil fruits and vegetables or cause disease. Others are used in making bread and alcoholic drinks.

The following terms appear in the section containing experiments with time:

Balance spring-the hairspring, a long, fine, spiral spring that determines the time of the swing of the balance.

Constellation—a cluster of stars that make up a pattern. Ancient peoples saw these as pictures, giving them names like Big Bear, Leo the Lion, Orion the Hunter, etc.

Diode—an electronic device that has two terminals and converts alternating current to direct current.

Earth's Axis—an imaginary line from the North to South Pole. It takes a day for the Earth to make a complete turn on its axis.

Equinox—the days when the Sun is directly above the equator and day and night are of equal length. March 21 is called the vernal equinox, September 21 is the autumnal equinox.

Escapement—a device that regulates the speed of the train of gear wheels of a clock or watch. It usually consists of a wheel with teeth and an anchor that releases one tooth on the heel at a given interval.

Frequency—the number of complete cycles or swings per second.

Gears—toothed wheels that intermesh so that one wheel turns to drive the other. A screw (a worm) or a toothed shaft (a rack) may replace one of the wheels.

Hertz (HZ)—a unit of frequency equal to one cycle per second, named for physicist Heinrich Hertz.

Horologists—clock-makers.

L.A.T.—local apparent time, which is time measured by the actual movement of Earth and the Sun and differs from season to season and from place to place. It is the time measured by the sundial.

Latitude—the distance in degrees of a point on Earth from the equator.

LCD (liquid crystal display)—an alphanumeric display on digital watches and calculators made up of a liquid sandwiched between layers of glass or plastic. It becomes opaque when an electric current is passed through it. The contrast between the opaque and transparent areas forms visible characters.

LED (light emitting diode)—a semi-conductor electron tube that converts electric power (applied voltage) to light and is used in digital displays, as a digital watch or a calculator.

L.M.T.—local mean time, which measures the average speed at which the Moon moves in its ellipse and Earth spins in its orbit. Our clocks and watches show local mean time.

Longitude—the distance east or west on Earth's surface, measured in degrees up to 180í, or the difference in time between the meridian passing through a particular place and the prime meridian at Greenwich, England.

Megahertz (MHZ)—one million cycles per second.

Meridians—imaginary lines running along Earth's surface from the North to the South Pole.

Oscillator—an instrument that produces a steady rhythm of swings or vibrations.

Piezoelectric effect—electricity created by pressure or pressure created by electricity, especially in a crystal like quartz.

Planetarium—an optical device for projecting astronomical images; a model or representation of the solar system.

Summer solstice—longest day because the tilt of Earth lets the Sun shine longest (June 21 in the Northern Hemisphere, December 21 in the Southern Hemisphere).

INDEX

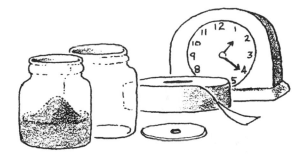

D

M

N

O

P

Q

R

T